For my dear Mum and Dad, with much gratitude.

Also by Dr Libby Weaver

Accidentally Overweight

Rushing Woman's Syndrome

Dr Libby's Real Food Chef, with Chef Cynthia Louise

Beauty from the Inside Out

Dr Libby's Real Food Kitchen, with Chef Cynthia Louise

The Calorie Fallacy

Sweet Food Story, with Chef Cynthia Louise

Registered Reader

Congratulations on purchasing *Exhausted to Energized*. The science and understanding of the impact that nutrition and lifestyle choices have on our bodies is constantly changing as colleagues in the research world continue to make breakthroughs.

By purchasing this book you qualify for our Registered Reader program. Our aim with this Registered Reader program is to ensure that we are able to keep you abreast of the latest developments in health and wellbeing, as well as provide you with a touch point to continue to motivate you to achieve the goals you desire for your health and body.

Please become a Registered Reader by visiting:
www.drlibby.com/registered-reader

Contents

★

My mission is to educate and inspire, enhancing people's health and happiness, igniting a ripple effect that transforms the world.

en·er·gy *noun*
: ability to be active : the physical or mental strength that allows you to do things
: natural enthusiasm and effort
: usable power that comes from heat, electricity, etc
plural **en·er·gies**

Full definition of ENERGY
1a : dynamic quality <narrative energy>
1b : the capacity of acting or being active <intellectual energy>
1c : a usually positive spiritual force <the energy flowing through all people>
2: vigorous exertion of power: effort <investing time and energy>
3: a fundamental entity of Nature that is transferred between parts of a system in the production of physical change within the system and usually regarded as the capacity for doing work
4: usable power (as heat or electricity); also : the resources for producing such power

Examples of ENERGY
The kids are always so full of **energy**.
They devoted all their **energy** to the completion of the project.

She puts a lot of **energy** into her work.
The newer appliances conserve more **energy**.

Origin of ENERGY
Late Latin **energia**, from Greek **energeia** activity, from **energos** active, from **en** in + **ergon** work — more at work
First known use: 1599

Related to ENERGY
Synonyms
aura, chi (*or* ch'i *also* qi), ki, vibe(s), vibration(s)
Antonyms
lethargy, listlessness, sluggishness, torpidity

en·er·gy **noun**
(Medical Dictionary)

Medical definition of ENERGY
1: the force driving and sustaining mental activity <in psychoanalytic theory the source of psychic **energy** is the id>
2: the capacity for doing work
Merriam-Webster's
Collegiate Dictionary

*E*nergy cannot be created or destroyed,
it can only be changed from one form to another.

Albert Einstein

Energy: Where Does It Begin?

For too long, people in the Western world have used weight as a marker of health and assessed themselves against this benchmark. Yet both science and clinical experience demonstrate that when you focus on weight you are more likely to regain anything you lose — plus more. A far more powerful insight into our level of wellbeing is energy, so much so that I want it to be seen as the true health currency. I want people to be curious about *why* they are tired, and passionate about resolving it. Because, let's face it, everything is more difficult when we are exhausted.

Each of us comes into this world endowed with a fundamental energy. On a physical level, the health of the ova (egg) and sperm that create you play a significant role in this original energy. This energy operates as a kind of bank account and supplies us with the power to function, grow, heal and regenerate ourselves daily. We are designed, however, to supplement this original endowment of energy with what we generate from eating, breathing, sleeping, working, playing, learning and relationships. Each day we make withdrawals and deposits; we invest or deplete. And when the balance of the scales tips in the direction of us using more than we put back in, we begin to live in the red, with the potential of falling further and further behind.

To keep the currency analogy going, we are then forced to dip into our savings. When we continuously withdraw from our savings account, alarm bells can begin to sound, telling us that our survival is being challenged. These alarms present to us as symptoms in the body, often of the type that don't initially lead us to stay home from work ... so we soldier on and often do nothing about them. Or the medicating — rather than the resolving — of these symptoms begins. For example, if you get a headache every afternoon at 3pm, it is not a deficiency of painkillers that has led to the headache, yet many people treat the headache as if it is due to such a deficiency.

Some of the symptoms of dipping into our energy savings accounts include fatigue, low mood, anxious feelings, apathy, unrefreshed sleep or insomnia, brain fog, lowered resistance to infections, stiffness, digestive system problems, "unexplained" changes in body fat levels, and signs of rapid aging. These are just some of the ways our body might choose to let us know that we are physically, mentally and/or emotionally exhausted.

The symptoms themselves don't have a voice to let us know what they want us to do. It is up to us to decipher them. And when we are running on empty, our body does its best to let us know that it is time to slow down, rest, better support and enhance detoxification pathways, repair, replenish and restore. Yet too many people ignore this, throw down another pill, or write it off as "I must be getting old". As an aside, I have had 25-year-olds tell me that they are really tired, believing it must be because they are getting old. And my reply is "Hashtag you're joking!" If you are 25 and exhausted, you need to do something NOW to get to the heart of why that is! Your energy is supposed to be strong, consistent and boundless.

When we begin to take a bigger perspective on life and what your ancestors innately did with their bodies — before marketing started instructing our way of life — you can see, when we stand in the common-sense, corner that our bodies are not built to be sedentary or to run marathons. We are not designed to live without adequate sunshine or be separate from Nature and her rhythms. We were not made to exist on very little sleep, or eat man-made "numbers" pretending to be food, or weird combinations of processed foods. We are not built to subsist on no-fat or no-carb diets. Nor are our brains wired to handle consistent and profound amounts of mental and emotional stress. We are also not designed to live without fresh air, yet I regularly meet people who wake up in air-conditioning, catch an elevator to their basement carpark to get into their air-conditioned car, drive to work where they park underneath the air-conditioned office in which they will spend their day, before catching the elevator back to the office basement carpark for the drive home to their air-conditioned house or apartment in their air-conditioned car.

We cannot fight our biology, yet too many people live as if they are trying to. And a deep, unrelenting fatigue can be one of the symptoms your body gifts you — yes, gifts you — guiding you to eat, drink, move, think, breathe, believe or perceive in a new way. Trouble is, without energy, it can be incredibly difficult to approach life with this curiosity, because you are too exhausted to lift your head beyond the bare necessities and conjure the resources you need for such a transition. I hope this book offers you the resources you need.

Science suggests that humans have been on the planet for about 150,000 years. Over that time we have evolved with each generation and, up until the very recent past, we have been beings who lived and worked in harmony with the seasons — we had no other choice. From this way of living, many interior bodily rhythms were created, one of which is our circadian rhythm. This rhythm contributes to the governance of many systems and processes inside the body, including the release of hormones, digestive enzymes, neurotransmitters, body temperature, sleep–wake cycles, and other important bodily functions. Circadian rhythms (out of rhythm) have been linked to various sleep disorders, including insomnia. Abnormal circadian rhythms have also been associated with obesity, type 2 diabetes, depressed mood, bipolar disorder, and seasonal affective disorder.

The "master clock" that controls circadian rhythms consists of a group of nerve cells in the brain called the suprachiasmatic nucleus (SCN). The SCN contains about 20,000 nerve cells and it is located in the hypothalamus, an area of the brain just above where the optic nerves from the eyes cross.

Circadian rhythms are important in determining human sleep patterns. The SCN controls the production of melatonin, one of our sleep hormones. Since it is located just above the optic nerves, which relay information from the eyes to the brain, the SCN receives information about incoming light. When there is less light, which is what is supposed to occur at night, the SCN tells the brain to make more melatonin so you get drowsy. Trouble is, too many people live each night exposed to too much light too late into the evening. And when we live our lives in a way that drives our surroundings and the environment in which we live to communicate messages to our internal assessors (essentially, our endocrine system), the cascading effect of those signals can disrupt our most basic and essential of rhythms. This book is about sharing the steps you can take to support these processes and, as a result, restore or enhance your energy.

Consider energy as a marker of health, and view poor energy as a sign that there are body systems that are off-track, body systems receiving messages that are unsupportive to their optimal function. This book is designed to help you identify the parameters that play a role in you experiencing energy — parameters that may be in need of your attention. Start to see energy in this way as you read this book.

For example, when the alarm goes off in the morning, do you bound out of bed, grateful for a new day, excited to get into all that lies ahead? Or do you groan, press snooze, and wonder how on Earth it can be time to get up already? If it is the latter scenario, do you also feel like you have pressed snooze on aspects of your life?

Despite being free from disease, and in the prime of their life, people in their twenties, thirties, forties and fifties are exhausted, overwhelmed, and have body aches and stiffness, and a mind that can't recall things. They don't wake up feeling refreshed from sleep, and they have no energy to live the lives they want to lead. And it doesn't need to be this way. It's time people understood what levers to pull to get their energy back. It's time to make our own personal energy our highest priority, for, without it, we cannot be, do or experience anything to the degree that we could if we had energy.

Without doubt, energy is not just the result of physical attributes or actions. Sleep, food intake and movement patterns make up a huge part of the physicality that allows us to experience energy, and all of these are explored across these pages. But a sense of purpose also rears its head here, too, as a major factor in our experiencing energy. For if you look beyond the everydayness of commuting, drinking coffee, working, drinking more coffee, replying to emails, forwarding emails, going through the bills you can or cannot pay this month … if you look past the grind, you will find truths about how and why you get up in the morning, and what infuses colour into the black and white of your reality. And energy helps us experience the colour. Passion, originality, risk, vulnerability, courage, empathy, optimism, humour, wisdom from others … these are just some of the forces that drive our decisions, how we define success, and whether we perceive *now* or in the end, if our life adds up to a fulfilling whole. So we look at purpose in here too.

While I was researching and writing this book, I spent time in: Burleigh Heads, Australia (beach); Tamworth, Australia (countryside); Auckland, New Zealand (small city); Necker Island, British Virgin Islands (island); and New York City, USA (large city). All of these places have an energy all of their own. Not only was I fortunate to have the opportunity to be in all of these places witnessing the impact of their energy on me, as well as the surroundings, but it also created the opportunity to ask people from all walks of life what they believed led to poor energy.

Here are some of the most common responses in the language they used:

⁂ lack of sleep

⁂ poor-quality sleep

⁂ toxic food

⁂ processed food

⁂ preservatives

⁂ dehydration

⁂ air-conditioning

⁂ lack of sunlight

⁂ stress

having young children
studying
long commutes
money worries
boring job
not having any time to myself
having no purpose
almost all, if not all, of the above!

The "having no purpose" sentiment was expressed time and time again, and to everyone who gave me this answer, in response I asked them whether they felt like they had a purpose. And it was mostly people who felt they didn't know their purpose, and wanted one, who felt this had a negative impact on their energy. And I made a note in my research book that said:

> There are people low on energy because they believe they have to find their purpose to live fully. And although people with a purpose, with a mission to make a difference no matter how big or small, say this fuels their fire and gives them energy, those who don't have one, or haven't identified it, don't need to suffer. Because worrying about not having a purpose can be draining in itself and messing people up. What people perceive to be social pressure to find their purpose, find their passion, and know what it is that they want to do can have its own impact on energy. It is perfectly fine — and in fact recommended — to simply live each of your moments fully and marvel at it all. What if that is the purpose? Many small and large passions and purposes may enter and leave your life, all of them awakening something within you, allowing you to grow. For many people, I don't think there is some elusive purpose out there. It's here, within them, because they have senses to experience all of this. There doesn't have to be a big realization, or bliss to follow, or a major moment of discovery of your life's purpose. Sure, for some this is their path, but for those for whom that isn't their way, it isn't sad, it's just what

is. So maybe for a while, stop trying to find the forest and just enjoy the trees. And observe what that does to your energy.

⋆　⋆　⋆

You have to be healthy to have energy. And if you don't have energy, rather than get frustrated with the fatigue, see it as feedback — your body asking you to eat, drink, move, think, breathe, believe or perceive in a new way. It can be a gift if we choose to see it this way, a gift asking us to bring curiosity to the question: Why am I so tired?

And when you feel as though there is something that you don't have and you need that for you to be fulfilled, then that alone can deplete you of energy. Sure, if you feel like you have a purpose, it can give you a reason to get out of bed in the morning. But what about life itself being a reason to get out of bed in the morning? What about the gift of being alive? You have senses to experience everything here on Earth and one day that experience, that opportunity will end. As you will see in this book, there are distinct *physical* reasons that energy can be low, and we will explore those. But there can be mental or emotional reasons as well, and I want to challenge people's perception of not having anything to get up for. For you have the opportunity to get up for life. And I want this book to enliven you with opportunities and choices to create and experience more energy within you, so you feel physically able to get up for life.

This book is not a scientific manual on personal energy. (I say "personal", because when people have asked what I am writing my latest book about, and I replied "energy", most of them thought of electricity. But the term "personal energy" cleared that up.) This is not a thorough exploration and explanation of each of the biochemical pathways that lead to energy creation. There is a small portion of that, but not bucket-loads, because I don't want to risk your getting bored and not finishing the book!

While I was doing my PhD, each year the biological sciences faculty had a conference and each PhD candidate had to do a presentation on where they were up to with their research and explain the design and results of their work. The audience was made up of other PhD students and the faculty staff, including a group of doctors and professors. One year, after I'd presented the nitty-gritty detail of my experiments, I was asked to give a layperson's version of my findings to date; to pretend I was being interviewed on television and that the general public would be watching rather than a group of scientists. And so I did. And at the end of that impromptu delivery, I didn't just see, but I *experienced* the vital importance of making scientific information relevant and accessible to everyone, not just those in scientific fields.

Sure, this book is built on my three-pillars approach to health: the biochemical, the nutritional and the emotional. So of course there is some biochemistry, but not detailed descriptions of each and every biochemical pathway that creates energy. Most of you would literally fall asleep! My intention has been to create a book that you can understand, and that enables you to identify with factors that may be contributing to why you are exhausted, and to offer practical ideas about how you can cultivate more personal energy. Everything is more difficult in life if you are exhausted, so use this book to identify the factors that need addressing in your life so that you can shift from being *Exhausted to Energized*.

As Pema Chodron so eloquently says:

Our life's work is to use what we have been given to wake up. If there were two people who were exactly the same — same body, same speech, same mind, same mother, same father, same house, same food, everything the same — one of them could use what he has to wake up and the other could use it to become more resentful, bitter, and sour. It doesn't matter what you're given, whether it's physical deformity or enormous wealth or poverty, beauty or ugliness, mental stability or mental instability, life in the middle of a madhouse or life in the middle of a peaceful, silent desert. Whatever you're given can wake you up or put you to sleep.

That's the challenge of now: what are you going to do with what you have already — your body, your speech, your mind?

For every moment, we get to choose what we focus on. So the real question is: do you feel the desire, the need or the longing to live in a different way? To live with ease and spaciousness and more energy. To stop punishing yourself or shaming yourself or telling yourself that you are a failure and are not okay the way you are. The punishment of yourself has to stop, not only in your relationship with food and lifestyle choices, such as sleep, but in your relationship with other people, with work, with money, and, most importantly, with yourself. And if you do, then that gives you a choice about what to do, how to eat, what you put your attention on, what your priorities are, how you perceive yourself, how you live. And it is your way of life that this book is about. My intention with this book is to help you live a life with a reservoir of, and a daily experience of, great energy, allowing you to experience all that is on offer to you, and allowing you to share your gifts.

*B*e responsible for the energy you bring.

Dr Libby

Guide To Using This Book

Energy is essential to life. Without it we wither and our life on Earth would be no longer. It is to be treasured, nourished, nurtured, supported and appreciated. Yet why do so few people do this, not realizing the importance of their energy until it is so low? Why is energy not a main method of health assessment? It is not until we are so weary that we wake up to the treasure that it is. As I described in the introduction, this book is designed to educate you and to lift your spirits, so that if you are on the exhausted spectrum it will give you hope that things don't have to remain this way. I want this book to give you insights into what may be leading you to experience poor energy, and what I offer will be based on the three pillars of my approach: the biochemical (body systems), the nutritional, and the emotional, looking at our beliefs and subsequent behaviours. Each chapter appears in an order designed to be a journey that fulfils both your head and your heart. The book begins predominantly with the science (biochemistry), nutritional information is peppered throughout, and numerous emotional factors related to energy are explored to conclude. If you find the science hard going or boring, please don't let that opening information put you off this journey into energy.

I want you to truly appreciate that energy is a treasured measure of wellbeing — a health currency — and that every-thing is more difficult without it. So as you read this book, mark up the points that resonate for you, and allow them to ignite hope in your heart so that you don't have to drag yourself through life for much longer if you take the steps, even small steps, to live in a new way, with a new level of self-care that restores you. For some of you, this will mean altering your priorities; for others, what you focus on. For others still, it will mean taking steps to change how you feed yourself; while for some, it will be all about making new decisions. Some of you may need support and guidance from a health professional experienced in restoring energy to get the outcomes you seek. But my hope with the book is that you will highlight or bend pages when something jumps out at you as an area to address, so that you have new insights, new options and renewed energy to live your best life.

*W*ithout passion man is a mere latent force and possibility,
like the flint which awaits the shock of the iron
before it can give forth its spark.

Henri-Frédéric Amiel

The Krebs Cycle

The biochemistry of energy is a big topic, and one which involves a host of pathways within you that are truly magnificent. And none of them runs without nutrients. I am opening this book with a description of some energy science, and some words and concepts I need you to know before we get to some of the juicier pieces of the energy picture.

A cycle known as the Krebs cycle — also called the citric acid cycle — is one of these, and I share it with you primarily to introduce you to the name of energy that is made in the body: *adenosine triphosphate*, or *ATP*.

Inside your body the Krebs cycle is the central metabolic pathway. It is in all aerobic (oxygen-utilizing) organisms. The cycle is a series of eight reactions that occur in the part of the cell known as the mitochondria, which will be explored further in a later section. The best way to imagine this is that you are made up of trillions of tiny little circles (cells) and that inside each cell is a mouse on a treadmill (mitochondria), generating energy.

These reactions take a two-carbon molecule called acetate, and completely oxidize it to carbon dioxide. The cycle is summarized in the following chemical equation:

$$\text{Acetyl CoA} + 3\text{ NAD} + \text{FAD} + \text{ADP} + \text{HPO}_4^{-2} \longrightarrow$$
$$2\text{ CO}_2 + \text{CoA} + 3\text{ NADH}^+ + \text{FADH}^+ + \text{ATP}$$

Please do not worry for a second if that is all gobbledy-goop to you. I simply wanted you know the name of energy made in the body: ATP. And to see what an ATP-yielding equation looked like ... in case you were interested!

Essentially, the Krebs cycle is part of the pathway for the breakdown of all metabolites, including glucose and other sugars, amino acids and fatty acids. All of these we obtain from our food. Each of these groups of molecules has a pathway that feeds into the Krebs cycle, and, once they have been "processed", energy is yielded. Visually it looks like this:

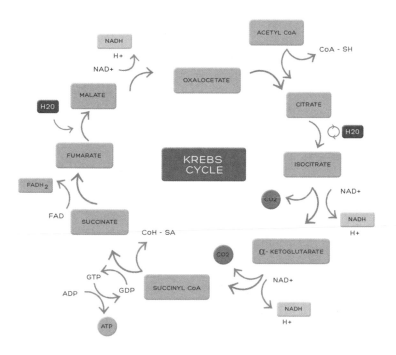

The Krebs cycle: Energy — ATP — is yielded from these reactions.

Again, please don't worry if the science is not your cup of tea. I simply want you to know that the foods you eat enter this cycle and then yield the physical energy you experience — so long as other processes are working optimally, as you will soon see. For example, carbohydrates are converted into acetyl CoA by a set of reactions known as glycolysis, whereas fatty acids are converted into acetyl CoA by the *beta* oxidation pathway. In each case, the molecules are converted into products that enter the Krebs cycle. In addition, intermediates from the Krebs cycle can go in the other direction and be used to synthesize molecules such as amino acids and fatty acids. For example, acetyl CoA can be used to synthesize fatty acids.

The challenge for so many people, however, is that they eat but do not feel energized by what they are eating. They may as well be eating air, their food does so little for them. And too many people eat — particularly in the middle of the afternoon or early evening — in a desperate search of energy, trying to haul themselves through until bedtime, yet no amount of lollies or sweet biscuits gives them the energy they are seeking.

So just because your body is running this reaction — and it is, every split second — doesn't mean you get to feel the effects. So how can it be that, although this most basic and essential part of your chemistry is yielding ATP, you aren't full of beans? The answer might be in your mitochondria.

When you have exhausted all possibilities,
remember this: you haven't.

Thomas Edison

The Mighty Mitochondria

This is the last of the hefty science sections in this book, so bear with me. All you need to know from this section is that the mitochondria are tiny little subsections inside a cell. And you are made up of about 50 trillion cells, a number that can so easily go over our head in its enormity. However, I will use the example of time to demonstrate just how large that number is. One million seconds ago was 12 days ago. One billion seconds ago was 32 years ago. But one trillion seconds ago was 32,000 years ago! And you have about 50 trillion cells that make you up.

As I outlined in the previous chapter, the best way to imagine a cell is as a tiny circle. And inside that circle there are numerous smaller components, including your DNA, as well as mitochondria. They are where the energy is made. So their health and function really, really matter. I will always think of the mitochondria as a mouse, peddling away furiously on his bicycle, creating energy for you and your body to enjoy. Trouble is, there is plenty in our world today that can engulf our mice in fumes, disrupting their ability to do their work efficiently, or sometimes at all. The function of the mitochondria matter very much for how you feel and function each day, so let's take a more in-depth look.

What are mitochondria?

Mitochondria are cellular organelles that function as power plants within a cell — the mouse within the circle. In the same way that a local power plant produces electricity for an entire city, mitochondria are responsible for the production of energy derived from the breakdown of carbohydrates and fatty acids. Mitochondria oxidize or "burn" carbohydrates, amino acids and fatty acids for energy, yielding ATP. As you now know, ATP is the cellular form of energy utilized by cellular processes all throughout the body, providing the energy to pump your heart, power neurons in your brain, contract muscles, exchange gases in your lungs, extract nutrients from food and regulate body temperature, just to name a few.

Simply stated, mitochondria produce ATP, and ATP is 100 per cent essential for survival. Without a sufficient generation of ATP, life would cease to exist.

Where are mitochondria found?

Mitochondria are located in every cell type and tissue in the human body, from your brain to your thyroid gland to the tendons around your knees. In short, trillions of mitochondria are distributed throughout your body with the sole purpose of generating ATP. Red blood cells are the only cell type that does not contain mitochondria.

Muscles contain the highest mitochondrial content of any tissue in your body, in order to provide large amounts of ATP for movement. Muscle is generally divided into three types: white muscle, red muscle and mixed muscle. The terms "red" and "white" are derived from the way these muscles appear during surgery or autopsies, but largely refer to the mitochondrial content of the muscle itself.

Red muscles contain a large quantity of mitochondria, white muscles contain fewer mitochondria, and mixed muscles contain both red and white muscle fibre types. Whereas a single cell (circle) contains one nucleus, muscle cells often contain hundreds or even thousands of mitochondria so that they can support the generation of large quantities of ATP during exercise.

It is no coincidence that mitochondria are located close to one another within the muscle cell. They do that to share the fuels of glucose, amino acids and fatty acids with the purpose of distributing the production of ATP across a well-coordinated, intricately linked network. Isn't the body truly amazing?

Mitochondria can replicate themselves

A process known as *mitochondrial biogenesis* was first described in the field of exercise physiology. It was found that certain types of exercise could induce large increases in muscle mitochondrial content, and thereby increased the ability of muscles to take up glucose during and after exercise, a very positive and important process.

The term "mitochondrial biogenesis" simply refers to the process of replicating mitochondria within a cell, with the sole purpose of increasing ATP production in response to an increased demand for energy.

The result of mitochondrial biogenesis is an expansion of the network of mitochondria within a cell, as well as an increase in the maximal amount of ATP that can be generated during intense exercise. In short, more mitochondria essentially mean more ATP production. Can you sense the importance of maintaining or preferably building muscle mass for great energy? Remember muscle mass naturally declines from about the age of 30 onwards unless you do something to counteract this.

> *R*emember muscle mass naturally declines from about age 30 onwards unless you do something to counteract this.

Another reason to embrace consistent movement

Sedentary lifestyles, chronic disuse of muscle, and aging (processes of degeneration known as oxidation, inflammation, and glycation) each independently result in a decline in mitochondrial content and function, leading to the production of free radicals and cell death. Think about that. If a cell dies, you lose a mouse. That means you lose energy-producing capacity.

The muscle tissue of people with type 2 diabetes has been extensively studied, revealing gross defects in mitochondrial number and function. Although the cause-and-effect remains unknown, muscle tissue from people with type 2 diabetes is often associated with reduced aerobic capacity, insulin resistance and deficient mitochondrial biogenesis. Studies have also shown that defective mitochondrial biogenesis in the heart can predispose individuals to cardiovascular complications, heart disease and metabolic syndrome.

Fortunately, reversing the effects of aging, type 2 diabetes and cardiovascular disease via increased mitochondrial biogenesis is as simple as exercising more. Truly, if exercise were a pill, everyone would take it! Studies have shown that if aged individuals with existing metabolic disease resume an active lifestyle, they can significantly improve pre-existing cellular damage and promote gains in muscle mass, as well as activating mitochondrial biogenesis.

Exercise is the most effective way to make new mitochondria

Exercise is the most potent signal for the increased production of mitochondria in muscle, by increasing the ability of the muscle to burn carbohydrates and fatty acids for ATP. That is a win–win for all parties!

This next bit might be a bit much — so park it if it is. But for some of you, it will spin your tyres. It is not essential that you really know this part — I'm sharing it because I love it! When you exercise, muscle cells generate a low-energy signal known as *adenosine monophosphate* (AMP), and the accumulation of AMP over time signals for increased ATP production. An increasing AMP to ATP ratio initiates a cascade of signals within the muscle tissue to produce more ATP to protect against an energy deficit. At the same time, during periods of sustained muscle contraction, calcium is released from storage, resulting in a 300 per cent to 10,000 per cent increase in intracellular calcium. Increased calcium and AMP are powerful signals for the production of more mitochondria, which occurs in the resting state immediately following exercise.

In response to a large demand for ATP production, muscle cells respond by overcompensating in their ability to produce energy for the next round of exercise, by inducing mitochondrial biogenesis in the resting state. By doing this, mitochondria are able to consume larger amounts of oxygen, carbohydrates and fatty acids, the fuels needed to power the production of ATP. That means you tend to eat more so you can fuel yourself well and feel the benefits. This is partly why, the greater your muscle mass, the higher your metabolic rate is and the less likely you are to gain body fat. The ability of muscles to overcompensate for exercise "stress" is a major reason why frequent exercise also results in increased strength, endurance, resistance to fatigue and overall fitness.

So the next time you exercise, imagine the work that your mitochondria are doing to keep up with the "stress" you create. I assure you, the behind-the-scenes work is nothing short of magical.

We are never so disposed to quarrel with others as when we are dissatisfied with ourselves, and being exhausted contributes to this. Great energy helps foster fulfilling human interactions.

Dr Libby

Antioxidant Defence Mechanisms

Our antioxidant defence mechanism is another superb aspect of our chemistry. In this journey to understand and resolve fatigue, we need to explore the role that free radicals play in the degenerative processes that go on inside us. When you read about "aging", essentially that term is referring to the biochemical processes that occur to drive degeneration. They are oxidation, inflammation and glycation, and I explore them in detail in my book *Beauty from the Inside Out.* All I need you to know here, however, is how oxidation works, because if degenerative processes occur at rapid rates, energy levels can suffer.

Humans stay alive through a process called *respiration*, meaning that we breathe in oxygen, and we exhale carbon dioxide. If you could see oxygen in space, it is two Os (oxygen molecules) stuck together. The diagram below illustrates what I am about to describe.

O_2

$O = O$

O^- (free radical)

A/O (antioxidant/donator)

$O = O$

O_2

Free radical protection from antioxidants: The oxygen donation of antioxidants.

When we breathe, oxygen splits apart, forming two single oxygen molecules. Known as *free radicals*, they have the potential to damage your tissues. One of the major ways the body defends itself from damage by a free radical is through the consumption of antioxidants. Antioxidant-rich foods are found in our coloured plant foods. Blueberries, green tea and chocolate (cacao) are rich in antioxidants, and are the most common antioxidant-rich foods called out at my live events when I ask the audience for ideas. That antioxidants are found in our coloured plant foods is one of the major reasons why people like me bark on and on about the importance of amping up the plant content of your diet.

The way it works is as follows. The antioxidant donates one of its oxygens back to the free radical, and they pair up. Oxygen is then content again as it has its buddy back, and damage to your tissues is avoided. We generate more free radicals in response to our exposure to pollutants and anything that increases respiration.

To understand one powerful way free radicals can damage our tissues, imagine a blood vessel leading to your heart. A free radical zips about through the blood and suddenly does a dive-bomb and makes an indentation in the wall of the vessel. It resembles the divot in the grass beneath a golf swing that has taken too much soil with it. The damaged vessel sends out a cry for help, signalling that it is damaged, and, in this case, cholesterol wants to be the hero. Cholesterol behaves like a band-aid in this situation, and it comes along and sticks itself on top of the injured site. It then sends out a message to all of its cholesterol friends to join the band-aid party, and they come along and stick themselves over the top of the first cholesterol globule that arrived. The cholesterol piles up, and it oxidizes and hardens. This is called atherosclerosis or plaque, and it narrows the interior of the arteries. Where once the blood could flow through a wide, open vessel, it now has a very narrow, restricted path to weave. Your blood is the only way oxygen and nutrients get around your body. Your heart is a muscle, and it needs both oxygen and nutrients to survive. If it is starved of either of these for long enough, this is one mechanism that can lead to a heart attack. Please note, "rubbish" can also accumulate in the walls of the vascular system, creating a major risk for heart disease and stroke, not just inside the vessels.

The good news, though, is that there is much you can do to reverse the buildup. The hardened, built-up cholesterol is, in part, *LDL cholesterol*, which is why it is commonly known as "bad" cholesterol. "Good" cholesterol (*HDL cholesterol*) comes along and unsticks each globule of cholesterol and carries it off to the liver, which, as you will see in a future section of this book, plays a significant role in the energy we experience, as well as cholesterol management. The best way to imagine this all occurring is this: the cholesterol that was unstuck from the pile within the blood vessel arrives at the front door of the liver to undergo its detoxification process, and, when the liver is functioning well, the cholesterol is processed, excreted and gone forever. However, if the liver is loaded up with substances that it *must* prioritize higher up the detoxification order than boring old, homemade cholesterol, then the cholesterol is only partially detoxified, and instead of being excreted, it is re-absorbed back into the blood supply. This is one mechanism through which our blood cholesterol goes up and up and up. Cholesterol can also be elevated when thyroid function is poor.

> *E*nhance the detoxification processes that allow the cholesterol to be eliminated when the body determines it is time for it to leave.

I don't consider elevated total blood cholesterol a problem in itself, although there is certainly evidence to suggest that the ratio of small to large particle cholesterol is an important consideration in the management of excellent heart and vascular health. However, I do use blood cholesterol as a marker for liver health, and also to give me insight into whether the body is efficiently converting cholesterol into steroid (sex) hormones, which are also critical for energy. If blood cholesterol suddenly increases, to me this indicates that something has changed with the way the body is managing its level of blood cholesterol, and it is this mechanism that must be identified, as this is what needs correcting. The cholesterol then comes back down to the level that that this individual's body functions best at. Your body has the most incredible capacity to heal and regulate itself — you just need to know which levers to pull.

To demonstrate the power of an optimally functioning liver, in the 17 years I have been working with people there is not one person whose blood cholesterol I have not been able to lower back into the "normal" range simply by focusing on liver support and enhancing the detoxification processes that allow the cholesterol to be eliminated when the body determines it is time for it to leave. After all, if any substance — cholesterol included — has been sent to the liver, it has been sent there because your body has decided it is in your best interest to eliminate it from your body.

★

Sometimes the most important thing in a whole day
is the rest we take between two deep breaths.

Etty Hillesum

Energy and Coenzyme Q_{10}: Prepare for Ignition!

As you now know, every cell (circle) in your body is powered by small organelles called *mitochondria* (mice). They are essentially the energy factories of the human body. They take glucose from the food you eat and oxygen from the air you breathe and convert them into the energy in your cells.

Mitochondria are one of the most important components of a cell. Without them, many crucial biochemical processes simply would not happen. Not only do they host cellular respiration, the process by which our bodies convert food into energy for the cell, they also send signals to other components of the cell.

As they are so intricately involved in many different biochemical reactions, they tend to generate free radicals as by-products. While free radicals do have some important benefits when present in the right numbers, the overproduction of free radicals can lead to the cell being damaged. Unfortunately, in this current world of ours, overproduction commonly occurs — to put it simply — due to "pollution". Pollution that we breathe, eat and drink, and that we absorb through our skin. Essentially, the aging process, exposure to environmental toxins, nasty chemicals and pollution, as well as a poor diet can all lead to increased levels of free radicals in the body. Alternatively, this pollution can cause or lead to an underproduction of our body's own antioxidants, such as coenzyme Q_{10} (Co Q_{10}). When these free radicals are left unchecked — or if they are not neutralized by the antioxidant substances we obtain predominantly from our coloured plant foods (as you saw in the previous chapter) — this can lead to a scenario known as *oxidative stress*. Hello, degeneration. Hello, illness. Hello, fatigue.

CoQ_{10} is a vitamin-like substance found throughout the body, but it is particularly concentrated in the heart, liver, kidney and pancreas, which are the organs with the highest energy requirements (other than the brain). It can be found in small amounts in meat, seafood, and the oils in grapeseeds and olives. It can also be consumed as a supplement, typically in the form of ubiquinol.

CoQ_{10}'s primary function is in mitochondria, the energy factories of cells. It's here that the food we eat is finally transformed into ATP, usable energy for our body. CoQ_{10} is needed for a crucial step in this process, where it transports energy-carrying electrons. CoQ_{10} also functions as an antioxidant (by binding to damaging free radicals) in the body, and hence may improve blood vessel tone and even help to reduce blood pressure. It is particularly important for those who take statin medication, as statins can deplete CoQ_{10}. More and more research is being conducted into the role that specific doses of CoQ_{10} can play to reduce the risk of heart disease, and stroke in particular.

If the science doesn't make sense or doesn't interest you, all you need to know from this section is that CoQ_{10} is an essential nutrient-like substance that helps the body to yield energy from the food we eat. It appears to become depleted with age and also with a poor-quality diet. Exposure to pollutants increases our need for CoQ_{10}, and sadly, in today's world, exposure to excessive amounts is far too common. In my practice, if clients start taking CoQ_{10} as a supplement, they regularly report noticing that their energy levels increase on the days they take CoQ_{10} as a good-quality supplement. Their mitochondria are clearly jumping for joy!

One of the simplest ways to generate more energy is to release those things that are not ours to fix.

Dr Libby

B Vitamins and Energy

Energy is essential to life, and when we don't feel energized we can't live our lives to the fullest. The food we eat plays many roles, but physically the two important ones are to provide us with nutrients to nourish our bodies, and to provide us with fuel to run the machine that is the human body. Micronutrients do the first job and macronutrients fulfil the second task. Nothing else on the planet can do this, and the foods we choose can either meet these needs, fall short, or completely disrupt them. I really want you to think about that.

Meeting our nutritional needs is essential for us to have great energy and health. If your nutritional needs fall short or you are consuming substances that disrupt the energy creation cycles of your body, then fatigue is a likely result. Nothing, nothing at all, can replace a real-food, wholefood, nutrient-dense way of eating. Nothing.

Once food is eaten, it follows intricate biochemical pathways before becoming the form of energy that the cells of our muscles, brain and other organs can use: ATP.

Many nutrients help the food we eat be be converted into ATP. The most important group of nutrients for the conversion of food into ATP are the B vitamins. There are many B vitamins, but three of them, in particular, are essential to allow the body to convert food into ATP. Thiamin (vitamin B_1), riboflavin (vitamin B_2) and niacin (vitamin B_3) are three B vitamins which assist with energy production. These three vitamins are critical for turning food into ATP. Without these helpers, known as *cofactors*, energy conversion can be slow or disrupted, leaving us feeling sluggish and tired.

B vitamins are water-soluble, meaning that whatever is not used by the body is then excreted. Therefore, B vitamins must be consumed every day, as we cannot store these three in particular. The best place to get B vitamins is from our food, as when vitamins are obtained through food they tend to be easily absorbed and utilized because there are other nutrients and substances unique to those foods that help with their absorption. Supplementation can also be highly beneifical for some individuals, as you will see.

B vitamins are found in a wide range of foods. Thiamin-rich foods include lentils, nuts and seeds, tuna and pork; if you eat pork, make sure it is free-range and organic. A significant amount of riboflavin is found in leafy green vegetables, tomatoes, almonds and eggs. Niacin is found in highest concentrations in meats such as beef, pork, chicken and fish. Some can also be found in wheat, peanuts and beans. Grains are also considered to be a good source of many of the B vitamins. If your digestive system handles them okay, including higher-quality grains such as spelt, oats and rye in your diet may be another way to boost your B vitamin intake. Quinoa is gluten-free and contains a variety of B vitamins, so some people may tolerate this "grain" better (botanically, it is actually a seed).

Many nutrients help the food we eat be converted into ATP. The most important group of nutrients for the conversion of food into ATP are the B vitamins.

Many people feel better without grains in their diet though, and hence we are seeing that some people are going gluten-free or grain-free. If your body gives you this feedback, with problematic symptoms being resolved when you eat this way, then for now eating this way serves you. And that is a great thing to know.

However, as grains are a significant source of B vitamins, for many people removing them from their diet can result in inadequate B vitamin levels, if they aren't sufficiently replaced by other foods. For example, very few people cut grains out and eat more liver — although more and more are! When excluding a type of food, it is important to ensure that the nutrients found in it are replaced by other foods in your diet. It may be worthwhile taking a good-quality multivitamin or a B-complex supplement to cover your vitamin needs, something best guided by an experienced health professional.

It is important to note that B vitamins are destroyed by heat and light, and the longer the time has been from when the food was picked or harvested, the lower the level of B vitamins. For example, if a food containing vitamins B_1, B_2 or B_3 is heated over 90° Celsius, research shows that the vitamins are destroyed, which is why when I was a nutrition student I couldn't get my head around why we were taught that grains are a good source of B vitamins; humans don't consume them raw.

Eating a varied and seasonal diet will help to ensure that your body gets a healthy amount of essential B vitamins. Increase your consumption of B vitamins by sprinkling salads with nuts and seeds or adding them to smoothies. Or eat an extra serving of leafy green vegetables each day. Eating foods rich in B vitamins with each meal will top up your B vitamin levels throughout the day, helping you to obtain the energy you need from the foods you eat.

Please remember that the B vitamins themselves don't contain energy. They allow the energy on offer in your food to be yielded; for you to obtain the energy from the foods you eat — essentially fats, proteins and carbohydrates, the macronutrients that we will explore next.

★

Let there be room for not knowing.
Some of the most beautiful chapters
in our lives won't have
a title until much later.
Don't let the uncertainty deplete you.
Embrace it and let the not knowing enliven you.

Dr Libby

Macronutrients:
Energy from Our Food

Where do we obtain energy from? The energy that goes on to yield ATP, supplying our cells with the energy they need to create our energy and vitality — what allows us to move our body, think, work and play? These are the macronutrients, which are:

fats

proteins, and

carbohydrates.

The macronutrients provide energy, and this form of energy is measured as calories or kilojoules: calories being the imperial and kilojoules being the metric way to measure energy. While each of these macronutrients provides calories, the amount of calories that each one provides varies. Alcohol actually falls into the macronutrient category as well, as it, too, provides energy (calories). However, many researchers do not class alcohol as a macronutrient because it is not needed for survival (despite what some people may think!) and it does not provide any nutritional value.

Macronutrients are substances needed for growth, metabolism and for many other body functions, and they allow us to experience energy in our daily lives, provided a host of other processes function optimally (as discussed throughout this book). Since "macro" means large, macronutrients are substances required in large amounts, while the micronutrients — vitamins and minerals — are needed in smaller amounts and don't contain energy themselves. You have already read how the B-group vitamins in particular contribute to us experiencing energy each day.

It is also important to note at this stage in the exploration of energy that there are only two fuels for the human body: *glucose* and *fat*. The body typically uses a combination of both, and the nervous system predominantly decides which fuel is most appropriate in each moment, explored in a later section.

Carbohydrates

Carbohydrates supply the body with glucose, the fuel you use first when you start to exercise, and the fuel that your brain, nervous system, kidneys and red blood cells prefer. One gram of carbohydrate supplies the body with four calories of energy. It is, however, important to note that when the number of calories a food contains is measured, it does not reflect what I refer to as the "metabolic consequences" of that food. For example, when you consume foods that contain carbohydrates, your pancreas secretes insulin to deal with the increase in blood glucose, and insulin signals to the body to store fat. Dietary fat, on the other hand, does not drive an insulin response, so the calories you obtain from foods rich in fats do not hormonally signal the body to store fat. The metabolic consequences and the fat-storing or burning signals the body receives are explored in detail in my book *The Calorie Fallacy*.

Science has attempted to distinguish carbohydrates from one another, as explained below. I simply want you to understand that the source of the carbohydrates matters, and I encourage you to obtain your carbohydrates from wholefoods as they come with a range of different nutrients, some of which contribute to their digestion and hence their ability to supply you with energy.

Carbohydrates can be sweet or starch-based. Simple and complex are two of the categories science has divided carbohydrates into, although this happens less often these days. Simple carbohydrates are sugars, lollies, soft drinks, fruit juice and other sweet products. Simple carbohydrates are usually quick energy; they enter your bloodstream quickly and are either used up or stored as fat, and typically offer little or no nutritional value. In fact, they may actually take away from your health. Complex carbohydrates, on the other hand, are sources of extended energy: sweet potato, brown rice and pumpkin all fall into this category. The energy from complex carbohydrates typically (although not always) takes longer to enter the bloodstream, and provides a more sustained form of energy.

The *glycaemic index* (*GI*) is another way of defining carbohydrates. This index is a scale based on how quickly the glucose from the food will hit the bloodstream. Essentially, the faster it gets to the bloodstream, the higher it appears on the index and the more insulin (a fat-storage hormone) is required. However, the GI does not take into account the amount of carbohydrate in a food. *Glycaemic load* (*GL*) is a better indicator of how a carbohydrate food will affect blood glucose levels. GL considers the actual amount of carbohydrate you eat in a sitting. For example, some types of carrots are considered a high GI carbohydrate, but are high in fibre, water, vitamins, minerals and protective phytonutrients, which alters the way they are digested and promotes excellent health. Their GL is low (a good thing). Worth noting is that both GI and GL are affected by the protein, fat and fibre content of a meal, as they all slow down the release of glucose into the blood and hence the requirement for insulin.

Many chocolate bars, on the other hand, are low GI yet they contain high levels of refined sugars, poor-quality fats, virtually no nutrients and are high GL. No wonder people feel confused and overwhelmed at times about dietary information! However, we don't need science to tell us that a carrot is a better food choice than a chocolate bar. Let's bring back common sense!

Fructose has a low GI too. In fact, the way fructose is digested and utilized by the body is different from glucose. It requires an enzyme from the liver to convert it into glucose. Only liver cells can take up fructose, whereas all cells in the body can utilize glucose, and the impact of excessive fructose consumption on liver health is finally coming to light. In other words, the GI can be highly misleading if that is all you use to guide your carbohydrate choices. Common sense is a better guide or simply embracing the statement "just eat real food".

Fibre refers to certain types of carbohydrates that our body cannot digest. These carbohydrates pass through the intestinal tract intact and help to move waste out of the body. Diets that are low in fibre can cause problems such as constipation and haemorrhoids, and may increase the risk of certain types of cancers such as colon cancer. Diets that contain more fibre have been shown to decrease the risk of colon cancer. However, again, I believe the source of the fibre matters. Wholefoods high in fibre that don't tend to aggravate the bowel include vegetables, some starchy carbohydrates, such as sweet potato, and some fruits, but not all. Over the 17 years I've worked with people in private practice, you see what works for people and what doesn't. And despite the mainstream advice for good bowel health encouraging high-fibre diets, based on symptoms, this can work against optimal bowel health for some people with specific bowel problems. Nutrition advice is truly best tailored to the individual.

You can see how complicated and confusing carbohydrate messages have been for consumers, which is why I opened this section with the reminder that when it comes to food, carbohydrates included, Nature gets it right and it is potentially human intervention (HI), that is, processing, that can get it so wrong. Choose low HI foods. Choose carbohydrates from wholefood sources.

Protein

A gram of protein offers the body four calories of energy, and it supplies the body with amino acids, substances that can become part of us. For example, the amino acids from foods go on to create the cells of your immune system, which helps defend you from colds and flus, as well as forming part of the anti-cancer response. Amino acids also create the neurotransmitters in your body, which influence your mood, and they create the muscles that provide us with the strength to carry our groceries and our children.

Of the 20 amino acids, 10 are considered essential (some research papers suggest nine are essential); in other words, you need to consume them in your diet as your body is unable to create them from other substances. A protein food that contains all of the essential amino acids is referred to as "complete". Most vegetable-based protein sources are "incomplete"; however, when you combine vegetable-based protein sources from different botanical families, you complete the protein, as the essential amino acid lacking in one of the foods will be high in the one from the other family. An example of this is adding sesame seeds to a vegetable stir-fry that you serve with brown rice: the seeds and the rice are from different families, and their amino acid profiles complete each other.

When people think about protein, many tend to think first of animal-based options. Chicken, beef, lamb and fish are all complete proteins. However, many people don't consume meat for a number of reasons, and many people would benefit from reducing their meat consumption. There is an array of non-meat foods out there that are also good sources of protein, as outlined below.

Keep in mind that no food in Nature is 100 per cent protein. Meat is 25 per cent protein, meaning that 100 grams of meat contains 25 grams of protein. Even the World Cancer Research Fund's (WCRF) position statement on the consumption of meat to reduce the risk of numerous cancers — in particular, breast cancer — is to "limit intake of red meat to no more than 300 grams per week". Yet I meet people who consume more than this every day. I personally don't believe the problem is the red meat itself. It can be part of a bigger health picture for a person, particularly if they don't have efficient bowel evacuation or liver detoxification pathways, or are what is known as "oestrogen-dominant", as discussed in a later section. Plus, they may be consuming meat from poorly raised animals, which have been fed poor-quality diets. Add to this the consistent lack of vegetable intake reported across many

Western diets, which means that too few cancer-protective substances are being consumed.

Given that this book is about energy, though, it is important to know that protein foods can supply the body with energy, although not directly. Proteins are broken down into amino acids, and those amino acids can be converted into glucose to be used for energy, if needed. The name of the main biochemical pathway responsible for this is *gluconeogenesis*. Because biochemically it is more efficient for the body to use glucose supplied as glucose — it is more labour-intensive for the body to convert amino acids into glucose — the body prefers to allow the amino acids to be used for their repair work, their neurotransmitter production work, muscle building and new cell building, as no other substances can do this.

Vegetarian sources of protein

Nuts and seeds

Nuts in general pack a mighty nutritional punch, providing protein and many essential vitamins, such as A and E, which are great for our skin and our heart health. They are also a good source of minerals (such as phosphorous and potassium), essential fatty acids and fibre. Raw nuts and seeds, or nut butter, are a fantastic addition to any meal, as the protein and good fats keep you feeling fuelled for longer. Nuts range in protein content from 18 to 25 grams per 100 grams.

Eggs

Egg protein is of great biological value — meaning it is easily absorbed and utilized by the body. Egg yolks contain vitamin B_{12}, which is important for vegetarians. Vitamin B_{12} improves your body's ability to use iron and generate red blood cells, which may help prevent anaemia, giving you more energy. Eggs make a fantastic breakfast option, especially served with extra greens, and they offer 12 grams of protein per 100 grams. They are not suitable for people on a vegan diet.

Quinoa

Quinoa is another good vegetarian source of protein. It is one of the only plant-based complete proteins. Remember, "complete" protein means that it contains all of the essential amino acids that are critical for the body to be able to make body proteins, like those listed above, and it provides you with about 14 grams of protein per 100 grams. It is also a wonderful option for people with coeliac disease or those with gluten sensitivity, as it is gluten-free. Botanically it is a seed, not a grain. As with all foods, let your body be your guide though, and if you notice it upsets your digestion, then park it.

Chickpeas

Chickpeas are a great vegetarian source of fibre and contain 13 grams of protein per 100 grams. Easy to incorporate into your diet in the form of hummus or falafels, they can also be used to make slow-cooked meals go further. They are easy to use in most meals as they don't have a strong flavour, and can be used with many different herbs and spices. If you have irritable bowel syndrome (IBS), they may not suit your digestive system until the IBS is resolved.

Green vegetables

Perhaps a surprise inclusion in this list, leafy green vegetables contain amino acids, the building blocks of protein. When you eat large quantities of green leaves you supply your body with these amino acids. There is compelling evidence showing that so-called "low-quality" plant protein actually allows for slow but steady synthesis of new proteins in the body — you only need to consider the muscle mass of gorillas for evidence of this. From a DNA perspective, gorillas are somewhat similar to humans. So the diet they naturally choose in the wild is of great interest to researchers, as their food choices haven't been influenced by marketing. Given that they have one of the highest strength ratios of any creature and their diet is 55 per cent green leaves, it shows you the power of the amino acids in the greens to contribute to muscle mass.

Lentils

Delicious, nutritious and super easy to prepare. Lentils can contain up to 18 grams of protein per 100 grams. Lentils also provide energy that is slowly released, again fuelling you for longer. Nutty and earthy in flavour, they are easy to combine into any meal. Always soak them and rinse them well before cooking.

Chia seeds

Chia seeds contain approximately 20 per cent protein and join quinoa as one of the few vegetarian sources of complete protein. They contain a wide range of nutrients, including potassium and omega-3 fats, and are great for your skin and hair, and for your vascular system. They are also a good source of fibre and can be used in place of eggs for vegan cooking.

Fat

Fats provide us with fatty acids, and they are an important source of energy. They offer us nine calories per gram. Ensuring your body is efficient at utilizing fats as a fuel source is an enormously powerful way to ensure a good and even supply of energy across your day. Too many people today are unable to efficiently use body fat as a fuel and rely predominantly on glucose. More on this later.

There are immense health and energy benefits from including fats from wholefood sources in the diet. However, one of the most commonly asked questions is: does eating fat make you fat?

I have met thousands of clients who are afraid of consuming fat. It is understandable, as for so many years the public was told that eating fat would make you fat. Sadly for the majority of the population, cutting out or eating less fat didn't make them any healthier or slimmer, for a multitude of reasons. The first thing to note is that there are different types of fat, so it is important not to generalize and say "avoid fat" or "consume fat" without first identifying and understanding which type of fat is being referenced.

There are three main categories of fats that serve your health — *saturated fats, monounsaturated fats* and *poly-unsaturated fats* — and all three fats can be obtained from eating wholefoods. And the fats that take away from your health? Most concerning are the *trans fats* and poor-quality vegetable oils, which are found mainly in processed foods, particularly deep-fried foods, processed cakes, biscuits and muesli bars, and foods with long shelf-lives. Trans fats are created when some types of polyunsaturated fats are damaged due to heat and processing.

The ratio of fats consumed can also be a problem. Within the polyunsaturated category, there are two types of fat — the omega-3s and the omega-6s — with the inflammation-promoting omega-6 fats typically too high in many people's diets.

The essential fatty acids: omega-3 and omega-6

The omega-3 fats that must be consumed daily are *eicosapentaenoic acid* (*EPA*) and *docosahexaenoic acid* (*DHA*), which the body can convert from another essential fatty acid called *alpha-linolenic acid* (*ALA*), which also must be consumed. However, the conversion of ALA into the critical EPA and DHA fats is inefficient in some people. Hence, it is wise to include adequate amounts of all of these fats in your diet. The health benefits of EPA and DHA are well documented, and they are powerful anti-inflammatories. They take up residence in the membrane (outside layer) of the cell and are able to exert their anti-inflammatory effects and keep the cells flexible. Due to their physical structure (which contains double bonds), they themselves, however, oxidize easily and are best consumed with an antioxidant-rich diet, which is one that is high in coloured plant foods.

The omega-6 essential fatty acid is called *linoleic acid* (*LA*), which the body elongates (converts) into the vital *gamma linolenic acid* (*GLA*). GLA can also be consumed, a necessary dietary action if people are inefficient at converting LA into GLA. This is usually true for people with eczema; their skin does better having the GLA supplied directly.

The typical Western diet is overabundant in omega-6 fatty acids — found in many processed foods, baked goods, and grains — and lacking in omega-3s. DHA is found in cold-water fish, such as salmon and mackerel, while the other omega-3 fat, EPA, is found in flaxseeds, chia seeds and walnuts. A good choice in the omega-6 EFA category is evening primrose oil, which contains GLA and has been shown to help people with eczema take up fat into their skin, allowing it to soften and be moisturized.

Medium-chain triglycerides
All fats and oils are composed of fat molecules called *fatty acids*, and there are two methods of classifying fatty acids. The one you are probably most familiar with is based on saturation. As outlined above, there are saturated fatty acids, monounsaturated fatty acids and polyunsaturated fatty acids. The second method of classification is based on molecular size or the length of the carbon chain (its backbone) in the fatty acid. There are *short-chain fatty acids* (*SCFAs*), *medium-chain fatty acids* (*MCFAs*) and *long-chain fatty acids* (*LCFAs*). Another term you will often see in reference to fatty acids is *triglyceride*. Three fatty acids joined together make a triglyceride, so you may have *short-chain triglycerides* (*SCTs*), *medium-chain triglycerides* (*MCTs*) or *long-chain triglycerides* (*LCTs*).

The vast majority of the fats and oils you eat — whether they are saturated or unsaturated, or come from an animal or a plant — are composed of long-chain triglycerides. Studies suggest that at least 98 per cent of all of the fats that most people eat consist of LCT. However, some food, such as coconut, is rather unique as it is composed

> *The typical Western diet is overabundant in omega-6 fatty acids — found in many processed foods, baked goods, and grains — and lacking in omega-3s.*

predominantly of MCT. Organic butter also contains some MCTs.

MCTs are broken down almost immediately by enzymes in the saliva and gastric juices, so that pancreatic fat-digesting enzymes are not even essential for their digestion, which is great for people who experience challenges with their digestive system. In the digestive system, MCTs are broken down into individual fatty acids (MCFAs). Unlike other fatty acids, MCFAs are absorbed directly from the intestines into the portal vein (a vein that goes straight to the liver) and sent immediately to the liver where they are, for the most part, burned as fuel. They can therefore offer the body an energy supply that is highly efficient ... provided your body gets the message from your nervous system that it is "safe" for you to use fat as a fuel. Like I said, more on this later.

Other fats require pancreatic enzymes to break them into smaller units. They are then absorbed into the intestinal wall and packaged into bundles of fat (lipid) and protein called *lipoproteins*. These lipoproteins are carried by the lymphatic system, bypassing the liver, and are dumped into the bloodstream, where they are circulated throughout the body. As they circulate in the blood, their fatty components are distributed to all the tissues of the body. The lipoproteins get smaller and smaller, until there is little left of them. At this time, they are picked up by the liver, broken apart, and used to produce energy or, if needed, repackaged into other lipoproteins and sent back into the bloodstream to be distributed throughout the body. Cholesterol, saturated fat, monounsaturated fat and polyunsaturated fat are all packaged together into lipoproteins and carried throughout the body in this way. In contrast, medium-chain fatty acids are not packaged into lipoproteins but go to the liver where they are converted into energy.

One MCFA deserves special mention and that is *lauric acid (LA)*. Both coconut and butter contain lauric acid, which is known for its contribution to a healthy gut bacteria profile. It has also been scientifically shown to have a stronger action against the bacteria often involved with acne than benzoyl peroxide, an ingredient in many medicated skin washes and some prescription acne medications. As an aside, butter from pasture-fed cows also contains *conjugated linoleic acid* (*CLA*), a relative of LA, which research has shown to have anti-cancer properties as well as anti-inflammatory actions.

An adequate consumption of healthy fats plays a crucial role in maintaining the health of your precious organs and great energy. Some wholefoods are composed of fatty acids that are essential for life, and fatty acids help the body to absorb the fat-soluble vitamins — vitamins A, D, E and K.

Even with that tip of the fat information iceberg, I hope you can begin to see that the "fat-free" fad took away a much-needed food, fuel and nourishment source from too many people. What is so sad is that "fat-free" mostly meant that the fat was replaced with refined sugars and, to mask the increase in sweetness in the food supply, a bucket-load of poor-quality salt was added! Through that low-fat era, the Western world ate more sugar and more salt than ever before in human history. The way to not get caught up in food and nutrition fads is to remember that when it comes to food, Nature gets it right and it is potentially HI that can get it so wrong.

Fat chosen from real-food and wholefood sources is impera-tive for great energy and optimal health. "Real-food fat" is satiating. It can help mediate inflammation in the body, is an integral part of a healthy immune system, is essential for the health of your skin, eyes, nails and hair, *and* you need to eat fat to help you to burn fat as an energy source. Consuming the right kind of fat will help you feel happy and content and fuller for longer. Most people also find that their desire for sweet food diminishes with more wholefood fat sources in their daily diet, again better at supporting great and even energy levels.

A breath of fresh air is a great thing to take —
and an even better thing to be.

Anon

The Nervous System and Fatigue

As I mentioned in the previous section, in any given moment the body is making a decision about which fuel to use. And it can only choose between glucose and fat, or a combination of both. The nervous system plays a major role in this decision-making, so it is a critical body system to understand when it comes to energy. This is because fat and glucose drive very different types of energy — sustained energy or a more crash-and-burn style. I have discussed the nervous system in some of my other books, but always in relation to the topic of that particular book — for example, weight loss or rushing — not in relation to energy. And this system can be such a vital piece of someone's energy health picture that it warrants a decent discussion here.

The nervous system makes countless decisions about so many things each day. And night. Fundamentally, we are hard-wired for survival. However, in this day and age, the messages from our environment can easily signal to our nervous system that our life is in danger when it isn't. And that can have significant consequences for our energy.

The autonomic nervous system

Everything in our internal and external environments, including the food we eat, the exercise we do (or not), and the thoughts we think, influences our nervous system. To understand this, we need to explore how the *autonomic nervous system (ANS)* works. The ANS "runs" our body behind the scenes and it is not under our conscious control. It regulates our heart rate, our respiration rate, our temperature control, and our immune and hormonal systems while we carry on with life. Don't you think it is truly miraculous that if you cut yourself the wound just heals? Don't you think it is amazing that you swallow food and your digestive system extracts the nutrients to nourish you so that you can stay alive? The human body is extraordinary and that's an understatement.

There are three parts to the ANS. They are the *sympathetic nervous system* (*SNS*), the *parasympathetic nervous system* (*PNS*), and the *enteric nervous system* (*ENS*). Here I will focus on the SNS, the "fight, flight or freeze" response, and the PNS, the "rest, digest and repair" arm, and their interaction.

In general, the SNS and the PNS have opposite functions. When we are under stress, the SNS raises our heart rate, increases our respiratory rate, releases stress hormones, and shunts blood away from the digestive tract to the muscles so that we can run away from or fight whatever is threatening us. If organ systems in the body are unhealthy and therefore stressed themselves, or if we are mentally or emotionally stressed, that increases the sympathetic load as well. The SNS by its very nature is catabolic, meaning that it breaks down muscle tissue due to the increased amounts of secreted cortisol (a stress hormone). High-intensity exercise is also sympathetic in nature: the heart rate goes up, as does respiration and body temperature, and cortisol is released into the blood. And over the course of this book, you will come to know the role cortisol plays in energy, both directly and indirectly, through the influence it exerts on other body systems, such as insulin.

Once the "threat" is dealt with (is it ever dealt with in the modern world?), the PNS slows our heart rate and respiration, and it brings the blood back to the digestive tract so that we can digest our food. It also works on repairing any tissues that have been damaged in our "battle" and allows libido to be restored. Your survival instinct doesn't want you thinking about reproduction when your body believes that your life is being threatened.

The PNS is able to do its wonderful work overnight, provided we go to bed early enough, because cortisol — a hormone linked to energy, body fat and inflammation, as you will soon see — naturally starts to rise around 2am. The SNS and the PNS are designed to balance each other out. We are not supposed to be "stuck" in SNS dominance, yet far too many people today do live in SNS dominance, which is damaging their health and energy.

When you live consistently in SNS dominance, your energy tends to be inconsistent. You fire up and then you crash, and the choices you make when you crash can set you up to fire up again, and quite often those choices are nutritionally of a poor quality. They will typically involve caffeine, sugars or starches, or all three, and be quick "fixes" out of packets based on convenience, rather than nutritional value. SNS dominance can be a reason why, even though you have good nutrition knowledge, it doesn't translate into you following through on that knowledge. Let's face it. You don't polish off a packet of chocolate biscuits thinking you are going to feel amazing afterwards. You don't do that from a lack of knowledge; you do it for biochemical or emotional reasons, or both. And one of the biochemical reasons can be living in an SNS-dominant state.

Anxiety is so incredibly common today, often as a result of relationship challenges, financial stress, a poor diet and its consequences, worries about health (your own or a loved one's) or weight, or whether you have upset someone. Yet a person may be in sympathetic overload and still not even mention feeling anxious, as they have become so accustomed to that state. Adrenalin — one of the hormones behind SNS dominance — is one of the major hormones that drives humans to feel anxious, and decreasing its production is key to shifting this. After a day or a week that was full of anxieties, are you energized or depleted? And when you start to think about energy as a currency — a currency of health, one which is far better and more accurate than weight — you want to do all you can for an even and sustained energy output.

What activates the SNS? Caffeine and our perception of pressure and urgency. What activates the PNS? Lengthening the exhalation of breath. And from PNS activation, energy is sustained, even, centred, focused and yet calm. Constant

SNS dominance is draining and unsustainable because of the hormones involved, but also because of the consequences that it drives.

Reducing the sympathetic load is essential for great energy if the SNS is dominant. Movement is important, but it is best approached from a gentle angle and with a nurturing attitude, rather than at a go-go-go speed. Far more effective exercise for SNS-dominant people is breath-focused and restorative, such as t'ai chi, qi gong, yoga, or any exercise that is done slowly and while being conscious of the breath. These types of exercise significantly assist in increasing PNS activity, which helps balance the ANS. Building muscle is also critically important to — among other things — metabolic rate, increasing and enhancing mitochondrial function and hence energy, and long-duration high-intensity workouts tend to break muscle down, not build it. Once the nervous system is better balanced, energy, sleep and mood quality will all improve, and you will most likely find that this concept is game-changing to the way you approach your body, your health and your energy.

The nervous system and body fat

The reason body fat information has to be included in a book about energy is that body fat is a major source of energy for the body. And when it isn't, significant problems with energy arise. Not only do your clothes stop fitting well, but, even more importantly, fatigue kicks in way sooner than it would if you were an efficient fat-burner. Here's how it works.

In any given moment the human body is making a decision about which fuel to use based on the information it is receiving from internal and external environments. The only two fuels for the human body are glucose ("sugar") and fat. Really think about that. You don't use protein for fuel. The body breaks proteins down into amino acids, which are then converted into glucose so the body can use that glucose as fuel (energy). As we learned earlier, the name of this biochemical pathway is *gluconeogenesis*. The body requires energy for everything it does, from walking to sleeping, laughing to blinking — it all requires fuel.

As you have learned, adrenalin communicates to every cell of your body that your life is in danger and it prepares you to fight or flee. However, you may be making adrenalin simply because you have to make a phone call that you would rather not make, or perhaps because you have gulped down three coffees already today. Or maybe your dad yelled at you a lot when you were a child, and so, even though you know now that your dad yelled a lot because that

> *T*he majority of stress for most people in the Western world today is psychological rather than physical, and it can be constant and relentless.

was how he coped with how stressed he felt (rather than it being about his lack of love for you), now when a male in your life raises their voice in your vicinity, you instinctively go into the fight-or-flight response. The majority of stress for most people in the Western world today is psychological rather than physical, and it can be constant and relentless.

You have also learned that stress activates the SNS, which has an intimate relationship with adrenalin. This fight-or-flight response, whether your thinking mind is telling you so or not, means that your body is saying you need a fast-burning fuel to get out of the stressful situation — and get out of there fast! So what fuel do you think your body will choose when it needs to flee, to get out of "danger" fast? Remember, its only choice is to either burn glucose or fat … In this scenario, it will choose glucose every time. The body thinks that it has to in order to save your life, and it's all about survival. The body doesn't feel "safe" enough to use fat, because fat offers a steady, slow-release form of energy, which is not what is needed in a time of danger. Fat can be burned effectively in a PNS-dominant state, because the body perceives it is safe when the PNS is activated. Yet, the PNS can never be the dominant arm of the ANS — it can never steer the ship — while the body perceives there may be a threat to your life. This alone can be a significant block to utilizing body fat as a fuel, and therefore to weight loss (if that is desirable), to a lovely sustained energy output, an even mood and good-quality sleep.

The glucose stored in our muscles and liver as glycogen is mobilized whenever our body gets the message that it is needed, when there is not enough glucose to fuel our escape left in our blood from our last meal. This mobilization of glycogen out of the muscles due to stress can, over time, impact the function, strength and appearance of our muscles, including allowing the onset of cellulite.

I believe that one of the most enormous health challenges of modern times is that the body can constantly be on the receiving end of the fight-or-flight message. There are so many stress factors, internal and external to us, that we have to begin to actively choose not to go there, not to get caught up in the rush. And to take steps in our daily lives to allow our nervous system to have some balance. Without this, using fat as a fuel can be an uphill battle, and feeling energized becomes a significant challenge.

Craving sugar

For many people today, they know they need to eat less sugar or cut it out completely. You would have to have had your head buried in the sand not to know that eating refined sugars does not serve your health in any way. Yet, even with a great understanding of this topic and even with the desire to change dietary sugar habits, many people describe it being a major challenge for them on their road to outstanding health. So why is it that so many people crave sugar so intensely?

One reason is certainly habit. Another is its infiltration into the food supply, even into savoury-tasting foods, and taste preferences for sweeter and sweeter foods is also playing a role. It is a case of more begets more. Very few people go back after dinner for a second helping of broccoli. Yet what most people are not familiar with is the impact of stress hormone production on sugar cravings.

As you now understand, there are only two fuels for the human body: glucose and fat. And when you are living on stress hormones because of too much caffeine or due to your perception of pressure and urgency, your body predominantly uses glucose as its fuel, not body fat. Glucose burns quickly, like petrol on the flames of a fire, while fat is more like a log of wood on a fire; both fuel the fire, but one gives out a sustained energy and the other is used up very quickly. This has major consequences to a host of processes, including the foods you might crave. A person weighing 70 kilograms has the capacity to store about 2,500 calories of glucose (as glycogen in their liver and muscles) and about 130,000 calories of fat. So the more your body thinks it needs to use glucose as your fuel to help you escape from danger, the more it needs to keep your "get out of danger" fuel tank full. So you crave it to support yet another survival mechanism.

For too many people in the Western world today, they regularly over-consume caffeine, feel pressured about their work, money, relationships or their body, feel like all of their tasks are urgent, like there aren't enough hours in the day and they scratch the itch of their "not enoughness" – feeling like whatever they do, it is never enough. Then they crave a glass or two of wine in the evenings for the sugar and to help them relax, even though underneath they are utterly exhausted. Many people have become so accustomed to living this way that they don't even notice how stressed they are anymore. Anxiety is rife, yet most people who experience it are not aware that caffeine intake leads them to make the very hormone that drives anxious feelings. If you experience such feelings, caffeine needs to be the first thing that goes.

When you live like this, your body will predominantly use glucose as a fuel, in preference to body fat, and it will only switch back to being an efficient fat-burner if you make some changes. You can start with the food — some people do — yet for others starting here is precisely why they have made no progress in decreasing or cutting out refined sugars and refined starches in their diet. (Both sugars and starches are all broken down to glucose in the digestive system.)

So if you know starting with the food is not your way, then park it. You can start by focusing on activating your PNS, which means embracing diaphragmatic breathing. This may take the form of a restorative, breath-focused practice, such as restorative yoga, t'ai chi, meditation, or simply regular intervals across the day where you commit to 20 long, slow breaths that move your belly as you breathe. It is a matter of retraining yourself to breathe in this way, instead of the short, sharp, shallow breaths in your upper chest that adrenalin drives. The calmer you feel, the more your PNS is activated, the less sugar your *body* will need to keep the glucose fuel tank full.

To breathe in this way, when you inhale through your nostrils, your tummy starts to stick out, don't hold your breath, simply pause and then as you slowly exhale, your tummy slowly shrinks back in. It can help to place your hands on top of each other just below your navel. That way, you can focus on moving your hands in and out as you breathe. Be patient with yourself, for if you have been breathing in a short, sharp shallow way for months, years or even decades, then it can take some time before your abdomen wants to move in and out with your breath. Some people describe to me a feeling that they can't get their breath past their heart. This is often the case if people have felt anxious for quite a while. Breath-work and also addressing any potential challenges with progesterone production (in females) can assist with this.

Increasing your intake of green vegetables and/or dietary fats from wholefood sources can also make a big difference to your desire for sugar. A high intake of green leafy vegetables for a minimum of 21 days starts to change your taste preferences, as greens have a bitter taste base. When it comes to fat, if you have lived through the "low-fat, high-carb" era and became conscious of your dietary fat intake, you may not be eating enough of it. Notice when you crave sugar and significantly increase your intake of fats at the meal prior to the typical craving time. For example, if the middle of the afternoon is your tough time — craving-wise and probably also with your energy — then eat more wholefood fat at lunchtime. Fat is incredibly satiating and you will notice it will fuel you for longer through your afternoon. Yet if you still have the mindset that counting calories is your only road to weight loss, you will never let yourself eat the fat, given that it has the highest number of calories per gram. However, when you eat carbohydrates it leads the body to make insulin, which signals the body to store fat, whereas when you eat dietary fat, no fat-storage-signalling hormones are released. Not all calories behave equally *inside* the body, a concept I explore in detail in my book *The Calorie Fallacy*.

Steps to address stress

So how do you support your nervous system for great and consistent energy?

* Embrace a restorative practice.
* Commit to regular diaphragmatic breathing.
* Instead of focusing on eating less sugar, focus on eating more dietary fats from wholefoods and/or green vegetables. Decrease or omit caffeine for four weeks (and keep on doing so if it makes you feel much calmer), or switch from coffee to green tea so that you consume smaller amounts of caffeine buffered by the effects of theanine in the green tea.
* Explore your perception of pressure and urgency. Have you made what you have to do each day full of pressure and urgency? Or is it a busy life, full of opportunity that is so ridiculously privileged because all of your basic needs are met? Of course there is real pressure and real urgency in this world. But save that perception for when you really need it, not your everyday existence. (This is explored in detail in my book *Rushing Woman's Syndrome*.)
* Explore your emotional landscape by reading books or seeing a psychologist or health professional experienced in this area, if feeling like you are not good enough resonates for you.

★

*E*nergy creates actions and actions
create habits and habits create outcomes.
And the momentum of this creates consistency
and that creates confidence.
It all starts with energy.

Dr Libby

Sleep: Its Role in Your Energy

We cannot fight our biology. The human body requires sleep so that an enormous array of processes are supported and repaired within. Plus it has a rejuvenation factor that allows you to bound out of bed with energy, ready for the day ahead. Has it been a while since you've felt this way? Sadly, yes it's true. Far too many people these days wake up just as exhausted as when they went to bed. So why has sleep stopped being refreshing for so many people? Let's explore this topic, which I feel incredibly passionate about for a huge number of reasons.

When you are exhausted, everything in life feels more difficult, so I want this section to give you very practical information, things you can actually apply to your life to make a really big difference in this area. However, before we discuss what to do about sleep that is not restorative, it is first important for you to understand *why* sleep can become disrupted and ineffective in its purpose of rest, repair and restoration. I also want to show you how common it is now to sleep poorly — common, but not normal, as I like to say.

In February 2013, my team and I conducted a survey asking people who read our Facebook page (facebook.com/ DrLibbyLive) about their sleep. Over 500 people answered our questions. Of those, 97 per cent shared with us that they wake up tired. Only three per cent of people reported waking up with energy.* Think about that. Waking unrefreshed is a

---

* Please note that this is not scientific research, but a survey. One could argue that people who are drawn to learn more about their body and/or who have challenges with sleep may be more likely to comment on a sleep survey. So I am simply pointing out that large numbers of people don't sleep restoratively.

really big deal with really big consequences. Furthermore, the majority of people who responded couldn't sleep through the night either, and this is an area that, once it is optimal, will make a significant difference to so many aspects of your health and energy. As I said, everything feels more difficult when we are exhausted. So let's get you sleeping restoratively.

Sleep, and the rest and repair it offers the body, is critical to life. With great sleep, we have improved memory, cognition and better immune function. Sometimes when I talk about immune function, I sense that the importance of this system doesn't fully register with some people. Many people simply link great immune function with minimizing how many colds and flus they get. Yet your immune function is critical in the prevention of cancer, as well as in the prevention of autoimmune diseases, such as multiple sclerosis, lupus, Hashimoto's thyroiditis, Graves' disease, and coeliac disease, all of which are on the rise. Taking great care of your immune system is of immense importance to your long-term health and quality of life, and sleep plays an enormous role in whether or not your immune system is able to function appropriately.

With restorative sleep, you have improved mood, enhanced physical and emotional resilience, increased physical endurance and better hormonal function. When your sleep cycles are disrupted, both your stress-hormone and your sex-hormone balances can be negatively impacted.

Everything works better with restorative sleep: your digestive system, sex hormone balance, your mood, your skin, and even your thyroid function. Clearly, energy is affected by sleep quality both directly and indirectly through some of these systems (such as thyroid hormone production). A recent clinical trial found that sleep quality impacts skin function and aging. If you have poor sleep quality or do not get enough sleep, your skin finds it harder to recover from free radical damage, such as sun exposure and environmental toxins.

I wanted to open this section by showing you just how far-reaching amazing sleep can be, because you may just think "Oh, I wake up tired most of the time, but isn't that normal?" No: it is common, but it is *not* normal. Many people blame age for why they start to feel more and more tired as the years go by, but it doesn't have to be this way. If low energy truly was down to age, then every 82-year-old I know would be exhausted, and they're not! You can make a really big difference to how you feel and function, on both the inside and the outside, through good-quality sleep.

Sleep required

How much sleep do you actually need? Requirements vary based on gender, age and individual physical demands. Some studies suggest that adults have a very basic sleep requirement of seven to eight hours per night. Other compelling studies show that eight to nine hours per night is actually critical for adults for all of the vital repair work that has to go on inside your body while you are asleep.

We are essentially the health of our cells, and cellular repair takes place during sleep. Everything from skin cells to the cells that make up your muscles need repair work overnight. When cells are working optimally, you look and feel your best. I want to remind you that we cannot fight our biology: our biology is our biology, and we need eight hours of sleep a night. When we are not getting that, all sorts of bodily functions can be disrupted, including energy systems.

Sleep requirements tend to be based somewhat on age. Newborn babies need a lot of sleep; although many of you may have experienced first-hand that some babies need more than others. Some like or need a lot of sleep, perhaps 18 hours a day, and then there are those who need somewhat less, perhaps 12 or 14 hours a day. Infants, toddlers and preschoolers need less sleep than newborns, but still substantially more than teenagers. Sleep needs continue to gradually decline, and by the time children are teenagers they need between about eight-and-a-half and nine-and-a-quarter hours per night. I have deep concerns, however, over what's happening for our teenagers, because many of them are taking back-lit devices to bed, such as iPads, laptops and cell phones. And the light that is omitted from these devices can significantly disrupt the production of the sleep hormone called melatonin. Light destroys melatonin, as you will learn more about in a moment, which is one reason why I have deep concerns for teens who may not be getting enough hours of sleep to do the vital growth and repair work that needs to happen. As mentioned above, an adult's biological requirement for sleep is essentially seven to nine hours of sleep per night.

If you have been jotting down things that resonate for you as you have gone through this book, now is a particularly important time to keep that paper close. Your willingness to open and consider new choices in all of the areas we have discussed so far begins with a good night's sleep. We are literally so tired without it.

Sleep attained

While I was gathering research for an online sleep seminar I created as well as for this book, I was curious about how much sleep people are truly getting. The data in the following graph shows sleep patterns for people in New Zealand from 1960 until 2002.

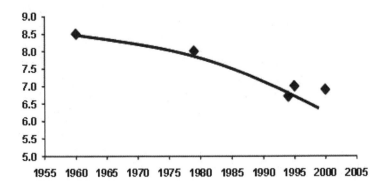

Self-reported number of hours of sleep per night. Note that the decline is a concern. (Source: Medscape)

In New Zealand in 1960, people reported that they were getting about eight-and-a-half hours of sleep each night. By

2002, the number of hours per night had dropped to six-and-a-half. If the graph continued on its current trajectory, you can see that by now, 2015, we would be down to more like five-and-a-half hours per night, which is of grave concern to our health, our longevity, how we feel, how we function, and how energized we are each day. And given that how you feel doesn't end with you — it has an impact on every single person you come into contact with — the ripple effect of lousy sleep can create additional challenges for not just your physical health but also your relationships.

Too many people aren't getting enough sleep. I also appreciate that many people make an enormous effort to get plenty of sleep but their body won't cooperate and let them sleep.

When I was working as the programme manager at the beautiful Gwinganna Lifestyle Retreat in Australia, it was a joy to look after people for a week of their lives in this gorgeous setting, full of incredible natural beauty. For those at the retreat, all meals were taken care of; the meals themselves were beautiful and also nourishing. Participants didn't have laundry to take care of or groceries to buy. Plush rooms, lovely spa treatments, and access to restorative movement ... the entire week was all about each individual having a transformative and restorative experience. At the end of each week, I always asked each group what they had loved the most during their stay. Countless people said that their favourite thing over the whole week was their sleep. This brought home to me just how invaluable sleep is. In the middle of a retreat, with every soul-nourishing amenity available, the best gift for so many was restorative sleep. It is amazing how you feel when you actually sleep well and for long enough.

Sleep as a priority

For many people to improve their sleep, it needs to become a priority. So many people today compromise their sleep to get more done in a day. They wake up earlier and go to bed later in an attempt to get more tasks done. Yet when you deeply appreciate how non-negotiable sleep is for your health and energy, you make it a priority. If you find you are someone who stays up later and later in an attempt to get more things crossed off your "to-do" list, then it may take an extreme question for you to follow through with making sleep a priority. Try asking yourself: "Will anyone die if I don't get this done?" If the answer is yes, then stay up later and do it. If the answer is no, go to bed! Some of you will have to go to this extreme to make sleep a priority. But I say this to you to bring home just how critical great-quality sleep is to outstanding energy.

Sleep stats and sleeping pills

This will help you see what a significant and widespread challenge good-quality, restorative sleep is. Many of the statistics are from New Zealand, but it is likely that the data would be relatively similar across most Western countries. Did you know:

* it takes a third of New Zealanders over 30 minutes to get to sleep?
* one complete night of sleep deprivation can be as impairing in a simulated driving test as a legally intoxicating blood-alcohol level?
* in New Zealand in 2012, almost 680,000 individual sleeping pill prescriptions were given, in a country with a total population (adults and children) of around 4.5 million?

What these statistics highlight to me is that sleep is an enormous issue for the 4.5 million people (not all of whom — obviously — are adults) who live in New Zealand and for those throughout the Western world. With 680,000 out of approximately 4.5 million citizens using sleeping pills to fall asleep and stay asleep, this shows that a significant percentage of a representative population struggles with sleep. Some people who use sleeping tablets may use them only occasionally, or for a brief time during a particularly trying time (after a bereavement, for example), while others will use them nightly. However, the numbers are still concerning. Why has such a fundamental function of our body that is essential for good energy become such a challenge?

A common scenario is that people go to their general practitioner (GP) and report that they are not sleeping well. The GP, who has more and more demands placed on them, is growing more and more time-poor. So when a patient comes in who is not sleeping well and the patient may even ask for sleeping pills just to get things back on track, the GP might just offer the prescription to support the patient in alleviating their sleep problem. And so people start to take the medication, without any real investigation done into *why* they aren't sleeping well, thinking they will only use the medication short term, just to get a good night's sleep. However, poor sleep can be just another sign the body gives you that the way you eat, drink, move, think, breathe, believe, or perceive needs to change.

What interferes with restorative sleep?

When sleeping pills are used as a bridge, as a short-term band-aid for sleep problems, there is potentially no problem. But until the deeper issue(s) that created the sleep issue in the first place are addressed, no progress will be made that allows the person to come off the sleeping pills and begin sleeping naturally again. So people come to rely on medication for their sleep, and it is this long-term use that I am concerned about. The deeper issue(s) must be addressed or other health challenges can potentially arise. I call it "getting to the heart of the matter". And sometimes the heart of the matter is physical (biochemical), such as too much caffeine or alcohol. It might be nutritional, such as a magnesium deficiency. And sometimes it is emotional. For example, you may lie awake at night worrying that you let someone down that day, or distressed at how much alcohol your partner seems to be drinking these days.

Another great thing to ask yourself is when the last time was that you slept well. If it was when you were on holiday, you can bet that stress is playing a major role in you not sleeping well in your usual life. If the last time you slept well was in a hotel, again it may be worthwhile to consider how stress may be involved, but also to look at what you are sleeping on. People often keep their beds for far too long; in a hotel, the beds tend to be newer, so it might simply be that the structural support that you are getting in a hotel allows you to rest easy. Pay attention to whether you sleep better when you have a small meal for dinner or even for some reason skip dinner. Seek help to resolve digestive system problems if this is the case for you. You might like to try omitting spicy food in the evening or eating smaller portions, as this may positively impact on your sleep and help you wake more refreshed.

Maybe the last time you slept well was after abstaining from alcohol. The reality is that alcohol disrupts rapid eye movement (REM) sleep, the fourth part of our sleep cycle, during which time the critical repair work is done inside our body. Even though alcohol actually tends to make people fall asleep quite quickly, it can disrupt sleep cycles by interfering with REM sleep. It can also lead people to wake up hot, typically between the hours of 2am and 4am. Notice how alcohol affects your sleep, and consider making changes.

The last time you slept well may have been before you had children. If you sleep quite well but your sleep is interrupted because little ones need you in the night, please remember that they are young for only a short amount of time and there will come a time when they sleep through the night. Worrying about your sleep, and disruptions that you can't do anything about, only serves to disrupt your sleep further. So I encourage you to accept that right now your sleep will be disrupted, and make the most of the nights when it is not!

Interference with melatonin production

Melatonin is your primary sleep hormone; it helps you fall asleep and stay asleep. Its production in your body is interfered with by light. Relatively speaking, it wasn't too long ago that we rose with the sun and rested soon after sundown. Obviously that changed with the invention of electricity.

When you expose your eyes to light too late into the evening through any means, including the use of back-lit devices, such as iPads, mobile phones and laptops, or you work until late under bright light or watch television, it can stop your body from producing the very hormone that is necessary for great sleep and hence is intimately linked to great energy. If you don't wake up refreshed, or particularly if you have trouble falling asleep, become very aware of how much light you are exposing your eyes to within two hours of bedtime. If sleep is a challenge for you, do what you can to only be in soft light in the lead-up to bedtime and make your bedroom a television- and wireless-device-free zone.

Another powerful way to help reset your body's own natural circadian rhythm is to get up at the same time each morning and expose your eyes to light. Preferably get up and go outside and exercise. If that is not practical for you — perhaps because you have young children who need you — then, on waking, get up and fling the curtains open and notice the day and Nature outside, exposing your eyes to light. Use this ritual to remind yourself to think of three things you are grateful for, allowing your eyes to gently be exposed to the light of this new day while you do. Commit to doing this for a week minimum, and notice if this ritual begins to make a difference to your quality of sleep and your energy.

Melatonin has an inverse relationship with serotonin, one of our happy, calm, content hormones. Inverse means that both substances can't be elevated at the same time. When one is high, the other tends to be low. Your circadian rhythm guides serotonin to be high during the day, helping you to feel good, while melatonin is designed to be high through the night, supporting your sleep.

The serotonin–melatonin seesaw, as I have come to call it, is I think one of the reasons why couples tend to have big conversations in the evening. Up until late afternoon, you may have been going along just fine, content, regardless of what was or wasn't going on in your life. Your serotonin level is still okay, and you aren't focused on anything you want. Then, if serotonin levels plummet instead of gradually falling away, you may start to feel like you want something, but you don't know what it is. Whenever you ask your brain a question, it always comes up with an answer, so be very aware of the quality of questions you ask yourself! Perhaps you say, "I feel like I want something. I'm not sure what it is, but I want something. A minute ago I felt fine and now I feel like I've got an itch I can't scratch and I want something. What do I want?!" If big things such as "I want ... to move house" or "I want ... to have a baby" don't surface, you will still be feeling like you want something, and you might decide it must be food that you want. So you will open the door of the pantry and stand there looking inside, as if the meaning of life is in that cupboard! You get what I mean.

The morning time can also prove to be a challenge for someone in this pattern, as serotonin can be slow to rise. As you now know, melatonin is destroyed by sunlight, which is partly why when you go outside and exercise in the morning you tend to feel better for much of the day than if you didn't do this. The melatonin plummets when the retina of your eyes is exposed to light and, as a result, your serotonin surges. On a day with that hormonal profile, you can cope with anything. The flip side, though, is not so appealing. If you have gone to bed after midnight, not slept well, and have children or work to get up for, or all of these factors, you may not want to rise with the sun, as you don't feel rested. If you don't have early-morning commitments and just wander out of bed at some point during the morning, your melatonin slowly seeps away, and your serotonin slowly rises. On a day like this, you may feel like you need a few coffees to get going.

If this tale is ringing true for you, step one is to start getting up at the same time each morning and going outside and moving. Or at least open the curtains and recognize that a new day has dawned. Welcome the day with t'ai chi, a walk, meditation, or a stretch — whatever feels right to your body. Commit to doing this for four weeks, every day. Your sleep, your serotonin and your energy will love you for it.

Sympathetic nervous system (SNS) dominance

Earlier we looked at SNS dominance, and now we look at how it can significantly interfere with sleep; a concept I go into great detail about in my *Rushing Woman's Syndrome* book and online programmes. Remember the SNS is behind the fight-or-flight response, driven predominantly by the stress hormone adrenalin, whereas the opposite part of the nervous system, the PNS, acts as the rest, digest, repair and reproduce arm. I could talk underwater for days about the vast impact your nervous system has on your level of wellbeing, but I'll keep the focus, this time, on sleep.

The challenge for so many people, and a major reason why they don't sleep well or feel their best, is that they are stuck in SNS dominance. I call it living from the "red zone". Historically, the only time we went into this alarm phase was when our life truly was in danger. However, today, anything that leads us to make adrenalin promotes this fight-or-flight response. And what leads us to make adrenalin? Caffeine and our perception of pressure. You'll notice that I used the word "perception" to describe pressure in the previous sentence. And that is because it is. You choose to see things this way. Too many people have made what they have to do each day full of pressure and urgency. And too many people have forgotten to see each day as one filled with ridiculous gifts, opportunities and a life that is so privileged because all of our basic needs are met, whereas, today, that is still not true for far too many people on the planet.

Your body doesn't understand that it is safe when you are churning out adrenalin, even if all you have done is had a few coffees and felt overwhelmed by how many emails you have. And some of you live on adrenalin and no longer even really feel stressed because you have become so used to it. It feels "normal" to you now. You tell yourself that it is just how life is these days. If that resonates with you, I cannot encourage you enough to read *Rushing Woman's Syndrome*. And if you don't have time to read the book — because you are in too much of a rush — do the *Rushing Woman's Syndrome Quick Start* course (at www.drlibby.com) to coach yourself out of the rush and back to living from the PNS "green zone" again.

Back to sleep. If you are churning out stress hormones and they are communicating to every cell in your body that you are not safe, your body does not want you to sleep deeply, as you need to be able to wake up quickly and save your own life. Your body has your best interests at heart. You just need to communicate to it that you are safe and that it is safe to sleep deeply and restoratively.

There is no more powerful way to activate the green zone, the PNS, than through the way that you breathe. The rest-and-digest arm of the nervous system is activated in response to diaphragmatic breathing. I know it might sound too simple to make a difference, but how you breathe consistently over a day — short, sharp, shallow breaths driven by adrenalin, or long, slow, tummy-moving diaphragmatic breaths — has an impact on your nervous system, your blood chemistry, your oxygenation, and hence your energy.

You might have noticed that many adults today breathe from the top of their chest. If you watch, this is the only part of them that moves in and out. Adrenalin drives those short, sharp breaths. Diaphragmatic breathing communicates safety to your body. It is the fastest way to decrease both adrenalin and cortisol. Simply investing some time each day in focusing on how you breathe can truly be game-changing. I believe that not too long ago we lived from PNS dominance, but now many people live in the "fight-or-flight" response for the majority of their days and years, and we actually have to schedule time to live from that calming, PNS green zone. Schedule diaphragmatic breathing. It truly is the cornerstone of calm, which is essential to restorative sleep and consistently great energy.

You can switch over to the rest-and-digest arm of the nervous system through how you breathe, and also by decreasing, or omitting, caffeine and beginning to identify where you perceive pressure in your life when you don't need to. These shifts will help the SNS lose its dominant position in your nervous system, which for some of you will help resolve your sleep challenges and help you wake with better energy.

Other factors

Any additional mechanisms that interfere with your body's ability to relax can lead to poor-quality sleep. Some of these additional factors include magnesium deficiency and worry.

Magnesium deficiency

Magnesium and other minerals are critical for the body to physically relax, particularly the muscles. However, many people today don't consume enough magnesium. The body's magnesium requirements fluctuate, too, for when we are stressed and producing adrenalin, each unit of adrenalin that is made utilizes extra magnesium. This can lead to the muscles not having enough magnesium for sufficient relaxation. For good-quality sleep, include optimal amounts of magnesium in your diet, found predominantly in green leafy vegetables, nuts and seeds. Some people's sleep and energy improve by taking a good-quality magnesium supplement.

Worry

Another factor that can play a role in not being able to sleep restoratively is worry. You might worry about paying the bills or about challenges your child is experiencing. You may be someone who worries about what others think. You may worry about things you have said or done over the day and what others said to you. You may worry about pleasing everyone in your life, and so you worry that you may have let someone down. What can you do about these things when you are lying in bed unable to sleep in the middle of the night? Nothing. Accepting while you lie there in the dark that in that restless moment there is absolutely nothing you can do to clarify or rectify a situation that may or may not even exist can be a great start. My dear mum gave me a wonderful piece of advice about worrying. She suggested: "Don't worry about anything until it is a problem." That is such good advice. You can take it one step further if you like. Even if something is a problem, worry still won't solve it. Breathe. Face the situation or the person with your authentic self and be present in that moment. Life asks this of us and we get to choose if we front up or turn away. Showing up leads to resolution, less worry and better sleep.

In some of my other books I have discussed in detail how the perceived need to keep the peace can also be a trait that leads to poor sleep. Here, I will simply say that it is important to bring curiosity to *why* you believe you have to do this — it is usually to be loved and to avoid rejection. I want to help you see *why* you do it so that you can change your response, if it is hurting your health, especially if the stress hormone production triggered by your subconscious emotional responses won't allow you to deeply rest. And I want you to truly learn: there is no peace when you have to keep the peace.

By trying to keep the peace, you have no peace, and the impact on your nervous system tension, of always living in the red zone, can take a significant toll on your health and energy. Realize that you don't have the peace you so desperately want by trying to keep the peace. With this new understanding you may find that you are able to gently and calmly have conversations with numerous people in your life that, before this insight, you would never have imagined yourself being able to do. Walking on eggshells doesn't serve you or the other person. Use your voice calmly and with good intention, as this may be your best sleep and energy tonic.

Resolve sleep challenges

If you currently don't sleep restoratively, decide to make resolving this your focus for the next 30 days. Hopefully you are making notes in your journal as you progress through this book and are capturing what speaks to you. Take action in the area(s) that resonated for you, as sleep is *critical* to every aspect of your health and energy.

Blood Oxygenation Is Critical To Great Energy

Oxygen is critical for energy creation within the body, and of course to the survival of our cells. Obviously, we, as humans, cannot survive without it. Blood carries oxygen to cells and tissues to support their metabolic activities, which includes energy creation. Low blood oxygen levels — also known as hypoxaemia — occur when the level of oxygen in arterial vessels is lower than 80 millimetres of mercury (written as mm Hg). If the oxygen level in the blood is too low, organs such as the brain and the heart can become hypoxic, meaning they are not receiving enough oxygen to function normally.

Hypoxia is a state in which the supply of oxygen is insufficient for essential life functions; hypoxaemia is a state where there is a low arterial oxygen supply — in some publications these terms are used interchangeably, just so we are clear on the use of these terms.

Mild hypoxaemia

The most common effects of low blood and tissue oxygen levels are related to the respiratory system. As a result, shortness of breath is generally one of the first symptoms. Anxiety, restlessness and headaches are also common symptoms of mild hypoxaemia. Fatigue is also a distinct symptom, yet this is often not investigated early on in someone experiencing fatigue.

It is even more important to have your GP check your blood oxygen saturation if you have a history of, for example, chronic ear infections, tonsillitis, asthma, croup, bronchitis, sinus congestion or sinus infections, and particularly if you predominantly mouth-breathe (as opposed to breathing through your nostrils with your mouth closed). Blood oxygen will likely be fine, but I raise it here as I have seen too many people with poor blood oxygenation as a major contributor to their fatigue.

In an effort to increase the amount of oxygen in the blood, the respiration rate may increase to more than 24 breaths per minute. Heart rate is also frequently elevated to above 100 beats per minute to help circulate oxygen to meet tissue demands.

Severe hypoxaemia

If hypoxaemia becomes more severe, brain function can become impaired, creating symptoms such as decreased attention span, confusion and disorientation. Breathing may become irregular, with cycles of deeper and shallower breathing occurring. Endurance for physical activity decreases further, and motor function, particularly for fine movements, can become impaired. Cyanosis, a bluish discolouration of the skin and mucous membranes, becomes visible. I have also seen this bluishness in iron-deficient children. They are not necessarily mildly (or severely) hypoxic, however, as iron is involved in the transportation of oxygen around the body in the blood; I simply use the bluishness as an indication to check for iron deficiency.

> Oxygen is critical for energy creation within the body, and of course to the survival of our cells. Obviously, we, as humans, cannot survive without it. Blood carries oxygen to cells and tissues to support their metabolic activities, which includes energy creation.

If hypoxaemia itself worsens, brachycardia (a heart rate of less than 60 beats per minute) and a drop in blood pressure may occur. Ultimately, coma and death can result from severe, untreated hypoxaemia. Please know that what I am describing here is not common but warrants description due to the crucial role blood oxygen levels play in fatigue.

Chronic hypoxaemia

A low blood oxygen level lasting for several days or longer is considered chronic hypoxaemia. The signs and symptoms will vary, depending on the severity and the duration. Fatigue, lethargy and irritability are common symptoms, as is impaired judgement. Respiratory patterns may be irregular, and arrhythmias (where the heart-beat pattern is disrupted) are also often present. Polycythaemia (an increase in the number of red blood cells) develops more slowly, accompanied by a ruddy complexion. Clubbing (a bulbous appearance to the fingertips and nails) may also occur.

Seek medical attention

Unexplained shortness of breath must always be discussed with a doctor, particularly if it occurs at rest or if it is associated with abrupt awakenings at night. This can be a potential sign of sleep apnoea, another condition that is important to understand in this exploration of energy.

Sleep Apnoea

The widely accepted definition of obstructive sleep apnoea (OSA) is a clinical condition in which there is intermittent and repeated upper airway collapse during sleep. This results in irregular breathing at night and excessive sleepiness during the day. It can be a major cause of fatigue, and one I feel must be explored here.

Complete apnoea is defined as a 10-second pause in breathing activity, while partial apnoea, also known as hypopnoea, is characterized by a 10-second period in which ventilation is reduced by at least 50 per cent. Less common than OSA is another form of sleep apnoea that results from miscommunication between the breathing muscles and the region of the brain responsible for controlling breathing.

Causes

In many people with OSA, airways become blocked due to excess body weight and a buildup of soft fatty tissue in the windpipe. It is estimated that about 70 per cent of all people with sleep apnoea are overweight. However, other issues, such as enlarged tonsils, can also contribute to sleep apnoea, as can a deviated septum or small or narrow airways in people's noses, throats or mouths. The narrowing can be structural or due to allergies that have never been diagnosed or treated, with the most common culprits being dust mites, animal hair and casein, found in dairy foods. It can also be due to an inability to retain adequate carbon dioxide in the blood, as carbon dioxide is a vasodilator, meaning one of its actions is to broaden blood vessels, thereby allowing more oxygen to be delivered throughout the body.

People who smoke and have high blood pressure are also at a higher risk of OSA, and it is more common in men. Interestingly, neck circumference can be a strong predictor of OSA. Less than 37 centimetres is considered to be low-risk, whereas a neck circumference greater than 48 centimetres has been found to be high-risk. An ear, nose and throat specialist, a GP or a dentist may also assess for the presence of nasal polyps, rhinitis or any deformity of the nose to determine the cause of any obstructions. After all, getting to the heart of sleep apnoea or low blood oxygenation and resolving them can make a world of difference to fatigue.

Symptoms of sleep apnoea

Since many sleep apnoea symptoms occur during sleep, it can initially be challenging to detect the disorder. One of the most common signs is loud, chronic snoring, often followed by choking or gasping. As sleep apnoea progresses, snoring may increase in volume and occur more frequently. However, not everyone who snores has sleep apnoea.

Other sleep apnoea symptoms include:

* daytime sleepiness
* morning headaches
* difficulty concentrating
* memory problems
* regular, repeated night-time urination
* irritability
* mood swings or symptoms of a depressed mood, and
* a dry throat on waking.

Your medical professional can conduct sleep studies, and if the above descriptions resonate for you or a loved one, and they experience significant daytime sleepiness, this is well worth investigating. The treatments are wide and varied, but all aim to ensure that adequate oxygen is entering the body, a process essential for great energy.

Energy-zapping Screen Time

As you now understand from the earlier discussion about circadian rhythms, light can disrupt the messages the body is supposed to receive to wind down and fall asleep. Certainly a major change in how many people live has occurred with the use of back-lit devices and the time we spend in front of screens, the television included.

In 2013, humans in the first world spent, on average, three hours a day in front of the television. To put this in perspective, if you watched this amount of television daily and lived to be 75 years of age you would have spent nine years of your life in front of a television. Really ponder that. Nine years of your entire and very precious life. Doesn't that seem excessive? And not only do people report feeling tired after watching a screen for extended periods, research has clearly shown this occurs.

When I am looking to help people make sustained changes to their lives, I first seek to understand what feelings or experiences the behaviour they want to change — quite often it is food-related — gives them. It might be "relaxation" or "to distract myself from my problems" or "fun". So if all I were to do was suggest that you change something — in this case, time spent in front of the television — and I didn't find out what gives you the feeling you are seeking from the screen, and help you find another way to obtain that, then you would most likely return to your original behaviour.

According to research, television viewing may not be as relaxing as you think. Yes, to an extent television can be relaxing, but only while you watch a show you enjoy. Once the show ends, people report feeling depleted of their energy and having lower levels of alertness.

Recent research found that study participants commonly reflected that television had somehow "absorbed or sucked out their energy", leaving them depleted. They said they had more difficulty concentrating after viewing than before, and that, in contrast, they rarely indicated such difficulty after reading. After playing sports or engaging in hobbies, people reported improvements in mood, yet after watching television, people's moods were about the same or worse than before they began viewing.

In addition, it has been found that people who watch a lot of television are more likely to be anxious and less happy than people who watch less television in situations where they have nothing to do.

But don't go putting your television out on the side of the road for rubbish collection just yet. Small amounts can be okay for us, depending on the topics you are watching. In small doses, some studies say it can even be beneficial. Problems with energy, however, begin to emerge when television viewing becomes excessive. And the three hours or more a day, mentioned above, is excessive.

Some of us are so unaware of how much time we spend in front of screens that it can help to keep a diary for a week to track your viewing habits. Placing a limit on how much television you watch is also a good idea. Try your best to be selective about the shows you watch rather than just watching whatever happens to be on.

And next time you are in front of the television, ask yourself this: are you watching television because you feel bored or lonely, or perhaps you have lost touch with other ways of relaxing? If this is the case, brainstorm all of the things you could do instead of watching television. For instance, you could create some real-food snacks to have ready for the days ahead, read a book, go for a walk, meditate, phone a friend you haven't spoken with for a while, watch your children sleep, or even start expanding on a new idea you have had or plan a trip away. By engaging in more active or restorative tasks, you may notice that your energy levels increase, and you are also more likely to feel happier, too.

★

*M*ost people have no idea how good
their body is designed to feel.

Anon

Dopamine, Infections and Energy

Is motivation involved in energy? Is it required for us to have energy to feel motivated, or is it the other way around — that feeling motivated gives us energy? Let's explore a key substance for motivation and see whether it is a chicken-or-egg scenario.

A host of neurotransmitters contribute to the regulation of pain, pleasure and motivational factors affecting human behaviour. Dopamine is one of them, and one which, in clinical practice, I have seen have a powerful impact on people's lives — both positively and negatively. Dopamine can make a significant difference to an individual's energy level, and its role in how motivated we feel — which is ultimately linked to energy — is also undeniable.

However, the widespread belief that dopamine regulates pleasure could be consigned to history with recent research results on the role of this neurotransmitter. Researchers have proved that dopamine regulates motivation, causing individuals to initiate and persevere to obtain something either positive or negative. It was believed that dopamine regulated pleasure and reward and that we release it when we obtain something that satisfies us, but in fact the latest scientific evidence shows that this neurotransmitter acts *before* that. It actually encourages us to act. In other words, dopamine is released in order to achieve something good or to avoid something "evil", as the researchers put it. Studies have shown that dopamine is released as a result of pleasurable sensations — keeping in mind that what is pleasurable to one person may not be to another — and its levels are also impacted by stress, pain or loss.

Dopamine levels are highly individual, and science shows that this can be linked to the reasons why some people are more persistent than others to achieve a goal. Dopamine leads humans to maintain a level of activity to achieve what they desire, which requires both motivation and energy. Think about a motivated person: do you picture them as energetic or lethargic? Typically they are energetic, and dopamine appears to play a role in this.

This in principle is positive; however, it will always depend on the stimuli that are sought — whether the goal is to be a good student or to drive a car too fast, for example. High levels of dopamine are also thought to contribute to, and partially explain, the behaviour of thrill-seekers, as they are more motivated to act.

Dopamine-related insights into depressed mood and addictions

To understand the neurobiological parameters that drive people to be motivated by something is important to many areas of life, such as work, education or health. Dopamine is now seen as a core neurotransmitter to address symptoms such as poor energy in general, but is particularly related to the lack of energy that occurs in states such as those which occur with a depressed mood. Science has shown that low dopamine levels are a major contributor to why people with low mood don't feel like doing anything. People with fibromyalgia report similar findings.

In the opposite scenario, dopamine may be involved in addictive behaviours leading to what has been described as "an attitude of compulsive perseverance". If dopamine production is excessive and somewhat unregulated, people can find themselves feeling out of control in seeking thrilling stimulation — anything that will create more dopamine to sustain their heightened state. This might show up as sky-diving, drug-taking, aggression, or a host of other behaviours.

When working with clients, I always seek to understand why someone expresses the behaviours they do. Of course, there are a wide range of reasons — genes, epigenetics, nutritional status, stress hormone production, family dynamics and relationships, trauma and even infections are just some of them.

Brain infection directly alters brain chemistry

Having done my PhD in a laboratory with exceptional brains who were experts and pioneers in biochemistry, immunology, microbiology and nutrition, I was exposed to ways of approaching dysfunction and disease in the body that has changed the course of my thinking and my approach to health, and the way I investigate and support people in their quest for healing from illness or for an improved level of wellbeing.

One of the major principles they taught me was that infections are potentially the cause of many currently inexplicable diseases. Not necessarily overt infections, but ones that are low-grade (not driving a fever) and chronic. If you can imagine that we probably know a drop-in-the-ocean number of infective organisms compared with the total number actually on the planet

> *I*nfection can potentially alter our chemistry, and thereby our behaviours, as well as disease development.

and that can take up residence inside the human body. Add to this, that we can only test for the ones we know about and, even then, some of the ones we know about we cannot yet test for. Time and research will continue to expand our knowledge and help more people obtain the appropriate assistance they require for recovery.

An example of this is from research published in 2011, which showed infection by the parasite *Toxoplasma gondii*, found in 10 to 20 per cent of the United Kingdom's population. In the United States, it is estimated that 22 per cent of the population carry the parasite as cysts, and it is likely to be similarly prevalent in other countries where cats are kept domestically.

(Cat faeces are the source of this particular parasite.) Toxo-plasmosis can be found on unwashed vegetables, and raw or undercooked infected meat. Most people with the parasite appear to be healthy and may truly be healthy, but for those who are immune-suppressed — and particularly for pregnant women — there are significant health risks.

If this parasite enters the brain — which it can — research shows that it can directly affect the production of dopamine. The parasite infects the brain by forming a cyst within its cells and produces an enzyme called *tyrosine hydroxylase*, which is needed to make dopamine. Dopamine's role in mood, sociability, attention, motivation and sleep patterns is well documented. The enzyme tyrosine hydroxylase is a crucial step in making L-DOPA (prescribed as levodopa for Parkinson's disease), a chemical that is readily converted to the neurotransmitter dopamine.

The research group mentioned above was the first to demonstrate that a parasite found in the brain of mammals can affect dopamine levels, providing particularly important and powerful insights for people with human neurological disorders that are dopamine-related, such as schizophrenia and Parkinson's disease, even though these conditions present very differently from one another. Please note, the researchers did not suggest the parasite infection was causal of these diseases. They simply showed that this parasite has the ability to impact dopamine production, which is involved in both schizophrenia and Parkinson's disease.

This research may explain how these parasites manipulate rodents' behaviour for their own advantage. Infected mice and rats lose their innate fear of cats, increasing the chances of their being caught and eaten, which enables the parasite to return to its main host (the cat) to complete its life cycle. In this study, the research team found that the parasite caused the production and release of many times the normal amount of dopamine in infected brain cells. People with known high levels of dopamine have been shown to be more likely to take risks, and perhaps this rodent research reflects that. We still have much to learn about these mechanisms.

Dopamine—being a chemical messenger (neurotransmitter) that relays messages in the brain — controls aspects of movement, cognition and behaviour. It helps control the brain's reward and pleasure centres, and helps to regulate emotional responses such as fear. The presence of a certain type of dopamine receptor is also associated with sensation-seeking, whereas dopamine deficiency, or perhaps altered dopamine metabolism, in humans is involved in conditions such as Parkinson's disease.

These findings build on earlier studies which showed that the parasite actually encodes the enzyme for producing dopamine in its genome, meaning that *T. gondii* can orchestrate a significant increase in dopamine production in neural cells. Humans are accidental hosts to *T. gondii*, and the parasite can end up anywhere in the body, including the brain, so human symptoms of toxoplasmosis infection may depend on where the parasite ends up. This may explain the observed statistical link between incidences of schizophrenia and toxoplasmosis infection.

What has this got to do with energy? Infection can potentially alter our chemistry, and thereby our behaviours, and even disease development. Infection may simply be yet another pathway to poor energy, as the infective organism(s) divert resources away from the human utilization of them, for their own use. Therefore, supporting our immune system must be a priority for great energy and optimal health, even though it is not a system commonly linked to attaining and maintaining great energy.

To do this requires a focus on real, wholefood to provide optimal nutrition (and a lack of "pollutants" as a result), with a particular focus on vitamin C and zinc (and herbal medicine-wise I love good-quality echinacea). Adequate rest and good-quality sleep are also essential, alongside movement which is suited to you (based on what you learnt in the section about the nervous system). However, most of our immune system lines our gut, so a robust immune system must begin with good digestion.

Digestion: The Foundation of Energy

If someone is tired, the first thing I explore to help support them is their sleep patterns. Second, their digestion. Third, adrenal health and stress. When people think of fixing their low energy levels or their tiredness, I have found that they mostly try to fix it by sleeping more. And for many people, this doesn't pay off. They wake up just as tired as when they went to bed. Of course sleep will help your energy if you aren't getting enough, or improving its quality will help you feel better if your sleep quality is currently poor. But sleep won't resolve your personal energy deficit if your tiredness is the result of dysfunction in another body system, a nutrient deficiency, or emotional grief or sadness, for example. And poor digestion is at the heart of lousy energy for many. Without good digestion, nothing works properly, including your experience of energy. As digestion is the nourishment basis from which springs all of our other body processes — and thereby ensures optimum or compromised performance — we will be looking at digestion in depth. This chapter is therefore a biggie!

The foundation of nourishment

I have included a chapter about digestion in each of my previous four paperbacks; a page of information about this topic even appears in my cookbooks. I have to include it here as well, because it is central to every aspect of health and energy, including influencing what calories are worth, via the types of gut bacteria that inhabit our large intestine. If you have read my other books, feel free to skip this section, although it might be worth re-reading this material to help you really understand the concepts and then be able to apply them. This is particularly important if your energy is low.

You may be someone who has intermittent challenges with your bowel or upper gastrointestinal system. If so, you may notice that when your digestive system is not behaving you feel fatigued. To understand how good digestion is critical to good energy, let's first explore how the digestive system works.

The digestive system

When making changes to optimize your energy, improving your digestion is a key place to start. We all know that it is best to build a house on a strong foundation, and building a robust digestive system is much the same. Gut issues are widespread, with one in five women in many Western countries reportedly suffering from IBS. You only have to look at the amount of advertising targeted at improving gut health to see the prevalence of this problem. Improving digestion can have the most profound effect on your overall health and appearance. With simple, easy steps, you can experience radical changes.

It never ceases to amaze me how magnificent and how clever our bodies really are, and it astounds me how many processes go on inside the body without us having to give them any thought. Digestion is one of those processes, and it is central to every aspect of our wellbeing; it is the way we get all of the goodness out of our food, and the nourishment we get as a result of good digestion is an extraordinary gift without which we would not survive.

Digestion is intricate and complex, and yet relatively robust. And it is intimately connected to how you feel and function every single day, from your energy level to the fat you burn, from the texture and appearance of your skin to whether you have a bloated tummy, right down to your mood. Digestion is responsible for so much that goes on inside us. If it is a body system that gives you grief, if you are bloated most evenings, if you have intermittent diarrhoea and/or constipation, or if you get reflux, you can reach a point where you feel as though this is how life is always going to be. It must just be how you are. Perhaps you believe it is "in the family". Well, bowel challenges do *not* have to be your reality.

After sleep quality and hygiene, digestion is the first place to start for amazing energy. It can be a challenge to balance hormones, for example, if your digestion is the bane of your life. Likewise, if the gut is not working optimally, it will often show up in the skin, as the skin is just another pathway of elimination for the body. Some of the information in this section may make you grin or screw your face up ... it can be a challenge to find the right words to describe our stools. And some of the advice may at first seem obvious and too simple to make much of a difference. But reflect on your own eating habits and digestive system functions as you read on, and be ready to take your vitality to a new level.

How the digestive system works

Digestion sustains us. It is the process of breaking down food so that we can absorb and utilize it for energy, and to maintain life. Food is simply broken down into smaller components. For example, as we saw earlier, proteins are broken down into amino acids, and it is through this breakdown of food, and our absorption of these smaller substances, that we are nourished and our life is maintained.

The digestive system is made up of a digestive tract — a big, long tube (like a hose) — and numerous ancillary organs, including the liver, the gallbladder and the pancreas. The following illustration gives you an idea of what it looks like and how it works. The big, long tube begins at your mouth, moves down the oesophagus, then through a valve and into your stomach. The food then moves through a valve on the bottom side of the stomach and into the small intestine, through the small intestine and ileocaecal valve into the large intestine, and from there any waste is excreted out of the other end. When this process works well, you look and feel fantastic. When it is in any way impaired, the opposite can be true, and correcting it can change your life.

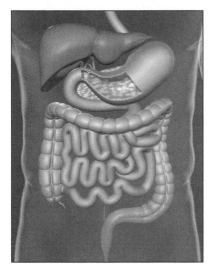

The human digestive system: The oesophagus enters the stomach (a cut-away section is shown above). The tube continues into the small intestine (the smooth tube above) and then into the large intestine (the indented tube section above). Finally, the waste is excreted. The liver is shown high on the left, the gallbladder is tucked in underneath the liver on the left, and the pancreas appears to sit behind the stomach pouch in the centre of the upper third of the image.

Supporting digestion

While digestion usually takes place without you being aware of it, there are ways in which you can help the process be efficient. As digestion is about breaking food down to extract nutrients and expelling what is not needed, you can help the process by selecting what food you give it to work with, and by making the breaking-down process easier. The following are some ways in which you can support your digestive system and begin to experience better energy as a result.

Chew your food

Food enters the mouth and moves down the oesophagus into the stomach. But what do we do to our food before it reaches the stomach? We chew it — or, in some cases, inhale it! There are no more teeth beyond the mouth: we can't chew food once it has left our mouth. Yet so many people eat as though their oesophagus is lined with teeth. Many of us are in such a hurry with our meals, or we are so excited by the flavour of our food, that we might chew each mouthful four times if we are lucky. It is a case of chew, chew, chew, chew, mmmm yum, next forkful in, chew, chew, oh gosh my mouth is so full, better swallow some food. So we swallow some partially chewed food and some not-at-all-chewed food — and we do this day in, day out, year after year. And somehow we expect our stomach to cope. This alone can be the basis of digestive system problems, such as bloating, that appear further along the tract.

The chewing action also sends a message to the brain to send a message to the stomach to let it know that food is on its way. When we inhale our food, this doesn't happen. The stomach can get to a point where it doesn't like the rules by which you are playing anymore, and it finds it difficult to operate efficiently. So, slow down! Chew your food!

If you are a food inhaler, try this: put food into your mouth, chew it really well, and then swallow it before you put the next mouthful in. I know that sounds simple, but try it. It can take an enormous amount of concentration for food inhalers to change their eating behaviours. Put your fork or spoon down between each mouthful if that helps. Engage in conversation between mouthfuls if you are eating with others. Savour the flavours, and the flavour combinations. Or think of your own technique to slow yourself down, if you rush your food. You need to pay attention when you eat to *how* you eat.

Watch portion size

Now, back to the stomach, the first place food lands after you swallow it. Make a fist and observe its size. That is how big your stomach is without any food in it. Tiny, isn't it? So, think about what happens when you pile your plate high in the evening and swallow that big mountain of food. Your stomach has to stretch to accommodate it. And food sits in the stomach for a minimum of 30 minutes to allow the stomach acid and other digestive juices to keep breaking down the food.

Once your stomach gets used to being stretched, it expects to do so every day, and this stretching is the reason why, if you decide to eat less or go on a "diet", you tend to feel hungry after your meals for around four days, as it can take a few days for the nerve endings around your stomach pouch to shrink back.

The nerves fire when they reach a certain stretching point, and then send a message to the brain to let you know you have eaten.

This is one of the numerous mechanisms we have that have the potential to tell us to stop eating, that we have had enough. The trouble is that for some of us the stomach is so used to being stretched that, by the time the nerves fire, we may have already over-eaten, started to feel lousy, and begun to berate ourselves.

The process described above is how carbohydrates let us know we have eaten. With fat and protein, however, as soon as we start to chew, messages are already being sent from the mouth to the satiety centre of the brain to let us know we are eating. These signals usually reach the brain within five minutes of chewing, while the stomach-stretch method can take more like 20 minutes. This explains why it is important to include fats and/or protein with each meal, as you are likely to eat less and be satisfied with less total food for that meal than if you simply ate carbohydrates on their own.

A rough guide to the amount of food you need to eat at each meal is approximately two fist-sized servings of concentrated food, such as proteins, fats and/or carbohydrates. You can, and need to, add to that as many water-based vegetables, such as green leafy vegies (non-starch vegetables), as you like. Although greens have a high nutrient content, they are mostly water. There is nothing wrong with starchy vegetables — potato, sweet potato, pumpkin, etc. They are packed with nourishment and are great to include, but bear in mind that they are more concentrated foods (with a lower water content) than water-based vegetables such as spinach and broccoli.

Wake up your stomach acid pH

Food arrives at the stomach after you chew and swallow it. The aroma of food, but particularly the chewing action itself, stimulates stomach acid production, which is an exceptionally important substance when it comes to great digestion. (In the past, we took much longer to prepare our meals, and the slow-cooking processes generated an aroma of the upcoming meal, signalling to the stomach that food was on its way.) Stomach acid's role is to break food down. Imagine your food is a big, long string of circles, as shown in the first row of the illustration below. It is the job of the stomach acid to go chop, chop, chop, and break the circles apart into smaller bunches, as the second row illustrates.

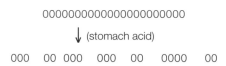

Digestion: The action of stomach acid on wholefoods breaks them down into their smaller components.

There are specific, ideal pH ranges for each tissue and fluid in the body. In scientific terms, pH refers to the concentration of hydrogen ions present, but you don't need to worry about that to understand this very important process.

pH is a measure of acidity or alkalinity. Its range is based on a scale of 0 to 14, with 0 being the acid end of the spectrum and 14 being the alkaline end; 7 is neutral. Every fluid, every tissue, every cell of your body has a pH, or pH range, at which it performs optimally. The optimal pH of stomach acid is around 1.9, which is so acidic that it would burn you if it touched your skin. But it doesn't burn you while it is nicely housed inside your stomach, as the cells that line the stomach itself not only produce stomach acid but are also designed to withstand the super-acidic conditions.

For many people, though, the pH of the stomach acid is not acidic enough, and it may have a pH far greater than 1.9, which is not ideal for digestion. This can mean the difference between a flat abdomen and a bloated abdomen after a meal. A professor in the United States has been researching the pH of stomach acid in various groups of people who have been diagnosed with specific conditions, such as children with autism spectrum disorder (ASD). Many children with ASD have been found to have a stomach acid pH of around 4, far too high to effectively digest many foods, particularly those rich in proteins.

Adults with reflux or indigestion tend to assume that the burning sensation they experience with heartburn means they are producing too much acid, when the opposite is usually true. They are usually not making enough stomach acid and/or the pH of it is too high. To understand this, remember the food-as-a-string-of-circles analogy and that stomach acid plays a vital role in breaking the circles apart. A pH that is much higher than 1.9 cannot effectively break the circles apart, and larger segments of, for example, seven circles in length may be the result. The body knows that if something seven circles in length continues along the digestive tract, it is not going to be able to further digest these partially broken-down circles. Rather than allowing that food to proceed down into the small intestine for the next part of its journey, the body regurgitates the food in an attempt to get rid of it, which is when you experience the acid burn. It "burns" you, because anything with a pH that is too acidic for the tissue to which it is exposed will create a burning sensation. When the acid is contained inside the stomach pouch, all is well; however, when it escapes out of this area, the lining of the oesophagus and the first part of the small intestine are not designed to cope with such acidic contents. Many people with reflux respond well to the stimulation of stomach acid and/or omitting problematic foods, and experience much fewer symptoms as a result. As a result of being better nourished, and also most likely due to experiencing less inflammation, energy levels tend to improve with the resolution of these symptoms.

Lemon juice and apple cider vinegar (ACV) physically stimulate the production of stomach acid. If you haven't consumed either of these before, it is best to initially dilute them and ideally consume them five to 20 minutes before breakfast (or all of your main meals if that appeals). For example, you might begin with half a teaspoon of ACV in as much water as you like. Over the coming days and weeks, you could gradually work up to having one tablespoon of ACV while you gradually decrease (or not) the amount of water.

If you prefer lemon juice, start with the juice of half a lemon diluted to your taste with warm water, and gradually work up to having the juice of a whole lemon in less warm water. Or enjoy the juice of a whole lemon in a mug of warm water as your first drink for the day.

If you use lemon juice, it can be a good idea to brush your teeth about 20 minutes after your meals to prevent any potential problems with tooth enamel in the future. Use these tips to wake up your stomach acid before you eat, because, if this area of the digestive system is not working optimally, it can have a significant impact not only locally, but further along the digestive system, and systemically on everything from energy to mood, from fat burning to restorative sleep.

The potential effect of drinking water with meals

We need the pH of our stomach acid to sit at around 1.9. Water has a pH of 7 (neutral pH) or above, depending on the mineral content — the higher the mineral content, the higher/more alkaline the pH. When you add a liquid with a pH of 7 or more to one with a pH of 1.9, what do you potentially do to the stomach acid? You dilute it. And we need all of the digestive fire we can muster to get the maximum nourishment out of our food and the best out of us. In my ideal world, we wouldn't drink water for 30 minutes on either side of eating.

You do not need to be concerned about the water content of food, nor do you need to focus on omitting all beverages at every meal. Simply aim to drink water between meals rather than with meals. It can be a challenging habit to break. Set yourself a goal of not drinking with meals for one week, and then preferably keep the new habit going. Alternatively, you can add a squeeze of fresh lemon juice if you want water during your meal, but it is preferable not to have water, particularly if you want to resolve gut challenges. Better to trial cutting it out for a week, and see whether you feel any different.

Stimulate the pH gradient of the digestive system

Once food has been partially broken down in the stomach, it moves through the pyloric sphincter, a one-way valve leading into the duodenum, which is the beginning of the small intestine. In your body this valve is located in the middle, or just slightly on the left, of the chest, just below the bra line.

While food is in the stomach, messages are sent to the pancreas to secrete sodium bicarbonate, which has a highly alkaline pH, along with digestive enzymes. The bicarbonate is designed to protect the lining of the first part of the small intestine, while allowing digestion to continue. What is known as a "pH gradient" is established all the way along the digestive tract, and each region of the big long tube has an ideal pH. When the pH gradient is not established in the stomach — that is, when the pH is higher than ideal — digestion problems are likely further along the tract. These may be symptoms of the small or large intestine, such as bloating, pain or excessive wind. The absorption of nutrients may also be compromised, another factor in this process that can interfere with good energy production. Insufficient pancreatic bicarbonate production may also cause digestive symptoms, such as a burning sensation underneath the stomach in the valve area described above. Pain in this area can also indicate that the gallbladder needs some support or investigation. It is best to consult with your health professional about this if you regularly feel discomfort in this area.

The best way to let the pancreas know that it needs to jump to action and produce bicarbonate and digestive enzymes is to have good stomach acid production at optimal pH. The digestive system runs off a cascade of signals from one organ or area to the next, via the brain. Use the suggested strategies, especially chewing food well, to stimulate the pancreas to fulfil its role.

There are occasions when I have suggested that clients use supplements of pancreatic enzymes, and this is appropriate if there is a genuine lack of digestive enzymes, rather than simply poor stomach acid conditions. I usually suggest the aforementioned strategies (chewing, taking lemon juice or ACV, and not having water with meals) before trialling these supplements; however, when symptoms are severe, and once other causes have been ruled out, a gastroenterologist may measure pancreatic enzyme levels. If enzyme production is low, people are often deeply fatigued and the fatigue starts to lift once enzyme production improves or support is added.

Promote absorption

As food moves through the small bowel, digestive enzymes are secreted from the pancreas and the brush border, or lining, of the small intestine. The role of these enzymes is to continue what the stomach acid began, which is to continue to break down the food that has been eaten into its smallest, most basic components. It is in the small intestine where you absorb all of the goodness (ie, vitamins and minerals) out of your food. Think about that. All of the nutrients that keep you alive are drawn out of your food in the gut and move across into your blood so that your body can use those nutrients to do all of their life-sustaining jobs. The small intestine is where the nutrients in your food move from the tube that is your digestive tract into the blood, which is obviously a different set of tubes. This is how we are nourished, and it is how we stay alive. And if this process is disrupted, inefficient or compromised in any way, you will feel like your energy underperforms every day.

Alcohol and vitamin B_{12} are virtually the only substances you absorb directly out of your stomach into your blood, rather than via your small intestine. Alcohol tends to be in your blood within five minutes of consuming it, which is why you may get tipsy if you drink on an empty stomach.

Just because you eat something, though, doesn't mean you get all of the goodness out of it. For example, if a food contains five milligrams of zinc, you don't necessarily absorb the whole amount when you eat it. The absorption of nutrients is dependent on a whole host of factors, some of which have been discussed above. If you inhale your food, drink water with your meals, or have poor stomach acid production, for example, you may absorb very little of the goodness in your food. Fibre interferes with the absorption of some nutrients, such as zinc. Some nutrients compete for absorption with each other, such as iron and calcium. In this case, calcium always wins, because it is a bigger structure. Some people are iron-deficient, for example, because they consume calcium-rich foods with iron-rich meals. There are many mechanisms through which someone can become iron-deficient, and, because iron is so highly linked to energy, it has a section in this book all of its own.

Nutrients are essential for life, and the *way* you are eating — let alone the foods you might be choosing — may be robbing you of some of the goodness your food provides, which can have an impact on every body system, including your energy. Give yourself the best opportunity to absorb as much goodness out of your food as possible by applying the tips above. It may add energy to your years, and years to your life.

Address niggling pain

Many clients describe an on-again, off-again pain that hits them quite low down on the right-hand side of their abdomen. If you place your little finger on your right hip bone and use your thumb to find your navel, this pain tends to be located about halfway in between on that diagonal line. This is the *ileocaecal valve*, where the small intestine meets the large intestine. Many people have mistaken ileocaecal valve pain for appendicitis, as the appendix is located not far from this area. Always see a medical professional to diagnose your pain.

For many, pain begins in this area after food poisoning or a stomach bug (infection), after travelling, usually overseas, or camping. When you had the bug, you might have had bouts of diarrhoea. Even though the obvious symptoms of the causative infection have long since gone, it is as though the nasty little critters that caused the original upset tummy have taken up residence in the valve. Or perhaps they have changed its function or led to other bacteria inhabiting this area that don't belong there.

To remedy this pain, there are numerous options to try. One is to release the reflex connected to this valve by rubbing the area with your fingertips 20 times in an anticlockwise circular motion with reasonable pressure; not so it hurts you, but also not with super-soft fingers. Another option is to use anti-parasitic herbs, such as Chinese wormwood and black walnut, every day for six to eight weeks, before each main meal, under the guidance of a health professional.

Promote good gut bacteria

Once the food gets to the large intestine, can you guess what lives there? Bacteria. On average, an adult will have three to four kilograms of bacteria living in their colon. So, just as an aside, every time you weigh yourself remember that three to four of the kilos you see in that number on the scales is made up of gut bacteria that are essential for life; another reason why it is crazy that we weigh ourselves.

Some of the bacteria in your large bowel (colon) are good guys, and some are bad guys. You want more good guys than bad guys. The role of the gut bacteria is to ferment whatever you give them. To come back to the circle concept of food illustrated previously, gut bugs love it when you give them something that is one or even two circles in size. They know what to do with that. But if a previous digestive process was not completed sufficiently, the bacteria in your colon may be presented with fragments of food that are five or even seven circles in size, and all they know to do with such fragments of food is ferment it.

What word springs to mind when you think of fermentation? I love asking this question at my seminars, as the answers usually amuse me as well as the audience. People will often say "beer", "wine", "sauerkraut"! But usually I eventually get the answer I am after, which is gas. Fermentation involves bacterial action on a food source, and the subsequent production of gas. Some gases are essential to the health of the cells that line our gut, while others irritate the gut and give us a bloated, uncomfortable stomach as the day progresses, whether we have eaten in a healthy way or not. These unfriendly gases may disrupt gut permeability, and they also add a load to the liver, so they could be deemed a problematic substance for the body; an additional liver-loader that we don't need in a world with too many of these already.

The trouble with a bloated stomach — for women in particular — is that it messes with their brain. When they look down and see a swollen tummy, something inside immediately communicates to every cell of their body that they have gained weight, whether they consciously think this thought or not. Many of my clients go up a size around the waist as the day progresses, even though they feel they have eaten with their health in mind. This can add a layer of stress to a woman's life that they just don't need or understand. It is especially stressful because they can't fathom why it is happening. Sometimes it is the foods and drinks they are choosing. Sometimes it is the bugs that live in their colon. Sometimes it is because of poor digestion further up the process, such as insufficient stomach acid. In traditional Chinese medicine (TCM), bloating is often considered a spleen and/or liver picture, and a TCM practitioner is likely to use acupuncture and/or herbs to support the spleen and liver. See more on this, below. Sometimes bloating is due to drinking too much coffee, or to a food sensitivity (not a true "allergy", but a food you are reacting to), or fructose malabsorption, or from stress and living on adrenalin.

Address stress

Poor digestion can be due to stress or, more precisely, adrenalin, a stress hormone. The perception of stress or real stress drives the body to make adrenalin, which diverts the blood supply away from digestive processes and concentrates the blood in your periphery, your arms and legs, allowing you to escape from the danger you are supposedly in. If blood were still concentrated on the digestive system, there is a risk you would be distracted by food or hunger, thus putting your survival at risk. These concepts are explored in detail throughout the book, as a variety of the consequences of stress can have an impact on energy.

Ensure complete bowel evacuation

In dealing with clients one-on-one, I have had to work out ways to extract information from people using words that accurately describe what is going on for that person. Many years ago, one of the questions I originally found difficult to phrase was around how empty someone felt after they had used their bowels. I tried to dream up ways to phrase this question so that it would not make clients feel uncomfortable, but also so that I could gain greater insight into how their bowel was functioning. As with many things, a client turned out to have the answer. While asking him about his bowel habits, he said, "You know what? My greatest discomfort comes from incomplete evacuation." There they were. The words I needed. So, early on in my consultation work with people, I started asking about feelings of incomplete evacuation. For some, it is not an issue at all, and they have no idea what I am talking about when I mention it. For others, they are so excited that someone has finally given them the words to describe such frustrating discomfort. They wouldn't answer "yes" if I asked them if they were constipated, as they may use their bowels every day. It is just that when they do go to the toilet, they feel like there is more to come but it doesn't eventuate and evacuate.

This feeling can be the result of numerous scenarios. It may be insufficient digestive processes as outlined previously. It may be inadequate production of digestive enzymes due to poor signalling, or a damaged or inflamed brush border. It may be a food allergy or intolerance. It could be undiagnosed coeliac disease. It could be related to fibre or dehydration. It can be stress hormones causing the muscles surrounding the bowel to contract and hold onto waste. It may be a magnesium deficiency not allowing the walls of the bowel to relax and allow the thorough passage of waste. Or the thyroid gland may not be working optimally. TCM teaches us that it is insufficient spleen and/or liver energy. The list of scenarios is almost endless, but finding those specific for you can change your health, your waistline, your energy and the way you experience life.

Dietary change: dietary trials
One option to help improve incomplete evacuation or other digestive system challenges is to have a health professional help you get to the heart of it and remedy the situation using dietary change(s). You might increase your green vegetable intake and omit processed foods in your diet for a week, and see whether that makes a difference, especially given that green vegetables are good sources of magnesium, water and fibre, amongst other things. Plus, in eliminating processed foods for this trial period, you will be missing out on artificial substances such as preservatives and colourings, and this alone may make a difference. Science has shown omitting specific preservatives from children's diets can improve behaviour and concentration; however, I believe we have only just begun to have demonstrated in scientific research some of the issues these substances may contribute to.

You may be suspicious that a food or a group of foods is causing this feeling for you, but because you love this food you are reluctant to remove it. I cannot encourage you enough to remove a suspicious food from your diet for a *trial* period of four weeks. Four little weeks out of your very long life — an expression I use regularly with clients to highlight the relatively short time period necessary to potentially offer enormous insight into their health challenges. For some, however, a longer trial of three months is necessary, and a longer trial must be done under the guidance of a health professional to ensure that you are getting all of the nutrients you need. You may get an answer to your challenge over the trial period; if not, you can relax and thoroughly enjoy this food without silently worrying. But I can hear you already asking: "What if it works? What does that mean? Will I never eat that food again?" My answer is always that this is your choice.

I have witnessed people be resistant to dietary change, but after a time feel so different, so much better, that they have no desire to ever go back to the way they used to eat. I have met others who, even though they may feel better, still miss a food terribly. In the latter scenario, I suggest to them after the trial that it is a good thing that now they know the culprit. It is no longer a mystery to them why they feel this way. Then they are in control. Unless the problem is a true allergy, I find that when people are strong — meaning when they are very robust from a digestion perspective — their gut will tolerate this food better than if they are stressed. Either way, once you know, you are in control and it is your choice. Unless the food is a true allergy for you, your tolerance of it may change and improve over time, especially with a focus on gut healing and stress management. Don't think that because it hurts you today it always will. Your body changes and renews itself constantly. Just know there is a reason for your symptom(s). It is simply a matter of finding your answers. And as you uncover them, a renewed energy and vitality are usually on offer.

Softening waste

One of the reasons I am so concerned with bowel evacuation is that, if this process is inefficient, waste can remain inside the bowel for too long. While it is there, it is fermenting. This can give the liver additional and unnecessary toxins to process, as well as "suffocate" the cells that line the colon. No one has studied the impact of this on how energized you feel. Common sense, though, suggests that it won't be doing your vitality any favours.

The waste can also dry out and harden, sticking itself to the lining of the bowel wall, narrowing the tube through which the new waste can flow. If you have ever seen soil in the middle of a drought — cracked, dried-out and unable to absorb a brief shower of rain — that is the way hardened faeces can behave in your colon.

If this scenario occurs, waste can move only through the middle of this newly formed, faeces-lined tube, and the efficiency of waste elimination is decreased. The old, hard, compacted faecal matter remains. When the cells that line the bowel are coated with hard faeces, they are unable to "breathe", and a process that was once described in medical textbooks as *auto-intoxication* can ensue. To remedy this, chamomile is one of the best things you can take. Either drink plenty of chamomile tea, take capsules, or have the medicinal liquid herb prescribed and have it with each meal. Once the waste has dried out, it is difficult to rehydrate it so that it can move through and be excreted. Chamomile softens the waste and helps the bowel wall relax.

Colonics
Another potential remedy is one about which many people have very strong opinions: colon hydrotherapy, or colonics. This process involves a tube being inserted into a person's rectum through which warm or cool water gently flows. This allows the hardened faecal matter to soften, like heavy, consistent rain on dried-out soil, allowing the large bowel to empty fully, often getting rid of built-up waste that may have been there for a very long time. I have had clients tell me that the waste they excreted during their first colonic was black, inferring that it may have been there for many years, interfering with healthy bowel function. I had a lady once tell me she saw popcorn in the viewing pipe during her colonic — and she knew that the last time she had eaten popcorn was at the movies over six months beforehand!

Colonics polarize people. The idea either appeals to you or it doesn't. There is no middle ground with people's love or dislike of colon hydrotherapy. I encourage you, though, not to lose sight of the effect that trends have had on medicine. Up until the early 1900s, colonics were accepted as part of general medicine. Doctors understood the importance of good bowel evacuation, and considered colonics to be a normal treatment method for a host of health conditions, not just bowel issues. Coffee enemas were actually cited in the *Merck Manual for Doctors* for liver detoxification until 1972.

With a well-functioning bowel, an enormous load is taken off not only the digestive system but also the liver, one of the organs primarily responsible for toxin transformation, helping keep the body "clean". Help prevent bowel cancer by ensuring efficient bowel evacuation using methods that suit you. Always seek advice from a health professional before undertaking colon hydrotherapy, if that option appeals to you. I have witnessed well-supported colonic therapy energize and revitalize people in a relatively short period of time and in a remarkable way.

Gut integrity and opioid effects

An additional concept within digestive health is not only fascinating but has wide-ranging effects on how we feel and function, including gut transit time (ie, how quickly food moves through the digestive system), mood, concentration and, potentially, food addictions. This concept is known as the *opioid excess theory*.

Gut integrity

The cells that line a healthy small intestine look like a row of bricks with finger-like projections (called *villi*), neatly stacked side-by-side as demonstrated in the picture below.

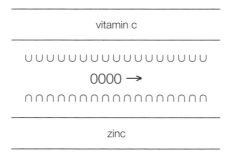

A healthy gut: Food (represented here by the circles) travelling through a healthy mature intestine move straight ahead. Only nutrients (for example, vitamin C and zinc) enter the blood vessels that closely follow the intestines.

In a healthy gut, only the tiny nutrients (vitamins and minerals) diffuse (move) or are transported across the gut wall into the blood, and this is the remarkable process through which we are nourished and stay alive. However, the cells that line the gut can come apart, as if the bricks have gaps between them, as illustrated below. This is also how our gut is when we are born.

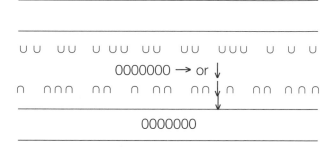

A "leaky" gut: Food (represented here by the circles) travels through an immature gut or a "leaky" intestine. Microscopic, poorly digested fragments of food can escape out of the gut and enter the blood.

When we are born, the cells that line our digestive system are a distance apart, which is why we can't feed all foods to newborns; foods must be gradually introduced to a child over time as the gut matures, in part to help prevent allergies developing. The gut is immature when we are born, and it slowly matures from birth until reaching full maturity somewhere between the ages of two and five, depending on the individual child and their health and life experiences in the early years. Sadly, for some this maturation process may be stunted by constant ill health, such as recurrent infections, until gut health is addressed.

The cells that line the gut can, however, also come apart during adulthood as a result of a gastrointestinal infection or stress. The chronic production of stress hormones can compromise the integrity of the gut cells and signal to them that they need to move further apart so that more nutrition can get through to the blood, as nutrient requirements increase during times of stress. Everything about us is geared for survival.

When food travels through a gut with good cell-lining integrity, it can only go straight ahead. However, if it travels through a gut in which the cells have come apart, it may go straight ahead or it may move out of the gut and into the blood. Fragments of food are not intended to enter the blood. Nutrients — the vitamins and minerals from food — are. So if fragments of food enter the bloodstream, the immune system, which is what protects you from infection, thinks that the food fragment is a germ and it mounts an immune response against it. This is one way adults develop food sensitivities, and is, I believe, a process that contributes to exhaustion in some people.

Poor gut integrity is also described as "leaky gut". Once you were able to eat anything without a problem and now certain foods seem to cause you grief. This process can be healed by minimizing irritation to the gut lining, which can mean avoiding some foods or ingredients for a period of time, while also working on gut integrity. Aloe vera juice to start the day can also assist an irritated gut. Formal studies have not been done on the impact of increased gut permeability on energy.

Given fragments of food that are too large end up in the blood supply in a leaky-gut state, I consider this to be extra "stress" on the body, or perhaps an addition to the toxin load, and it can certainly create conditions of inflammation. And, as you will see throughout the pages of this book, all of these factors potentially influence whether you bound out of bed full of beans each morning or press the snooze button a handful of times, groaning that a new day has begun already.

Often people are able to tolerate the foods that cause them grief once we have worked out why they have leaky-gut symptoms in the first place and corrected them. Did the problem begin as a result of stress or an infection? The power to heal the symptoms is always in the "why".

The opioid effect

The blood supply into which the food fragments flow is the same blood supply that goes to your brain. Humans have what is known as the blood–brain barrier, a semi-permeable layer separating the peripheral blood supply from that of the brain. The blood–brain barrier was always considered to be a highly selective membrane that only allowed substances into the brain that would be of benefit to it. However, research has now shown that this is not the case. In cases where gut permeability is increased, the blood–brain barrier is often suspected of having the same increased permeability.

If we could see the food fragments, their structure is very similar to that of opioids. Opioids are substances that help humans feel good. They also help modulate pain. We have our own natural feel-good hormones, endorphins, which have an opioid-based structure. In our brain, and in our gut, we have what are called *opioid receptors*. To review: just because your body makes a substance (ie, a chemical messenger or hormone), that doesn't mean you necessarily experience the effects of that substance. For you to get the effect generated by that hormone, the substance must bind to a receptor, just like a lock and a key fitting together. In this case, when we make endorphins and they bind to the opioid receptors, we feel pleasure. Heroin and morphine are opioids, and they, too, bind to the opioid receptors in the brain. Anything that gives a human pleasure has the potential to be addictive, hence the aforementioned drugs. You can also see from this example how someone might become addicted to exercise. Activity tends to generate endorphins. So whenever you partake in or experience something that gives you pleasure — like a sunset, a spin class, a tennis game, a butterfly, or a child's laughter — you make endorphins which bind to opioid receptors, and you feel pleasure.

How does this relate to food, body fat, over-eating and energy? Some of the fragments of food that can escape out of a leaky gut into the bloodstream can also have an opioid structure. These include beta-casomorphine and gluteomorphine. They are partially digested fragments of casein (a major protein in cow's milk products) and gluten (a major protein in wheat, rye, barley, oats and triticale). Just like endorphins, these opioids from food also have the capacity to bind to the opioid receptors in the brain and very subtly make us feel good. The effect is not usually noticed as an enormous boost in mood, but the person will often feel as though they can't live without this food, and they will feel as though they *have* to eat it in some form daily or even at every meal. Sometimes they start eating it and they can't stop, although this can be due to numerous reasons, not just an opioid effect.

I have seen this to be the case with countless clients. If a patient has a set of symptoms that warrants them omitting a food from their diet for a trial period to see whether it will make a difference, some people have no problem. There is no resistance. Others will beg me not to take them off a food for a trial, yet they are seeing me because they want results, and all I am asking is four measly weeks of omitting a particular food that may just give them the answer to some of their health concerns! I am not judging someone who responds in this way; I am simply pointing out to you that the power food can have over an individual can be just like an addiction. And it can be making them feel exhausted. An individual's connection to a certain food is often highly emotional, and also potentially physical, through this opioid mechanism.

Food was never intended to fill these roles for humans. However, on a physical level, where there is a leaky gut, it is possible that the opioid effect, which some foods have the potential to generate, might be one of the factors behind food addictions, and, hence for some, over-eating or eating and not feeling like you can stop. This is an area that deserves much more research, time and money, as the opioid excess theory may be involved in numerous health conditions as well as obesity. Much research has already been done in relation to children with autism and adults with schizophrenia, where these *exorphins* (opioids from an exogenous source — that is, consumed rather than made by the body) have been found to play a role in the expression of symptoms of these conditions.

Food not only has the capacity to affect our energy, sleep, skin, body shape and size, but also our mood. Our digestion of some foods may also be incomplete, leading to the generation of an opioid effect and addiction to particular foods. If you suspect this process is going on for you, consult a nutrition professional experienced in this area and have them guide you to omit all sources of that dietary component (eg, gluten and/or casein) for a trial period of four weeks. The first four to seven days will be the most difficult, but persevere. The results may be enormously worth it.

Support the spleen — the TCM perspective

The spleen rules digestion in TCM. In TCM, each organ is considered to have its own vital energy, as well as there being whole-body energy. If spleen energy is down, you will feel your usual hunger for meals, but as soon as you eat even a small amount you will feel full and possibly bloated. Your short-term memory is likely to not be what it once was, and you may possibly feel like you eat like a bird yet your weight continues to escalate. You can eat and exercise with a real commitment, but if spleen energy is low, from a TCM perspective, you won't feel like your best self, and you will likely feel that, no matter what you do, you can't lose weight or feel energized.

According to TCM principles, supporting spleen energy can make a real difference. Acupuncture will do this, as will specific herbs. Warming foods (referring to the unique properties foods have, according to TCM, as well as temperature) also help, as can adding warming spices, such as ginger, cumin and turmeric, to dishes. It is also believed in TCM that spleen energy can become low from "overthinking". The busy mind, relentlessly thinking of the next thing you need to do, takes energy away from the vital process of digestion every day, according to TCM principles. The spleen may also lose some of its strength if liver or kidney energy is overbearing or low. (The adrenals, which produce stress hormones — along with other hormones — sit on top of the kidneys.) Working with a wonderful TCM practitioner can also help you heal your gut, which in turn helps every aspect of your wellbeing, including your energy and vitality.

> *F*ood not only has the capacity to affect our energy, sleep, skin, body shape and size, but also our mood.

Consider food combining

Food combining can be a wonderful approach to eating that can enhance digestion, energy and vitality, and it can be a great way to combat a bloated tummy. It involves a few simple principles, including eating animal protein separately from starchy carbohydrates. In practice, that means no meat and potatoes on the same plate. It means that if you eat meat, chicken or fish, you eat it with high-water vegetables and no starchy vegetables, such as potato, sweet potato, pumpkin and corn, or any other starchy foods, such as pasta, bread or rice. If you eat vegetable protein, such as one of the many types of lentils, chickpeas or beans, then, using food-combining principles, you do not eat meat with these foods, but instead any vegetable at all, including starchy ones if they appeal. If you feel like eating rice, then with food combining it needs to be a vegetarian meal. Oils and other foods rich in fats, including avocado, can be eaten with either animal-based meals or starch-based meals.

Another principle of food combining is that fruit is only consumed as your first meal and not again during the day. For some, instead of digesting it, it ferments, which can lead to a range of gut symptoms and low energy. You are also encouraged to omit all refined sugar and processed foods, as the main goal of food combining is to support the health of your blood, given that it does all of the nutrient-dissemination work within the body.

I know people who live by the concept of food combining and feel spectacular. They are brimming with energy and vitality. For others, for whom food combining seems extreme, but who still want to try it, I suggest they apply the *zigzag principle*. This means that most of the time they follow food-combining principles (zig), while one day a week, or two to three meals a week, they relax the principles and they zag. This approach is more sustainable for some; you are still able to dine out and enjoy all foods, whatever combination arrives on your plate, but just not every day. It is important to note that this latter statement is *not* applicable to true food allergies — they must be strictly omitted from the diet.

Food combining is a structured way of eating that allows some individuals to thrive. I have seen this approach to food truly change people's lives. For others, eating this way might take every aspect of joy out of their life. If this is the case for you, then focusing on food combining is not for you — right now or ever — or perhaps the zigzag concept might appeal. I am certainly not prescribing this for you. I simply want to offer you options to help you experience your best health and a new way of looking at how you fuel your body in a way that serves you.

Why eat real food?

Scientists have created a tiny camera that sits inside a capsule (not unlike a dietary supplement capsule), which research participants swallow, thereby providing about 16 hours of footage from inside the digestive system. Researchers gave one group of study participants a real-food meal, where they made noodles from scratch, from flour and water, and served it in a broth made from water, salt and vegetables. The other group was given a ready-meal bought from the supermarket: ramen noodles with 15 different ingredients on the label, along with a blue "sports" drink. After four hours, the camera footage showed that those in the real-food group had only tiny, white pieces of fluff remaining in their digestive tract; the food was well broken down. For those in the bought-food group four hours after ingestion, you could still see the teeth marks in the noodles where the participants had bitten into them. There were still long strings of noodles remaining intact four hours after eating. In addition to this, the noodles and part of the lining of the intestine had been dyed blue from the drink. This is the result of the dye in the drink being petroleum-based, and humans have no capability — no enzymes — to break down petrol.

Eat real food. Your body has the equipment (ie, digestive enzymes) to break it down and provide you with the nourishment your body needs to function optimally. That includes energy. You have to be healthy to have energy. And if you don't, rather than get frustrated with the fatigue, see it as feedback — your body asking you to eat, drink, move, think, breathe, believe or perceive in a new way. It can be a gift if you choose to see it this way, a gift asking you to bring curiosity to the question: why am I so tired?

Remember ...

Digestion is central and essential to every process in our body, which is why, when exploring the way the body creates energy and the way we experience it, it is the base from which we build. As around 80 per cent of your immune system lines your gut, when gut function is impaired it can have a significant impact on the immune system, with more and more research suggesting that this is where some autoimmune conditions originate.

So, whether your focus is optimizing your health and wellbeing, and/or improving a challenging or diseased gut, supporting your immune system, body fat management, resolving congested skin, or restoring energy, understanding your digestive system is a crucial step in your big-picture knowledge of how the body works and how energy is extracted (or not) from the food we consume, allowing you to have an energized life.

Part of supporting that process involves becoming aware of the potentially "problematic substances" we are exposed to and that we ask our body to digest and detoxify. For if that can't happen efficiently, those problematic substances can be stored inside the body, hindering our personal energy.

Toxicity, Body Fat and Energy

We store energy — fuel — in our body for later use, in case we miss a meal or a famine strikes, so that we will have enough fuel to support the inner workings of the body that keep us alive. We store calories that are not used straight away, in the form of glycogen (which is stored glucose), fat and proteins. Proteins, when needed, can be broken down into amino acids and converted into glucose to be used as fuel. Remember when we were discussing sugar cravings we learnt that a person weighing 70 kilograms can store about 2,500 calories as glycogen and about 130,000 calories as fat.

The fat we store in our body is not, however, just fuel for later. It fulfils many roles. Adipose tissue (fat cells) acts as an endocrine gland, which is a gland that secretes hormones. In the case of our fat cells, they secrete oestrogen in both men and women, boys and girls. Oestrogen itself is a fat-storage hormone, so the more fat cells we have and the larger they are, the more they make a hormone that signals fat storage, adding to the oestrogen being produced. (As an aside, this is one of many vicious cycles that need to be interrupted for weight loss to occur, as discussed in *The Calorie Fallacy*.)

An additional function of body fat is that it is a storage house for what I call "problematic substances". I could refer to them as "toxins", but that is a term that is often misused and misunderstood. Nonetheless, for ease of language I will use both terms. For example, some substances are outright toxins, such as the pesticide DDT was shown to be, whereas others are detrimental to an individual only when they accumulate, if the detoxification pathways and waste-disposal systems of the body cannot keep up with the load, such as may occur with oestrogen. Other substances behave like a toxin based on an individual's health picture, in the way that gluten does for people with coeliac disease and others whose digestive systems present with adverse symptoms when they eat gluten, despite an array of tests having not yet been developed to determine the precise mechanisms behind such sensitivity. A problematic substance for your individual body might be something you ingest, inhale or absorb.

While their road into the body might vary, once they are in the blood the body has to deal with them, as problematic substances cannot be allowed to accumulate in the blood. So the body shunts them to the liver and the kidneys for detoxification (transformation into something less harmful that can be excreted), filtration and then excretion. For the liver and kidneys to perform their critical work, nutrients are required.

But here's the thing: if the load arriving at the front door of either of these organs is too much for it to deal with at the time, due to the previous ongoing loads being too much or too regular, or due to a lack of detoxification enzymes being available due to nutrient deficiencies (as specific nutrients are essential for the production of detoxification enzymes), the problematic substances still need to be removed from the blood so that they don't harm you. In such cases they are moved to the fatty tissues of your body (unfortunately some are stored in bone or brain as well), away from the vital organs. The fat cells thus become storage houses for toxins; substances that the body sent to the liver, for example, to be changed so that they could be excreted, yet instead are recycled.

They were sent to the liver because your body deemed them unsuitable to stay. In fact your body may have identified them as substances that may put your health at risk if they stayed. But because the liver didn't have the capacity to handle what arrived (due to the reasons outlined above), the problematic substances were slightly (not completely) changed, becoming more reactive and problematic than they were in their original form that entered the liver. And once they ended up back out in your blood, your body knew they would be even more of a problem for you if they stayed there! So to get them (literally) out of circulation, they are sent to your body fat to be stored until some more resources (usually nutrients) are available to fully detoxify them. Only then can they depart your body for good. But most people are never taught this approach to their health, and as a result are never taught or supported to create the space (consume fewer "liver-loaders") and enhance the resources (consume more nutrients) so that these problematic substances can be released from storage and excreted. Instead, they stay there and more and more body fat and more and more fatigue results.

As I have said before, your body is geared for survival. To burn the stored fat as fuel and hence lose weight, you will also need to release these stored toxins, and your body can only do that when it has the required detoxification and filtration capacity. This means you need to put fewer problematic substances in, and enhance your nutritional status through increasing the nutrient density of your diet. Not eat fewer calories. Moreover, if the low-calorie foods come out of packets, they potentially contain some problematic substances, adding to your load.

If you don't create the space for your liver to have to do less detoxification work by decreasing the loaders going in, and you don't increase the nutrients you ingest to allow the liver to create more of the enzymes required for the critical detoxification work, then fat won't be burnt and energy won't be enhanced, as you are not freeing up the required detoxification capacity.

It is not a pleasant thing to consider, nor for the people who experience this, but essentially people are getting more and more toxic due to their lifestyle choices, and due to a lack of awareness about the chemical load going into their bodies via what they eat, drink, inhale from the air, or absorb through the skin. The more rubbish we store inside our bodies, the more lethargic we feel.

For some people, their inability to lose weight despite eating fewer calories than they burn — but particularly when the calories going in are not from whole, real, nutrient-dense foods — is due to these mechanisms. The body will still not have the resources to allow you to burn your body fat and enable you to lose weight. For to do so risks dumping the problematic substances back into your blood, which could harm you in a minor or major way. And your body is so clever it won't allow this to happen, so instead it continues to store the toxins until it can process them. And the lethargy that can stem from this is often debilitating.

The gallbladder

Another key factor to the body being able to detoxify and eliminate potentially problematic substances is the efficiency of the gallbladder to release bile. The liver produces bile, which the gallbladder then stores until it is needed. Many toxins are fat-soluble, and bile is essential for them to be metabolized, detoxified and eliminated.

Good bile production and release occurs as part of the cascade of signals that is generated from good digestion. If stomach acid production is poor or if the pH is too high (not acidic enough to initiate the pH gradient of the digestive tract), bile release from the gallbladder can be compromised. Gallstones can be another reason for the gallbladder not working optimally. Bitter foods and herbs stimulate bile production, which is not a flavour many people seek out. Globe artichoke and St Mary's thistle are two medicinal herbs that can be highly beneficial to efficient bile production, and a medical herbalist can advise you whether these would be suitable for you personally if this appeals.

For those who have had their gallbladder removed, the liver has to continue to make the bile the gallbladder is no longer available to store, asking the liver to jump to action more frequently and accomplish yet another task on its long list. Producing bile is not the liver's only job, plus it cannot make as much bile without the gallbladder as there is nowhere to store it. This means that those who have had their gallbladder removed need to take extra good care of their liver, so that it can be highly responsive to the need for bile, to enable poor-quality fats and fat-based toxins to be detoxified and eliminated efficiently from the body.

If someone has a fatty liver (explained in detail in the liver section), they can follow a plan of action designed for them by a health professional experienced in this area, to allow the liver to start to release some of the stored fat. It will come away in bowel motions as a fatty film, or globules of oil may be visible after a motion. (I know it's no fun to talk about this, but I want this information to be clear.)

All of the above is partly why whenever someone seeks me out for assistance with weight loss or to improve their energy, I don't focus on the weight or the energy themselves. I focus on the body systems that need support, based on the symptoms an individual is presenting with. This is also why with any weight loss programme anyone ever undertakes in this world we now live in, it needs to be accompanied by liver support, either through a high plant way of eating, green drinks, nutrient supplementation and/or herbal medicine. The enhanced energy someone experiences, as their fatty liver improves or as a result of weight loss, is also, I believe, the result of less of a toxic burden within the body, allowing energy systems to operate more efficiently. So let's get to know the liver a whole lot better.

> *B*itter foods and herbs stimulate bile production, which is not a flavour many people seek out.

Liver Detoxification and Fatigue

The health and efficiency of the liver plays a significant role in whether we feel energized or not. I believe that the ways in which our liver functions are some of the most critical to our health and longevity, and how spritely we feel across our life span. You'll see how in a moment.

When it comes to every aspect of our health — your energy, vitality, hormonal balance, fat loss, the clarity of your skin and eyes, just to name a few — the liver packs a powerful punch. In conjunction with the gallbladder, the liver works endlessly to help us excrete substances that the body no longer needs, including old hormones, pesticides and stored body fat. And if these substances are allowed to accumulate (as described in the toxicity section), energy can be significantly hampered.

Physiologically, the liver sits behind your right ribcage. Its primary role is detoxification, a concept that has had much confusion surrounding it — confusion that I want to resolve for you.

How the liver works and signs of poor functioning

A simple way to imagine the detoxification power of the liver is to picture a triangle shape: inside that triangle are billions and billions of little circles, each one of them a liver cell. Imagine that inside each liver cell is a wheel, spinning and spinning and spinning, with each turn of the billions of little wheels driving your liver function. When we treat our liver unkindly, a circle can die, and for a time the liver can regenerate a new cell to replace the dead cell, but after a while this is no longer possible, and a globule of fat can take up residence where once that fat-burning little "wheel" was working. The liver cannot now keep up with the load coming its way, as it could before, and, now that it has less function — with liver cells dying — it has even less function. So how will it keep up with the load if the load doesn't change? The answer is that it won't, and the fatty deposits will continue to be made.

When many fat globules take over (a situation known as "fatty liver"), our health and energy can suffer significantly. Less efficient detoxification processes can lead to poor thyroid function, sex hormone imbalances, congested skin, lousy cholesterol profiles, and impaired blood glucose management, which often show up as sugar cravings. Moreover, where our body wants to lay down body fat can also shift. For the first time people may notice that they have a fat roll quite high up on their abdomen. For women this is just below their bra line, and for men, just beneath their pectoral muscles. It can come and go, and sometimes there is a point right in the centre of the torso that is tender. I will always suggest ways to support the liver based on the presence of a fat roll in that position, and gallbladder support based on that tender point. Sometimes both organs need support.

In the not-too-distant past, only people who regularly over-consumed alcohol developed fatty liver disease, but now we are seeing teenagers develop it simply from eating diets high in processed foods and drinks. This has become so common that a new disease has been named, called "non-alcoholic fatty liver disease". Imagine a liver that looks just like one that has been chronically battered by alcohol, but instead processed food and drinks have created it.

Detoxification

It is important that you understand the mechanisms of detoxification and elimination that your body utilizes, because, when they are compromised, because when they are compromised, typically energy is as well. There are numerous organs and body systems involved in detoxification. They include:

＊ the *liver*, which transforms substances that if they were to accumulate would harm you, altering them into less harmful substances you can then excrete

★ the *colon* (digestive system), which contains bacteria that produce both healthy and unhealthy substances, so you want to keep your bowel moving regularly, as one of its roles is to release waste and problematic substances so they don't accumulate

★ the *kidneys*, which are constantly filtering your blood and getting rid of anything you don't need, including toxins, in urine

★ the *skin*, which not only protects and houses your organs, but allows problematic substances to leave the body via perspiration

★ the *respiratory system*, which plays a key role in the detoxification squad — even the hairs inside your nose help filter the air you breathe in — while the lungs are responsible for filtering out fumes, allergens, mould, and airborne toxins; when we are stressed, we tend to shift from slow belly-breathing to short, shallow upper-chest breaths, which in turn can reduce the lungs' ability to transport oxygen to all tissues; for those of you who know my work, you now know another reason (other than the nervous system and stress-hormone-lowering benefits) why diaphragmatic breathing is my number one health tip.

Detoxification is a process that goes on inside us all day, every day. The choices we make influence how efficiently the liver is able to do its job, and this significantly contributes to how we feel. Detoxification is essentially a transformation process. Any substance that would be harmful to you if it accumulated in your body must be changed into a less harmful form so that it can then be excreted safely from your body. To feel your best, you want this to be a highly efficient process.

There are two stages to the detoxification process, appropriately named phase 1 and phase 2 liver detoxification. Both phases require certain nutrients to function, and dietary choices can influence how efficiently each phase is able to work. The figure below illustrates the phases of detoxification, and you can see some of the nutrients that are required.

```
                Detoxification Pathways in the Liver

Toxins      →   Phase 1     →   Phase 2    →   Waste Products
(fat-soluble)   Required Nutrients  Required Nutrients  (water-soluble)
                                                        ↓
metabolic       B vitamins                      Eliminated from
  end products    including    sulphur            the body via

alcohol         folic acid     selenium                ↓

food additives  glutathione    amino acids,        Gallbladder

pesticides      antioxidants,  such as                ↓

drugs           such as Milk thistle  taurine    Skin       Kidneys

micro-organisms  vitamin C     glycine                ↓

pollutants      vitamin E      cysteine            Bile
                                                     ↓
contaminants    carotenoids    glutamine      Sweat Bowel Urine
                                                    actions
```

Liver detoxification pathways: Phase 1 and phase 2 liver detoxification pathways, and the nutrients essential to these vital processes.

Phase 1

For the first stage of detoxification, numerous nutrients, including B vitamins, are essential. As we discussed in the section about B vitamins, whole grains are supposed to be a rich source of these; however, many people feel much better with fewer or none of these foods in their diets. People decrease or cut grains out of their diets for a variety of reasons. Some people first experienced rapid weight loss with the advent of the high-protein, very low-carbohydrate diets, purported as the ultimate answer to weight-loss desires in the late 1990s, a repeat of the popular dietary concept from the 1970s, and a natural progression from the high-carbohydrate, low-fat guidelines that had preceded them. Others simply started to notice that foods made from grains induced reflux or made their tummy bloated, and they took action to change how they felt. If grains feel good for you and energize you, then enjoy them in wholefood form; some are best soaked prior to consumption. If they don't suit you, don't eat them. Your body knows best what works for you. Simply be aware that if you have a low intake of B vitamins, your phase 1 liver detoxification processes may not function optimally unless you are obtaining adequate B vitamins from other food sources, such as liver. You may choose to take a good quality supplement that contains a range of B vitamins.

Phase 2

There is one road into the liver and five pathways out of the liver. Just as for phase 1 reactions, phase 2 liver pathways also require certain nutrients to function; in particular, specific amino acids and sulphur.

We get our amino acids from protein foods. Think about this next statement: what we eat becomes part of us. Protein foods are broken down into amino acids, and they go on to create all of the cells of your immune system, which are what defends you from infection. Amino acids also go on to create the neurotransmitters in your brain that influence your mood and your clarity of thought, and also build your muscles. What you eat really does matter — your food becomes part of you.

For further phase 2 support we need sulphur, which we obtain from eggs, onion, garlic and shallots, as well as from the *Brassica* genus of vegetables, which includes broccoli, cabbage, kale, Brussels sprouts and cauliflower. The liver makes enzymes that are responsible for the transformation of each substance, and the rate of production of these essential enzymes determines how quickly each substance is processed. The load placed on the liver also determines how quickly things move through it, and you will see shortly how all of this has an impact on how you feel, as well as how your clothes fit you.

Liver-loaders

There is a group of substances I lovingly label "liver-loaders". They include:

alcohol

trans fats

refined sugars

synthetic substances, such as pesticides, medications, as well as conventional skin, laundry and cleaning products

infections — for example, viruses such as glandular fever (also known as Epstein–Barr virus (EBV), or mononucleosis)

caffeine; however, its mechanism of action on liver detoxification pathways differs from those above, as explained later in this section.

When we consider our exposure to synthetic substances we must consider skincare and cleaning products. We are crazy if we think that we don't absorb things through our skin. You only have to look at the way nicotine patches work to realize that the skin provides a direct route to our bloodstream, carrying the blood that the liver will need to "clean". There are plenty of wonderful skincare companies out there who do not use synthetic ingredients. Seek them out or even make your own. I love to suggest to people that it would be good if they could eat their skincare! You want to be able to recognize the words on the label of your skincare, just as you do with food. The same applies to the ingredients in laundry and cleaning products, which can enter through your skin or respiratory system.

It is also important to do what we can to minimize our exposure to, and consumption of, pesticides and herbicides. First, a number of these synthetic chemicals mimic oestrogen and can bind to the oestrogen receptors in the body, which has consequences for males and females of all ages. Research from the United States suggests that a significant and growing number of girls in this country are now starting to menstruate at the age of eight. It is difficult to explain how this is so without contemplating the role of environmental oestrogens.

Another concern with the consumption of pesticides and herbicides is the risk of their storage in the fatty tissue of our body (the mechanism was explained in the toxicity section). We don't know the long-term consequences of this, nor of being exposed to these substances for an entire lifetime, as we are essentially the first generation of people to be exposed to some of them for such a long period. Do we yet know the extent of their cumulative impact on our energy and metabolism, let alone other aspects of our health?

Caffeine

Often when I talk about caffeine, because I know how much people love coffee, I almost want to say "block your ears!" Some people's health and energy are definitely better without any caffeine, and, for those who need to decrease their adrenalin production, changes to their caffeine consumption are essential. And yes, sometimes that means none. For others, it means less. Or it means a single shot of coffee three days a week instead of a double shot three times a day, the latter being one of the most typical coffee consumption patterns I see. The best support for some people's nervous systems, depending on their symptoms, such as anxiety (explored already) or adrenal glands (explored in a later section) is without doubt none.

However, the liver has a role to play with caffeine as well, and decreasing the liver load can be another reason to cut back on caffeine intake or omit it. See what you think once you understand this mechanism, and see one of the reasons why some people tolerate caffeine better than others; why it can be some people's friend and another's foe.

Like the other liver-loaders listed above, caffeine arrives at the front door of the liver needing to be changed (detoxified). It is not, however, known to congest phase 2. Instead, it upregulates (increases the speed of) phase 1. Great, you might think, sounds like just what I need — faster liver detoxification processes. But here's the thing: for too many people today, their phase 2 is inefficient, congested or simply overwhelmed with the load, so imagine phase 2 moving slowly, like traffic crawling along a motorway. And now you have sped up phase 1 with the caffeine. So what seems to occur is that you process substances like oestrogen and cholesterol faster along phase 1, but they have nowhere to go because phase 2 is so overwhelmed, and they hit a road block. So you create a scenario where there are *more* partially changed substances being generated, and, because they cannot be taken straight into phase 2 processes to be fully detoxified, and then go on to be excreted, you wind up recycling even more problematic substances. And this can have major consequences for your health and your ability to prevent diseases, as well as for your energy. So if phase 2 is moving well, upregulating phase 1 seems to pose no real problem. But if phase 2 is congested, upregulating phase 1 adds to the problem. After you read about "recycled substances", later in this section, this will make even more sense.

The genes involved in the phase 1 and phase 2 liver detoxification pathways have also been highlighted as playing a role in what I have just described. However, I will never forget being in an audience at a medical conference where a professor of medicine bowled onto the stage exuding high energy at the spritely age of 76 and the first thing out of his mouth was: "We're all born with bad genes. It's what we do with them that matters." Certainly some conditions are 100 per cent genetic. But in many conditions, the interplay between our genes and our lifestyle choices is at work, and the only part of that dance that we can influence are the choices we make hundreds of times each day … "Will I go back for seconds?" "Will I eat a meat pie for the fourth time this week?" "Will I go for a walk now?" And this expression of genes based on environmental stimuli is known as *epigenetics*, a concept explored in the next section.

Internal stressors

However, it is not just infections or the things we consume or put on our skin that can place demands on the detoxification processes of the liver. Substances which your body makes itself also need transformation by the liver so that they can be excreted. These substances include:

cholesterol

steroid (sex) hormones, such as oestrogen

those created by or causing any short-fall in digestion, due to compromised digestive processes

those generated by untreated food sensitivities, and

metabolites produced in people eating gluten who have (undiagnosed) coeliac disease.

I have met countless people who have not consumed much in the way of liver-loaders, but have diabolical menstrual cycles or an ongoing challenge with irritable bowel syndrome or constipation, and often exhibit what I consider to be distinct signs that their liver needs support. Passing clots while menstruating is a classic liver-congestion sign, as are many skin conditions. More symptoms are listed below.

Indications your liver needs support
The following are symptoms that may indicate that your liver needs support:

liver roll

tender point in the centre of your torso (which can indicate gallbladder issues, past emotional heartbreak, or massive disappointment); if your gallbladder has been removed, your liver has to make the bile on demand as the gallbladder is no longer there to store it, so additional liver support is often required

short fuse or bad temper

episodes or feelings of intense anger

"liverish", gritty, impatient behaviour

premenstrual syndrome (PMS)

cellulite (lymphatic or cortisol-related also)

congested skin or skin outbreaks related to the menstrual cycle

- skin rashes
- eczema, rosacea
- overheating easily
- "floaters" in your vision (can also be a sign of iron deficiency)
- waking around 2am
- poor sleep on an evening you consume alcohol
- waking up hot during the night
- not hungry for breakfast when you first get up in the morning
- preference for coffee to start your day
- elevated cholesterol
- oestrogen-dominance symptoms
- bloating easily
- daily alcohol consumption, and
- daily long-term caffeine consumption (although tea and green tea are more favourable than coffee, soft drinks and energy drinks).

Recycled substances impacting energy

It is also important to understand another aspect of the role the liver plays in managing the levels of specific substances in the body via excretion following the complete detoxification of that substance. This occurs with substances the body makes as well as substances you might consume. Examples of the former include cholesterol and oestrogen. To understand an additional mechanism of fatigue, oestrogen metabolism needs to be explored — a process relevant to men, women, boys and girls. It is of particular importance for any females who identify with being oestrogen-dominant (described in detail in *Rushing Woman's Syndrome*).

When a liver-loader, either consumed (*exogenous*) or made as a result of internal chemistry (*endogenous*), arrives at the front door of the liver, it has arrived to be transformed. In the case of oestrogen, it may have originated from inside the body or come from the environment — plastics, pesticides and foods can contain substances that can bind to oestrogen receptors in the body. In menstruating women, oestrogen is made by the ovaries. But for everyone else (men, boys, girls and pre-pubertal or post-menopausal women) oestrogen is made by the adrenal glands and the fat cells. In other words, the more fat cells we have and the bigger they are, the more oestrogen we make, regardless of our gender. And this is a major problem for numerous aspects of our health, but also for energy levels.

When it comes to sex hormones, ratios are everything. When you have too much oestrogen — regardless of where it has come from or whether it is in its original form or the recycled version — an excess of oestrogen doesn't just put us at risk of ill health, it can also be debilitating to energy. Oestrogen dominance can drive a bone-weary tiredness that is like no other. So let's understand its metabolism better.

Oestrogen

The explanation that follows focuses on oestrogen as the liver-loader. When any of the liver-loaders arrive at the front door of the liver, they undergo their first stage of change (phase 1 liver detoxification). Between the front door and the middle of the liver, oestrogen is still oestrogen, but it has been altered somewhat. This slightly changed form of oestrogen then wants to go down one of the five phase 2 detox roads, and, once it has done that, it has been slightly altered again, and it is this substance that can then be excreted — expelled from your body forever.

Health problems can arise, however, when the traffic on the phase 2 pathways gets banked up like traffic on a motorway. After years of regularly consumed liver-loaders, and/or hormonal or bowel problems, the roads out of the liver can become congested. Conventional blood tests for liver function do not reveal this. The liver usually takes years of battering before conventional blood tests reflect the congestion that led to the liver function enzymes becoming elevated in the first place. When the traffic is banked up, the oestrogen undergoes its first stage of change and arrives in the middle of the liver, ready to go down the appropriate path for the second stage of transformation before excretion. If the phase 2 pathways are congested, the oestrogen sitting in the middle of the liver has nowhere to go. However, it cannot remain waiting in the middle of the liver, as there is more rubbish constantly coming through the front door of the liver. When this occurs, the liver releases the oestrogen back out into the blood, and it gets recycled. It is the recycling of these substances, not the substances themselves, that can potentially be harmful to human health, including our energy and our waistlines due to the metabolic effects that the increased levels generate. In addition, it is this recycled form of oestrogen that has been linked to numerous reproductive cancers, particularly oestrogen-sensitive breast cancer.

What organ can we take much better care of if we want to stop this recycling from happening? Our precious liver. Our livers need more support, and less of a load, for amazing energy, vitality, disease prevention and hence longevity.

Alcohol

Unfortunately alcohol is a depressant in its action on the nervous system. And in the aftermath of too much to drink, many people can identify with the fatigue that is present. Yet, if you wake up tired every morning and you tell me that you drink alcohol every day — even if it is only two glasses — I will tell you that this very habit might very easily be the thing robbing you of your get up and go. I don't say what I'm about to say lightly. I say it simply to report a fact. Alcohol is a poison to the human body. It is a poison because we cannot excrete it. We consume alcohol, but the liver has to transform (detoxify) that alcohol into another substance called *acetaldehyde*, which is what you are then able to excrete. This process utilizes energy and your body will prioritize this detoxification over-supplying you with energy with which to enjoy your day. It has to. For if alcohol is allowed to accumulate in your blood supply to an exceptionally high level, you will go into a coma. That is how it works and we cannot fight our biology.

So I could not conclude talking about liver detoxification without talking about alcohol. There is a reason it is at the top of the list above — I consider it one of the most pervasive substances impacting on too many livers today. I see people who might eat as green as can be, but at the same time consume alcohol daily. Alcohol is certainly a substance that can take away our energy and vitality, and sometimes the energy and vitality of those around us, particularly when it is regularly over-consumed. As a society, we need to get real about the dangers of the regular, over-consumption of alcohol. Weight that won't shift can be a major consequence, too, particularly if the routine consumption has been going on longer-term and this is not necessarily due to alcohol's calorie content. Because of the way alcohol is broken down in the body, requiring the liver to transform the alcohol into acetaldehyde before it can be excreted, it can lead to sex hormone imbalances due to oestrogen recycling; hello fatigue, anxieties and fat storage. Many alcoholic drinks are also very high in sugars (carbohydrates) and hence require insulin; hi, again, fatigue and body fat storage. It also leads to excess cortisol production and — you guessed it — another depleting and fat-storage signalling message to the body. You can see how many of the body systems involved in you feeling energized can be disrupted by alcohol.

The effects of the regular, over-consumption of alcohol are far-reaching. Whether it is less energy, increased body fat or cellulite, worse bouts of premenstrual syndrome (PMS), or mood fluctuations, or perhaps your get-up-and-go has got up and left ... the price of over-consumption is just not worth it. As fun as it can be at the time, alcohol can rob you of your clarity and purpose when it is regularly over-consumed.

January often sees people making big statements about their health, and many involve alcohol reduction or avoidance. Some wait until February to take a break, as they have worked out that it has the least number of days! I know others who do Dry July or Oct-sober. Others simply select the special occasions when they choose to imbibe, rather than making it part of every day, or totally go without.

We drink for a wide range of varied reasons. For some, it is the way they socialize, or the way they wind down from the day. Some use alcohol to distract themselves from thoughts and feelings they would rather avoid, and to numb themselves from registering that there are things about their life they would like to change. It can be a way for people to cope. Regardless of the reason, too many people over-drink without even realizing it. Yet to change the pattern, if this is something that you want to do — whether it be for better energy or emotional reasons — it is usually much easier a transition to less frequent alcohol if the underlying reason you use it every day is addressed.

To put all of this into perspective, based on current evidence-based medicine, a standard drink is 100 grams of alcohol, in whatever form that comes. In Australia and New Zealand, 100 grams of alcohol is a 330-millilitre bottle of 4 per cent beer, a 30-millilitre nip of spirits, 170 millilitres of champagne, or a measly 100 millilitres of wine — about four swallows! Next time you pour yourself a glass of wine, measure it, and see what your natural pour is. For most, it is considerably more than 100 millilitres, and, as a result, many people unknowingly over-drink.

The current recommendations provided by numerous heart foundations in concurrence with the National Health and Medical Research Council (NHMRC) now suggest for those who already drink alcohol it is safe to consume no more than two standard drinks per day, for both men and women, adding that the evidence suggests that this must include two alcohol-free days (AFDs) per week. However, I also encourage you to consider the position statement on alcohol endorsed by many of the cancer organizations from around the world, which says that if you have a family history of cancer, there is no safe level of alcohol consumption — which is a very powerful statement to contemplate. The link between the consistent over-consumption of alcohol and breast cancer is undeniable. Research has shown this time and time again and for many years now, yet we rarely hear about it.

I am not suggesting that you don't drink. Having a drink can be immensely pleasurable for those who partake on occasion. I simply want to appeal to you to get honest with yourself about how alcohol may affect you. You know in your heart whether you drink too much and when it is negatively impacting your health. Alcohol can affect the way we relate to those we love the most in the world, deplete our energy, and of course it affects how we feel about ourselves. So, if you drink, drink for the pleasure of it or to celebrate on occasion, rather than to escape from your daily life.

If you want to cut back or cut out alcohol for a while, or even if you just want to break your habit of regular drinking, still pour yourself a drink at the time you would normally have a drink, and do what you would normally do. Sit and chat to your partner, make dinner, talk on the phone to a friend. So often we have mentally linked the glass of wine to a pleasurable activity when it is actually the pleasurable activity that we don't want to miss out on! So have sparkling water in a wine glass, with some fresh lime or lemon if that appeals, and add a few more AFDs to your life.

Liver support

At the weekend events that I run, I help people understand the exhaustion and guilt that a vicious cycle of too much alcohol in the evenings, coffee to cope the next morning, and sugar cravings mid-afternoon drives. The guilt you feel tends to lead you back to that cycle, whereas if you saw it as a one-off and then returned to a higher level of self-care, it would have a much more minimal impact. Remember, it is what you do every day that impacts on your health, not what you do sometimes.

Be honest with yourself about the liver-loaders in your life. Focus on taking good care of yourself and nourishing yourself, rather than on what you may need to consume less of; as that in itself can feel overwhelming or exhausting and just another thing to do. As you have read, the liver plays a significant role in our experience of energy as well as in the metabolism of countless substances that are linked to whether the body gets the message to burn body fat or store it, not to mention disease prevention. We only have one liver. Love it accordingly.

Epigenetics: The Empowering New Movement in Science

In my opinion, epigenetics is one of the most empowering movements in science today. It may sound futuristic and complex, but the key concept is really quite simple. Epigenetics means you have the ability to control the expression of your genes, meaning you have the ability to control to what extent you "inherit" certain health conditions. Until fairly recently, science suggested that the genes you inherit from your parents — namely, the ones that code for disease — are the most common way to inherit risks for diseases like cancer and heart problems. But there is another way to pick up genetic changes that researchers are starting to pay closer attention to. And I love it, because it puts you back in the driver's seat of your health. Because, let's face it, when you believe something is genetic, do you feel like there is anything you can do about this? No. So you spend your life living in the cloud of false belief that you have to put up with your health picture, when there may be numerous options for you to employ to resolve a particular health challenge.

Most of us had our first taste of science and biology (whether we were awake or not!) at school. As part of the curriculum we learn that genes, made up of DNA, are essentially the blueprints that make us who we are. This DNA code we have is a unique combination of information from our mothers and fathers. Which genes we pick up from mum and which from dad is a somewhat random process. That genetic draw in turn helps to determine which diseases we're most at risk of developing during our lifetimes — well at least that's how we used to view it.

More recently, scientists have learned that DNA alone does not define our health destiny, and hence they have been focusing on another layer of genetic inheritance or potential called *epigenetics*. Epigenetics also plays an important role in determining what our DNA blueprints become. Epigenetic changes can be created by exposure to things like smoking, environmental pollutants and nutritional factors, as well as lifestyle behaviours. Essentially our environment has the ability to switch our genes on or off, which of course has significant implications when it comes to turning on or off the genes relating to disease. Furthermore, researchers have demonstrated how it is possible to pass on these epigenetic changes to your children. So how you eat, drink, move, think, breathe, believe and perceive literally has the ability to influence your genetic blueprint. It is truly mind-blowing.

This is particularly exciting, as we used to hear of people who were likely to have inherited disease risk factors feeling completely disempowered by their luck of the draw. We have moved from feeling "trapped" or "defined" by our genes to being empowered that the lifestyle we lead can literally alter the expression of these genes. The power is well and truly within our hands, or perhaps more accurately, on the end of our forks. The foods we choose and the nutrients they contain literally have the power to flick the switch on our genes.

Biology and belief

As this new movement in biology moves us away from the belief that we are victims of our genes and that life is controlled by them, we begin to understand to a greater extent how influential our thoughts, beliefs, and our behaviour are to the life we experience.

Many people are unaware of what drives their choices and behaviours. It is essentially our beliefs. The challenge is that most of us absorbed many of the beliefs that create our behaviours before we were old enough to talk. And unless this is something you have explored in your adult life, they will be creating the life you now have. Some beliefs serve us. Others limit us, and we outgrow many of them. The other tricky thing is that many beliefs are subconscious and, to understand just how important our beliefs are to our biology, we need to explore the subconscious as well as the conscious mind.

The conscious mind can think freely and create new ideas, and we are aware of this. However, the subconscious mind is more powerful and tends to be responsible for our pre-programmed behaviours, most of which we acquire before we reach the age of seven. It has been estimated that most of our decisions, actions, emotions and behaviour depend on the 95 per cent of brain activity that is beyond our conscious awareness, which means that 95 to 99 per cent of our life comes from the programming in our subconscious mind.

The subconscious mind struggles to move outside its fixed "ideas" — it also automatically reacts to situations with previously gathered behavioural responses. This is often why we can be unaware of our behaviour; in fact, most of the time we are not even aware that we are acting from our subconscious. Studies show that our brains begin to prepare for action just over a third of a second before we actually consciously decide to act. In other words, even when we "think" we are conscious, it is our subconscious mind making the decision for us.

If we interpret our interactions in a positive way, we start living better-quality lives, regardless of the genetic makeup we started with. So your attitudes, beliefs and perceptions — positive or negative — can actually influence the health, behaviour and structure of the cells in your body.

Becoming aware of your beliefs means accessing the behavioural programs in your subconscious mind so that you can change the underlying limiting or self-sabotaging thoughts that don't serve you. If this is difficult for you to identify, it may help to ask a close, wise friend. Often they can see things that we can't. Or you can see an experienced psychologist who can help you explore your patterns.

However, you may be aware of underlying negative thought patterns. Ones I often hear are "I'm not good enough", "I'm worthless", "I would like myself more if I lost weight", "I'm such a failure" … and the list goes on. While it is natural to have these thoughts from time to time, it can be incredibly destructive if this is your default programming. Trade your expectation for anticipation and your whole world will change instantly. If this subject is of particular interest to you, I cannot encourage you enough to explore the work of Dr Bruce Lipton, a cell biologist and epigenetics pioneer.

So what does it mean for you and me right now?

How do we know that one of the key determinants of our energy systems doesn't involve the expression of particular genes? And the short answer is that we don't!

The environment has the ability to alter the expression of our genes, and we can to a certain extent control our environment, from the foods we choose to the thoughts we think. We now know that some chemicals in our environment can damage DNA, so whenever possible I urge you to choose non-toxic options. Become aware of what you clean your house with and what you put on your skin, supporting companies that consider the environment and human health when they develop their products using non-toxic ingredients. From a nourishment perspective: move regularly, nourish your body with wholefoods, choose organic and free-range sources whenever possible, and address your limiting beliefs and behaviours that no longer serve you.

Let the quote from the previous chapter ("We're all born with bad genes. It's what we do with them that matters") empower you so that you have the ability to alter your health future. You are not a victim of whatever predisposition your genes say you might have — you can be an active participant in creating the life you want to live.

The price of anything is the amount
of life you exchange for it.

Henry David Thoreau

The Adrenal Glands

Stress has undoubtedly infiltrated many people's lives, and for some it feels relentless. Because stress and the adrenals are another of the major three factors at the top of the list of potentials involved in energy issues, this area will be looked at closely — another big section! Stress doesn't just play a role epigenetically (switching gene expression on or off); when it comes to energy, after sleep quality and digestion, the adrenal glands are the next major area to consider physically (as opposed to emotionally) when someone is tired, as stress hormones are produced by the adrenals.

The adrenal glands are part of the endocrine system, and they sit just on top of the kidneys. They produce an array of hormones (chemical messengers), which include our stress hormones, adrenalin and cortisol, sex hormones such as progesterone, hormones that help control blood pressure, fluid balance and salt retention in the body, just to name a few. When it comes to our vitality, they pack a major punch in helping to create this.

To understand the role they play in energy, we need first to look at their structure, as some of the fatigue people can experience can be coming from deficits in the actual structure of the gland itself, or as a result of the hormones the glands release. For example, low cortisol levels can lead to a deep, unrelenting fatigue.

The structure of the adrenal glands

The image below shows how small the adrenals are compared with the kidney (one sits on top of the left kidney and one on top of the right). They are about the size of a walnut. The image shows how there are different components to the gland, and that they secrete specific categories of hormones from each different part.

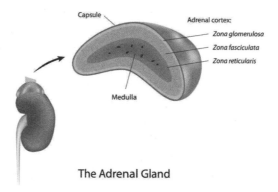

Capsule

Adrenal cortex:
Zona glomerulosa
Zona fasciculata
Zona reticularis

Medulla

The Adrenal Gland

The adrenal glands: Made up of a capsule, the cortex and the medulla. Within the cortex are distinct tissue types known as *Zona glomerulosa, Zona fasciculata and Zona reticularis.*

The *medulla* produces the *catecholamines*, such as adrenalin, while the *cortex* produces cortisol. So a person's symptoms — whether they demonstrate an elevation of adrenalin or cortisol, or low cortisol — will determine part of the road to restored energy. However, as mentioned above, the treatment needs to address the *consequences* of the hormones. For example, adrenalin contributes to sugar cravings, blood glucose dys-regulation, inflammation, elevations in blood pressure, as well as to anxious feelings, and these (consequences) must be treated. Yet if cortisol is low for an individual, they will have a host of debilitating symptoms, such as body pain, plus their adrenal cortex may also need support to improve its function.

Before we look at the specific stages of stress and how these relate to energy, as well as at useful nutritional and herbal medicine support for restoring vitality from an adrenal perspective, it is important to understand the role each stress hormone plays and the way it impacts on other body systems, as sometimes the consequences of the stress hormone are the biggest challenge for an individual.

Back to basics

The production of stress hormones can significantly influence a wide range of body systems all linked to health and energy, including the immune system, the nervous system, sex hormone balance, gut function, and whether your body gets the message that it needs to store body fat or burn it, just to name a few. The two main stress hormones the body makes are adrenalin and cortisol. They behave very differently from one another, and communicate different messages, but both have the power to influence whether you bounce out of bed full of vitality or wonder how it could be morning yet.

A US study published by the American Psychological Association in 2011, conducted with 1,226 people over the age of 18 years, found that the top five areas of stress (in descending order) were money, work, the economy, relationships (spouse, children, girl-/boyfriend), and family responsibilities.

In 2013, in a study conducted by the Australian Psychological Society, involving 21,000 people aged over 18 years of age who were working, Australians reported significantly lower levels of wellbeing and significantly higher levels of stress and distress than in 2012 and 2011. Almost three-quarters of Australians (73 per cent) reported that stress was having at least some impact, with almost one in five people (17 per cent) reporting that stress was having a strong to very strong impact on their physical health. Finances were the leading cause of stress for Australians, followed by family and health issues. I share these results with you to demonstrate how significantly stress has permeated our existence in the Western world, and, given it has such major metabolic and health consequences, these mechanisms need to be understood so people can be far more accurately guided with their health choices to obtain the outcomes they seek. Addressing stress hormone production can be a critical factor in modern-day energy creation as well as in weight loss. Of course we can argue that there has always been stress, but it has never before come in the constant, urgent avalanche that has become the norm for so many people in the Western world.

Stress hormones don't just impact on the energy system

directly. They can also interfere with other processes in the body that are vital to metabolic rate and energy levels, such as thyroid function, gut function and sex hormone balance. These body systems can also influence whether we feel calm or anxious, happy or sad, and these emotional states can also impact food choices and our level of self-care and self-esteem. There are ripple effects in action everywhere. Nothing in the body stands alone.

The three parts of the brain

As we learnt earlier, central to our response to stress is what is known as the *fight-or-flight response*: when faced with a perceived threat to our safety, we either stand our ground and meet the threat head-on, or we flee to safety. Our body's — and in particular our hormones' — response to perceived stress is influenced by the three integrated parts of the human brain, so we will briefly look at these before moving on to the stress hormones themselves.

The first part is the *brain stem*, or *reptile brain*. This is the *survival brain*. It controls the functions responsible for our survival, as an individual and as a species — things such as hunger, thirst, heartbeat, breathing, digestion, immunity and sex drive. It is the basic, primal part of us that is in all animals: give me food, give me shelter, let me reproduce. This part of the brain also *initiates* the fight-or-flight stress response.

> The production of stress hormones can significantly influence a wide range of body systems all linked to health and energy, including the immune system, the nervous system, sex hormone balance, gut function, and whether your body gets the message that it needs to store body fat or burn it, just to name a few.

The second part is the *limbic system*, or *mammalian brain*. All mammals have it, and it is composed of the amygdala, the hippocampus and the thalamus. This is our *emotional brain*. It controls all of the functions related to emotional aspects of survival, such as memory, behaviour, pleasure and pain responses, and our experience of all emotions. It *maintains* the fight-or-flight stress response.

The third part is the *cerebral cortex*, or *human brain*. Humans and some other mammals, such as apes, dolphins and whales, have this brain, and it is our *thinking brain*. It controls such things as decision-making, attention, awareness, language, judgement, reading and writing. It is the centre of higher thought, and it is *impaired* by the fight-or-flight stress response.

These comprise the mental processes that feed into our physiological response to life.

The adrenal glands

Let's look at what we ask of our body from an adrenal and stress hormone perspective when we live a high-stress, fast-paced lifestyle, or if we live life on an emotional roller-coaster. For those of you who have read *Accidentally Overweight, Rushing Woman's Syndrome, Beauty from the Inside Out,* or *The Calorie Fallacy*, some of this information was covered there, but this section has been expanded and is essential reading at this stage in your journey to understanding the way stress hormones can have an impact on your energy and vitality.

Adrenalin, sugar cravings and blood glucose

Adrenalin is your short-term, acute stress hormone. It is the one that is produced when you get a fright. If someone suddenly runs into the room and startles you, the feeling that follows is caused by adrenalin. Adrenalin is designed to get you out of danger — and get you out of danger fast. Historically, humans made adrenalin when their lives were threatened. The response, fuelled by adrenalin, was typically physical. If a tiger suddenly jumped out at you in the jungle, or perhaps a member of another tribe started chasing you with a spear, the body made adrenalin, promoting the fight-or-flight response.

When activated, the typically excellent blood supply to your digestive system is diverted away from your digestive system to your periphery, to your arms and your legs. This is necessary because you need a powerful blood supply to your arms and legs to get you out of danger. Hence digestion is compromised. This may not only create digestive system symptoms, but this alone can create low energy for an individual, as the section about digestion explains further.

You also need fuel to help you escape, and the most readily available, fastest-burning fuel inside the body is *glucose*, often referred to as sugar, a carbohydrate. Your liver and muscles store glucose in the form of *glycogen*, and adrenalin communicates to your liver and muscles when energy is required. Glycogen is converted back into glucose, and this glucose is released back into your blood. Your blood glucose (ie, sugar) subsequently shoots up, ready to fuel your self-defence or your escape. And you feel amped up, although many people today don't identify this, as they have become accustomed to it being their norm.

This cascade of events — and the biochemical changes that result — allows you to escape from danger in a very active way. Regardless of the outcome, regardless of whether you win that challenge or not (you escape, die, or win the fight), this stress, the threat to your life and the need for adrenalin are over quickly. The trouble is that, for many of us in the modern world, it is more often psychological stress that drives us to make adrenalin, and for many people today that stress is never switched off. Although our life may not literally be threatened, this hormone still communicates to every cell of our body that our life is indeed at risk. Adrenalin makes your heart race, your thoughts race, and gives you a jittery feeling that can make it difficult to feel calm and centred, despite your best efforts.

Psychological stress can come in many forms. It may be that you return from a week away from work to find 700 new emails in your in-box, and you wonder when on Earth you are going to find the time to deal with those. It may be that your landline rings, and while you take that call your mobile rings, and you feel that you can barely finish one conversation before demands come in to start another one. If you are sitting in front of your computer while all of this is going on, and a few emails arrive in your in-box while you juggle the incoming demands and noise, adrenalin tends to climb higher. Or perhaps you set your alarm for the morning, you press the snooze button … you keep pressing snooze … and suddenly you sit bolt upright in bed and realize that you are running late. Maybe you still have clothes to iron, lunches to prepare, little people to deliver to school, and, because you are leaving later than usual, you get stuck in traffic. Meanwhile, your mobile phone starts ringing, with people at the office wondering where you are, as you are supposed to be in a meeting, but you are stuck in rush-hour traffic, and your brain has gone into overdrive with the enormity of your morning. And you have only been up for an hour!

When you finally burst through the doors at work, all you can think about is how much you want a coffee. So all morning you have been making adrenalin, and now you are going to make even more adrenalin, as caffeine promotes its production. All you actually want from the coffee at this point in your day is a little breathing space, a moment in time just for you, so your brain can catch up with your morning. The reasons we crave a hot drink vary, but, without realizing it, sometimes it is just a chance to catch our breath. In those coffee-break moments, it is as though there is a bubble around us, and we are silently communicating, "Don't you dare come near me for the next three minutes!" I have had countless people tell me that coffee is the only peace they get in their day, which, if you look at the reality of it, is not true, as physically coffee is actually adding to the demand on the adrenal glands, pushing them to produce adrenalin to get you away from a danger that doesn't actually exist.

There is an important distinction to make between the past and the modern day. The biochemical changes generated by adrenalin, such as glucose being dumped into your blood to get you out of danger, serve a useful purpose when you are physically fighting or fleeing, but if you are sitting at your desk and sugar is being dumped into your blood, you make insulin to deal with that elevation in blood sugar. And insulin is one of our primary fat-storage hormones. It says "store fat, don't utilize it". Not only that, but it sets up your blood sugar to crash at a later stage, creating a fatigued state that makes you feel like only more caffeine or high-sugar food can fix it. You can already see how adrenalin might make you go for foods or drinks that you know don't serve your wellbeing. Remember, if you don't utilize the glucose in your blood as fuel, it gets stored as glycogen first, and then any left over is stored as body fat.

Caffeine

Consumption rates

Over 90 per cent of adults in the Western world consume caffeine daily. In Australia and New Zealand, studies suggest that caffeine consumption has more than tripled since the 1960s, and, although levels may not be on par with rates of consumption in the United States, they are rapidly rising, not only due to an increase in coffee consumption, but also due to the widespread use of caffeine as an ingredient in, for example, energy drinks. In the United States, 70 per cent of soft drinks contain caffeine. In a US study conducted in 2011, 28 per cent of coffee drinkers had their first cup within 15 minutes of waking and 68 per cent within an hour of waking, while 57 per cent added sugar or a sweetener to their brew. The level of caffeine consumption for far too many people is considered addictive by medical textbook standards, and I don't say that lightly.

Effect of caffeine

Here's what happens when you consume caffeine. Caffeine sends a message to the pituitary gland in your brain that it needs to send a message to the adrenal glands to make stress hormones: adrenalin and/or cortisol. When adrenalin is released, your blood sugar elevates to provide you with more energy (ie, fuel); your blood pressure and pulse rate rise to provide more oxygen to the muscles, which tense in preparation for action. Reproductive functions are down-regulated, since they use a lot of energy and are not necessary for your immediate survival, given the impending "threat". Plus, your body does not believe it is safe to bring a baby into what it perceives to be an unsafe world, as adrenalin is telling your body that your life is in danger, while cortisol communicates that there is no more food left in the world!

Adrenalin production can be the result of real or perceived stress, or simply the result of your caffeine intake. Caffeine, via stress hormones, and coupled with the signal to activate the fight-or-flight response, fires you up. Once triggered, in this state you have little hope of being calm and centred, and you initiate an energy roller-coaster.

In addition, this biochemical state puts all of its resources into saving your life rather than into what are considered non-vital processes, those inside you that allow the reproductive system to work optimally, as well as interfering with the nourishment of skin, hair and nails. Over time, the lack of resources available to these non-vital processes (ie, those not necessary to sustain your life) has significant consequences internally and externally. First, your skin, hair and nails won't receive the nutrients and other substances they need to look their best. Secondly, because the fuel that drives the fight-or-flight response is glucose (ie, sugar), you will crave sugar to constantly refill your fuel tank, and you won't utilize your fat stores often or easily. Also, with additional glucose in your blood, you will release insulin — a fat-storage hormone — and it will first convert unused glucose from your blood into glycogen and store it in your muscles, and then what is left over will be converted into body fat. Powerful, isn't it?

It is so important that you consider your caffeine habits and get honest with yourself about how it affects you. Does it dull your appetite, and so unconsciously you grab a coffee instead of eating? This is especially true for many women at lunchtime. Does it make your heart race, give you the shakes, or loosen your bowels? Does it elevate your blood pressure? Do you notice you want it more when you are stressed, and, if so, what story have you attached to what coffee gives you?

Do you have restless, poor-quality sleep because of how much caffeine you consume? Or does it lift your mood, make your brain function better, or nourish your soul with no ill effect whatsoever? My clients will tell you that, when it is warranted, I ask them to decrease or take a break from caffeine completely for a four-week trial period. They are often shocked by how much more energy they have without caffeine in their lives, not to mention having less or no anxiety! You know yourself better than anyone. Act on what you know is true for you.

A little note on tea
Not so long ago, tea was the major source of caffeine for people in Australia and New Zealand, before the coffee culture hit town. Tea contains caffeine, although how much depends on how long you brew it. An average cup of black tea contains 50 milligrams of caffeine, whereas green tea tends to contain about 30 milligrams per cup. Tea, however, also contains another substance called *theanine*, which acts as an antioxidant, but also helps buffer the effect of the caffeine. It makes you alert but not wired. Some people are actually highly caffeine-sensitive, and even green tea can impact on them negatively. However, many people tolerate tea and feel good drinking tea compared with coffee. They may not realize this until they take a break from coffee though. Do what serves your health and energy.

The pace of life

Think about all of these mechanisms. So many people run on adrenalin these days. Moment to moment, day to day, it is as though a light-switch has gone on, and it hasn't entirely switched off for a really long time. And it doesn't have to be traumatic stress and/or shocking situations that drive this process. It can simply be the pace at which we live our lives: being contactable 24/7; constant exposure to social media, unless we purposefully choose otherwise; the juggling act that leads so many people I meet, women in particular, to say that they want more "balance" in their lives, as they can't cope like this anymore. (I wrote *Rushing Woman's Syndrome* for women who feel like this, to help guide them out of the rush.)

The human body is incredibly resilient and, although we were not designed to withstand long-term stress (due to the way we are designed, we are healthier when it is short-lived), many bodies appear to tolerate, but not necessarily thrive on, years and years of living on adrenalin. Yet I have witnessed first-hand what the relentless production of this hormone can do to health, including its impact on fertility, the incidence and severity of PMS for women, its impact on digestive systems, skin, relationships, happiness, the shape and size of the body, and the energy they wake up with and are able to sustain each day. An additional challenge, however, is that once the body perceives that the stress has become long term, your dominant stress hormone can begin to change, and that can have significant consequences on your energy and metabolism.

Cortisol — the chronic stress hormone

Cortisol is your long-term (ie, chronic) stress hormone. Historically, the only long-term stress humans had, revolved around food being scarce. Long-term stress came in the form of floods, famines and wars. During such times, a person didn't know where the next meal was coming from. Today, in the Western world, our long-term stresses tend to be based more on financial situations, relationship concerns, challenges with friendships, particularly for teenage girls, and uncertainty or worries about our health or bodies. I can't tell you how many times I have heard women, in particular, say that they would "do anything" for a different body part — thinner thighs, less body hair, no cellulite — and for many women the part or parts of themselves that they dislike intensely become a silent fixation in their minds. For so many women, their first waking thoughts involve "What will I, or won't I, eat today?" or "How much exercise can I get done today?"

So many people zoom through their days with a pervasive not-good-enough or never-enough-time monologue running through their head. Day after day, this can easily lead to a chronic pattern of stress response, hence increased cortisol output. In turn, this can lead to a significant change in your metabolism, your energy and where you store fat on your body.

How cortisol works

It is important to understand how cortisol works, as it can be your friend or one of your worst nightmares. When made at optimum amounts, cortisol does numerous wonderful things for your health. It is one of the body's primary anti-inflammatory mediators, meaning that wherever there is inflammation in the body, which is a process involved in most disease states, cortisol, having been converted into cortisone, dampens down the effect of that inflammation and stops your body from feeling stiff, rigid or in pain. Many people, for example, describe feeling that they have suddenly aged as they come out of difficult times, and often this is the result of sub-optimal cortisol levels during such periods. In the right amount, cortisol is not only an anti-inflammatory, it also buffers the effect of insulin, meaning that optimum amounts of cortisol help you continue to burn body fat for energy while also maintaining stable (as opposed to rapidly fluctuating) blood sugar levels.

Cortisol levels change over the day. The right amount at the right time assists you with various bodily functions throughout the course of the day. Cortisol is designed to be high in the morning and, for the purpose of this discussion, let's say that 25 units at around 6am are ideal. Cortisol is one of the mechanisms that wake you up in the morning full of life.

By midday, optimum cortisol will sit at around 15 units, and, by 6pm, levels will ideally be at around four units. By 10pm, optimum cortisol levels are around two units, a level at which they are designed to stay until around 2am, when they slowly and very steadily begin to rise again.

The following graph illustrates this. So it is true what your mother told you — that one hour of sleep before midnight is worth two after — because cortisol starts to rise around 2am and the waking-up process gradually begins.

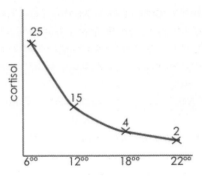

The optimal cortisol profile: Cortisol is nice and high in the morning, and falls away again by the evening.

As a stress response continues, its effect on the body begins to change. In the early stages of stress, one of the first challenges cortisol presents is that the evening level of the hormone starts to spike again rather than continue to decrease. At this stage, you still make optimum levels in the morning and are able to bounce out of bed and get on with your day with reasonable energy, but evening levels are creeping up. This is one mechanism through which good sleeping patterns can be interrupted. Research has shown that chronic sleep deprivation impairs concentration as much as what is considered an unsafe blood alcohol level.

When cortisol levels become elevated above optimal, other changes in body chemistry begin to unfold. It has been suggested that elevated cortisol is one of the common threads behind what we have come to describe as *metabolic syndrome*; that is, elevated blood pressure, elevated cholesterol, and insulin resistance. This last condition is a warning sign that, if nothing changes in the near future, type 2 diabetes is a likely consequence.

It is important to remember that we are completely geared for survival, and that elevated cortisol tells every cell of our body that food is scarce. This means that one of its roles is to slow down your metabolic rate. Cortisol's concern is that if you keep utilizing energy at a more rapid rate, you may become too thin and die. So it slows down your metabolism and tells your body to store fat, not burn it, in an attempt to put some more flesh on your bones so that you are more likely to survive the famine your body perceives you are facing. This, too, can promote a sense of lethargy, with less muscle mass and therefore less mitochondrial function.

One of the ways cortisol slows down your metabolic rate is by breaking down your muscles. Cortisol is what is known as a *catabolic hormone.* It breaks body proteins down into their building blocks, known as *amino acids,* and with less muscle mass you burn fewer calories. Remember, your muscles are made from proteins, and cortisol signals them to break down, as the body's perception is that fuel is needed. Additional amino acids are also needed in the blood to help repair tissues from this chronic stress you are enduring, even though you may be simply sitting on your bottom in front of the television, with your financial or relationship concerns milling around in your head. The amino acids released as a result of the catabolic signalling of cortisol can be converted, through a process called *gluconeogenesis,* back into glucose (sugar), which your body thinks may be useful to assist you in your stress. Yet, if you are not active, this increase in blood glucose will not be utilized, and insulin will have to be secreted to return blood glucose levels to normal by returning the glucose in the blood to storage. Remember that glucose is stored as glycogen in the muscles and the liver.

Over time, the catabolic signalling of cortisol itself may have broken down some of your muscles, so now there is less space for glucose storage. As a result, some of the blood glucose returns to the remaining muscles while the leftovers are converted into body fat. Keeping the glucose level of the blood within the normal, safe range is of more importance to your body than whether you have wobbly bits around your middle! This is also one of the mechanisms through which cellulite can appear, as where muscles once were, fat can now be deposited. This is also the process through which long-term stress can contribute to type 2 diabetes.

Because excess cortisol is produced after the stress in your life has been going on for a while, your body — not knowing any better — thinks that there is no more food left in your world, and it instinctively knows that it has a greater chance of survival if it holds onto some extra body fat. In modern times, when, for health reasons or vanity (or both), many people understand the importance of not carrying too much body fat, cortisol can provide a potential challenge to someone who believes that eating less (ie, a diet) is their only solution to body fat loss. Yet if you eat less when excess cortisol is already telling your body that there is no food left in the world, you will confirm to your body what it perceives to be true — that there is no food left in the world — and your metabolism will be slowed even further.

Feeling like you are fighting an uphill battle with your body can be an immense source of stress and fatigue, adding another layer of stress to an already busy life. It can also lead people to feel like their body is betraying them, for throughout this metabolic change they may (or not) be making great efforts with food and movement. In other words, they may be ensuring their calorie equation is skewed for weight loss, but they are not achieving weight loss as a result. If anything, their clothes continue to fit them the way they have for a while or they become tighter, despite great efforts. This alone can be incredibly disheartening. Going on a diet is never the right medicine.

Cortisol has a distinct fat deposition pattern. If cortisol is an issue for you, you typically lay it on around your tummy, and once again the reason for fat placement here is governed by the body's quest for survival. If food suddenly did run out, your major organs have easy access to fat that will keep you alive. You also tend to lay down fat on the back of the arms (you get "bingo wings"), and you grow what I lovingly call a back verandah. So what do most people do when they notice that their clothes are getting tighter? They go on a diet, which typically means eating less. Eating less, though, just confirms to your body what it perceives to be true — that food is scarce — and so slows down your metabolism even further. But food is not scarce; it is abundant for you. If you want a chocolate bar at 3am, you can get one.

Guilt and cortisol

When you feel grateful for the life you have, it is easy to feel guilty if you complain about anything. A common internal phrase might be "there are so many people worse off than me". Such thinking immediately makes you feel guilty, and you stop focusing on your source of stress, having not solved it or resolved to see it differently. Trouble is, although there *are* people worse off than you in this world, the minute you feel guilty you change your focus so that you don't ever get the opportunity to identify what is bothering you, and more importantly why. What is bothering you can offer an insightful road to the core of something bigger, if you follow it with curiosity, rather than judging yourself. Constantly feeling guilty can be exhausting in itself.

Many people have shared with me that they keep the peace to avoid stress. Yet there is no peace when you have to keep the peace. Think about that. Here is a common example to help you see how everyday life, because of the perceptions we bring to it, can lead to cortisol, from an emotional source, being a contributor to health challenges.

Basic psychology teaches us that humans will do more to avoid pain than they will ever do to experience pleasure. Some women, in particular, will do anything to keep the peace and avoid conflict. Inwardly, they become highly strung because they are always walking on eggshells around others, especially their intimate partner, doing all they can to help prevent those around them from losing their temper. If the man of the house has a tendency to communicate with explosive, angry outbursts that seem unpredictable — hello, silent stress hormone production! Some people avoid feeling emotional pain by eating too much or making other poor food or lifestyle choices; perhaps drinking bucket-loads of wine or chain-smoking cigarettes. Some go shopping and rack up credit card bills that will take months or years to pay off. Alternatively, some people might cope or explore their pain by writing in a journal, or going for a walk or a swim. Others will pray, meditate, or telephone a friend and chat to deal with emotional pain. Some of the ways we cope with or explore what is going on support our health.

Some potentially harm our health. And all of these activities may take place with or without a conscious understanding of why.

I want to help you see *why*, so that you can change your response, if it is hurting your health, especially if the stress hormone production triggered by your subconscious emotional responses is blocking you from experiencing the amazing human that you are — and is making you tired in the process. I love this quote by Marcus Aurelius, which may assist you if guilt or worry are patterns for you: "If you are troubled by external circumstances, it is not the circumstances that trouble you, but your own perception of them — and they are in your power to change at any time." Do something creative with that quote — stick it on your fridge if it helps.

Adrenal fatigue

The next biochemical stage of stress that can occur, especially if the stress has been prolonged, may involve cortisol levels falling low, and these days I see more and more of this in younger and younger people. If you have had a high level of cortisol output for many, many years, your adrenal glands may not be able to sustain this. They are not designed to withstand this kind of output, and so they "crash". In general terms, you burn out. Your energy crashes. You feel like you've been hit by a bus most days. It is worst in the mornings. In more recent times, this has become known as *adrenal fatigue*, because the major symptom is a deep, unrelenting fatigue.

Yet even with fatigue as the major symptom, what I have observed over the past decade is that, not only are people beyond tired, at the same time they can also be wired, although not always. And when you are tired but wired, you desire deeply restorative sleep more than ever, yet it rarely happens; your adrenal hormone production is usually at the heart of this. The pituitary gland in your brain regulates your adrenals (and the rest of your endocrine system), and, although treatment for adrenal fatigue usually involves a range of strategies that support the adrenals themselves, going one step further and assisting the pituitary gland can also be immensely powerful and highly beneficial to restoring your health and vitality.

In my opinion, a form of yoga known as restorative yoga, or Stillness Through Movement, is the most effective way to make progress in recovering from adrenal fatigue. Combined with dietary changes and herbal medicine, you can recover from this debilitating condition.

As you now understand, the adrenal hormone cortisol is supposed to be high in the morning, helping you to bounce out of bed. It plays a role in how vital you feel and helps the body combat any inflammatory processes that want to kick in. Stiffness is a key symptom of adrenal fatigue. For those with chronic stress, morning cortisol levels tend to be low; if 25 units is the ideal, with adrenal fatigue you may only get to 10 units, or even less. It can be very difficult to get out of bed with such low levels. By mid-afternoon it will be at an all-time low, and you will usually feel you need something sweet and/or something containing caffeine, and/or a nap to get you through your afternoon. (This can also be the result of low blood sugar or poor thyroid function, which are explored in other sections.) For an adrenally fatigued person, cortisol tends to be nice and low in the evenings, as it is supposed to be. But, if you don't go to bed before 10pm, you will typically get a second wind, and it will be much harder for you to fall asleep if you are still up at midnight, partly due to the body's natural next adrenalin surge (not cortisol) that tends to happen between 10.30pm and 11.30pm. The following graph illustrates this cortisol pattern.

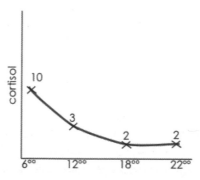

A typical cortisol profile of an adrenally fatigued person: Note, particularly, the low waking cortisol and low midday reading.

When cortisol drops low, it is likely that prior to this it was high (although not always) and body fat may have increased during this time. But just because cortisol is low does not necessarily mean easy access to body fat burning, due to cortisol's relationship to insulin, as described earlier. Plus, if cortisol was previously high, your muscle mass will likely be less, and as a result your metabolism is slower than it was previously, before the stress began.

Additionally, the fatigue you feel with this biochemical picture may make exercise the least appealing thing on the planet to you. You actually tend to feel worse after exercise when you are adrenally fatigued, whereas exercise typically energizes. When we are sedentary some enzymes necessary for fat-burning aspects of metabolism, as well as good energy production, are down-regulated too.

Humans were never designed to sustain long-term stress, and our individual bodies cope with it in different ways. For some, adrenalin seems to remain as the dominant stress hormone, while others flip over into a more cortisol-dominant stress response. If the stress response doesn't truly switch off, there is the potential that the adrenals will eventually run out of substances necessary to create the hormones they are being instructed to produce (by the pituitary, based on its perception that your life is in danger), and cortisol output is no longer optimum or elevated; it will be negligible.

At its extreme, this can become a condition called Addison's disease (although there can be antibodies involved in this condition). Yet if a person's cortisol level is extremely low but still falls just inside the "normal range", they will be told that they are fine. They may feel lousy, but all the tests they have always come back "normal". They feel anything but normal, and people who know and love them will often comment that they are a shell of their former selves.

Cortisol can also be rather sinister in that it can interfere with your steroid (sex) hormone metabolism, sleep patterns, your mood, insulin and blood glucose management, as well as thyroid function, all elements that influence energy, metabolism, and how you feel and function every day.

A typical stress pattern in adulthood

Something you weren't expecting happens: you lose your job, a relationship suddenly ends and you didn't want it to, someone you love passes away. Adrenalin production kicks in. You feel like you are in shock. You feel like you get more done — because you have to — and you sleep less. But you're not noticeably tired. If you stopped you would be; in fact, you worry that if you stopped you might never get up. But you can't stop, so you don't. You might also lose weight without trying. If the stress or the ramifications of the stress continue, your body can't sustain the output of adrenalin and all of its biochemical consequences (for example, inflammation). With the continuing stress your body has no choice but to start to make more cortisol than before, in an effort to dampen down the inflammation created by the ongoing, excess adrenalin.

You feel heavy in your body, perhaps lethargic, or just not as good as before when the stress was fresh. You may gain weight, a little or a lot. It doesn't seem to matter how little you eat or how often you exercise, nothing changes. You have thickened up through the middle, and it won't seem to budge. With the ongoing stress, you tend to drink alcohol each evening to avoid feeling the emotional pain, and so you wake up tired and start every day with coffee to get yourself going; two liver-loaders. This adds to the stress inside your body, takes away from the efficient production of energy, and over the long term can disrupt sex hormone balance, lead to fat accumulation in the liver, with energy continuing to decline and body fat continuing to increase.

No diet will resolve this. Resolving the emotional pain will. Resolving why you have stopped seeing and treating yourself as the precious human you are, will.

Strategies for adrenal support to restore energy

The importance of rest

At the heart of all of my strategies to support you adrenally, so that you can experience amazing health and energy, is the desire for you to rest and to rest well, in a restorative and revitalizing way. Rest must follow action for us to have optimal health, great energy, excellent fat burning, the ability to remain calm, and all those "non-vital" processes mentioned earlier, such as our skin, hair and nails getting all of the nourishment they need. And very few of us these days truly rest or live in a calm state, where productivity, creativity, patience and kindness tend to easily flow.

The importance of diaphragmatic breathing

Breathing is the only way we can consciously affect our ANS, the part of the nervous system from where the red and green zones stem (explored previously in the nervous system section). We cannot control our ANS with our thoughts; we cannot instruct it with what to do. How we breathe is our only road in there. Every time I write or say that out loud, I am reminded of just how magical and miraculous the human body is.

The impact of diaphragmatic breathing on the nervous system is one of the main reasons why it is the cornerstone of all my adrenal support solutions. If you take nothing else away from this book, I would like to encourage you with every ounce of my being to incorporate a ritual into your day that allows you to focus on breathing diaphragmatically. It is key to sustained energy as it allows you to utilize body fat as a fuel, rather than primarily glucose. You will have seen in the nervous system section how this means you fuel your fire with wood (fat), rather than petrol (glucose). And, sure, that means your clothes continue to fit you, but more importantly it means you don't hit the energy wall.

How can the breath drive such powerful shifts in your nervous system and your biochemistry? The role of the ANS is to perceive the external environment and, after processing the information in the central nervous system, regulate the function of your internal environment. The name *autonomic* implies that it is independent of the conscious mind. Think about a family of ducks and their newborn ducklings. Just like ducklings, the ANS will always follow the leader, and breathing is the *only* way that the ANS can be controlled consciously. Breathing is your only way to access and influence your ANS. Your breath leads. Your body follows. Breathing dominates your ANS, and because we breathe 5,000 to 30,000 times a day — or 200 million to 500 million times in a lifetime — it has the potential to influence us positively, or negatively, in many ways.

Nothing communicates to every cell of your body that you are safe better than diaphragmatic breathing. So, while we looked at this in the nervous system section, it is worth having another good look at it here, especially as it is the single most important thing to take away from this book. If you breathe in a shallow way, with short, sharp inhalations and exhalations, then you are communicating to your body via your ANS that your life is in danger. It then has to make adrenalin. Remember the cascade of hormonal events that follow such an alarm, and the role these hormones play, for one thing, in switching fat burning on or off, and depleting energy.

How you breathe can also be a fast-track to the symptoms of anxiety, and potentially panic attacks, regardless of what led you to breathe in a shallow way in the first place. Whether it was an event, a deadline, too much caffeine, the perception of pressure, the "need" to rush, or the lifetime habit of your nervous system, the result is the same. Long, slow breaths that move your diaphragm communicate the opposite message to your body — that you are very safe. Nothing down-regulates the production of the alarm signals within your body more powerfully. No practice restores your energy and vitality like regularly breathing this way. And I don't say that lightly.

Practice diaphragmatic breathing, making sure your tummy moves in and out as you breathe, as opposed to just your upper chest. You can begin your breath by allowing the lower part of your tummy to expand, and then imagine as the breath slowly continues that the expansion of your tummy has now extended into the area where you can feel it meet your ribcage. Keep the slow inhalation going until your upper chest feels like it is pushing your ribs out at the sides of your body. Then pause, rather than hold your breath, and slowly allow the exhalation to begin in the reverse order of the inhalation, with the top and side of the chest emptying first, followed by the middle of your abdomen and lastly your tummy. If that sounds or feels too tricky, just move your tummy (abdomen) in and out with each breath. Allow it to expand on the inhale and shrink back in on the exhale.

Be kind and patient with yourself, as this takes practice. You may feel unable to get your abdomen to engage at first, but in time and with practice the parts of you that have become disconnected will be thrilled to be back in touch.

At first, you will more than likely need to schedule regular diaphragmatic breathing time slots into your day, until it becomes your new way of breathing. Make appointments with yourself to breathe in this way. If it is peaceful each morning while you boil the kettle for the first time that day (to make your hot water with lemon, of course), instead of racing around and doing 80 jobs while the kettle boils, stand in your kitchen and breathe. Link breathing well to your daily routine, such as having a shower, or to a particular hour of the day, so that it quickly becomes a habit. Do it numerous times over the course of your day. Book a meeting into your calendar each afternoon at 3pm. If you work at a computer, have it pop up on the screen that it is time for your meeting with yourself to do 20 long, slow breaths. We keep appointments with other people, so be sure to keep the appointments you make with yourself.

Take part in movement that facilitates a focus on the breath, such as t'ai chi, qi gong, yoga, particularly restorative yoga, Stillness Through Movement, or walking quietly in Nature. Pilates can also be useful, but I have found that it is highly dependent on your attitude while you are doing the session, and also to some degree on the attitude of the instructor. Extending the length of the exhalation is the cornerstone of PNS activation, which means great energy, vitality, calm and readily burnt body fat. These practices allow us to still the stories, still the monkey mind, which can be one of the sources of daily stress.

The importance of laughter

Another free and powerful tool is laughter. If we see life as tough, and full of hard work, pain and drudgery, it will be precisely that. Even saying that out loud feels exhausting. Humans have the ability to see only their perspective in the world, rather than the world as it truly is. We see the world through filters, even though we often don't know they are there. I am not denying that life can be tough at times, or that being honest with ourselves if we do feel down and out about life is not a good thing. The problem comes when we see the world this way and believe that it will never be any different. A belief in permanence can create immeasurable stress.

Think about it. A belief in the permanence of doom is dangerous for every hormonal signal in your body. Do your absolute best to shift your thinking to see life as an adventure, a journey, a gift full of opportunity, and a process through which you can contribute. Some of the greatest, most moving stories I have ever heard involved someone turning a horrific hardship into their greatest opportunity, and a way to give back. Keep this in mind. Keep in mind, too, that you can choose to laugh at the calamity around you. I remember clearly witnessing this when my dearest friend had her third baby, and, with him not even a day old, countless well-wishers chattering away, a hospital staff member wanting to clear the food tray away, and her deliciously spirited two-year-old daughter not being too thrilled about this as she wanted the remaining apple juice — and all in one small room — my precious friend and her husband just shrugged and grinned at each other and laughed, internally clearly focused on the love in the room, rather than on anything else. What you focus on is what you feel.

The stages of stress

To complete this section about the adrenals, I offer you a summary of the stages of stress to help you identify where you may be, and some ideas to help you begin to heal your energy — and other — systems.

Stage 1

* The fight-, flight-or-freeze response
* Elevated and consistent adrenalin output
* High cortisol, attempting to dampen down the impact of the inflammation created by adrenalin
* High cortisol uses the resources that would typically go into making progesterone, so progesterone levels fall low and postmenstrual tension (PMT) begins
* Anxiety
* Panic
* Insomnia
* Irritability

Goals of treatment for this stage of stress are predominantly related to reducing adrenalin and cortisol levels. Please understand that the herbal medicines recommended below are not designed to replace the lifestyle changes that must occur. For example, you cannot continue to consume large amounts of caffeine — which drives the body to produce adrenalin — and then take herbal medicine still hoping to heal. Lifestyle strategies, including dietary, breathing, restorative movement, sleep and relationship-based support are likely to be needed. Two herbs that can highly useful, however, during this stage of stress are withania and Siberian ginseng.

Stage 2

* Cortisol is now low
* Deep fatigue
* Inflammation
* Body pain
* Injury
* Illness
* Muscle pain

* Feeling like you have been hit by a bus
* Depressed mood
* Fibromyalgia-type symptoms
* Clotty painful periods
* Exhaustion, but still agitation due to adrenalin

The goals of treatment at this stage of stress are mostly focused on restoring the function of the adrenal cells; essentially those of the adrenal cortex, or more specifically the zona glomerulosa, given that is where cortisol is produced. The goal is to help the body make appropriate amounts of cortisol again to increase energy and decrease inflammation. Again, other lifestyle work is essential — even more essential — at this stage of stress than at stage 1. Herbs that can help restore adrenal cortex function, however, include rehmannia and licorice. These can help energy and pain begin to lift. Rhodiola can be a highly useful herb in this stage as well, if a depressed mood is part of this health and low energy picture, as it can help increase dopamine production.

> *D*o your absolute best to shift your thinking to see life as an adventure, a journey, a gift full of opportunity, and a process through which you can contribute.

Stage 3

This is the recovery phase. You can now get out of bed. You are getting over colds faster. Your relationships are often improving at this stage. Your energy is improving. Challenges with the menstrual cycle are now improving too.

Along with continued lifestyle changes, a wide variety of herbs can be useful and important at this stage of recovery. The herbs a medical herbalist will select, however, are highly dependent on how the body is healing. Different people do better with different herbs at this stage. A wonderful herb for this stage, though, is usually skullcap, as it helps to balance the SNS and the PNS as someone is coming out of exhaustion into better energy.

Use the symptoms described to contemplate where you may be at. More than half of the clients we see in my clinic (or via phone/skype —we have clients from all over the world) are in one of these stages and various aspects of their health and energy are suffering. Having a health professional experienced at supporting and guiding people out of an adrenal-based fatigue condition, whether it is short term or has been long term, can be game-changing to their progress and to re-establishing their quality of life.

Daily Choices

Research and also my clinical experience show that even a profound threat to one's mortality is mostly a poor motivator for making better decisions today, and on a daily basis. Knowing that it may help prevent cancer several years down the road does not motivate most people to exercise daily. Most people don't stop before eating a takeaway dinner to contemplate how doing so regularly can increase their long-term risk of heart disease. Most people don't go to bed at a good time and catch an early-ish sleep train (the tired feeling that comes over you around 9pm and then again about 10pm) as they are hoping to get more done, even though they know a lack of rest has a host of consequences in their lives, including being snappy with their children, elevating blood pressure, and increasing their risk of heart disease and stroke. And it is what we do every day that impacts on our health, not what we do sometimes. If we only stayed up late and pushed on and worked later into the night on occasion rather than every day. "Occasionally" as opposed to "daily" creates a different health, energy and life experience. Same goes with the takeaways.

All of the knowledge about creating a healthy lifestyle does little good until it leads to a change in daily behaviour, a change to what you do *consistently*. Research and my experience from working with people to support their health has shown me that when an individual connects the better decisions they make with improvements in their daily energy, they are more likely to make them a new habit. Connecting their choices with better *daily* energy does more for people than anything they might learn about poor choices increasing their risk for major diseases. It is a huge reason why all of my health information is framed in the positive: it is about what you can experience, what life can be like if you make these changes, rather than threats of what may happen if you don't change.

For example, when Alice, a lawyer I worked with a few years ago, knew she had a particularly important day ahead, she would make sure she did some activity in the morning so that she was in a better mood and so that her thinking was sharper across her day. She based her decisions about what to eat for lunch on whether she knew the meal would help sustain her energy across the afternoon and into the evening. She knew that if she ate well and was active throughout the day, she would also have a better night's sleep, which set her up well for the following day.

> *All of the knowledge about creating a healthy lifestyle does little good until it leads to a change in daily behaviour, a change to what you do consistently.*

After I worked with her, she commented to me about how remarkable she found it that these small choices accumulated to create either a better day or a worse day for her. She found that if she had a breakfast of sweet or baked foods, it made it almost impossible for her to get back on track — energy-wise and choices-wise — for the rest of the day. She said she felt like she would chase her tail all day trying to feel better, and the food and drink options she wanted did not match the outcome she was seeking. When she had to fly or sit in a meeting for a few hours without moving, she felt physically and mentally wiped out, and put it down to the inactivity. She reported that a single night of poor sleep would lead her to feel grumpy the next day, and impaired her ability to work effectively and to be patient with other people. She was very clear that when she didn't make the choices that she knew served her health in any one of these three areas — food, movement or sleeping — it threw everything else off-course. A poor night of sleep would lead her to skip a workout, make poor food choices, become irritable with people, judge herself ... and on it went until she broke the cycle, usually with a commitment to a good sleep.

The good news is that doing just one of these things *consistently* well leads to an upward spiral in the other two areas. Think about how you are eating, moving and sleeping, and how they are impacting on each other each day. Doing all three consistently well is the key to having more energy throughout the day, as they are the physical foundations upon which great energy is built. Some people won't do this for themselves due to an underlying belief that they aren't worth looking after; that they aren't worthy of their own love and care that consistently healthy meals provide, for example. Years of working with people has shown me this day after day.

I encourage you to explore this within yourself. What is stopping you taking one step towards eating, moving or sleeping in a way that better serves your energy? For these are the most basic foundations of wellness and we cannot fight the needs of our biology; we must get seven to nine hours sleep per night (if you have little ones who need you during the night, I have covered that conundrum earlier, in the section on sleep); we must get plenty of nutrients from our food and little, if any, problematic substances from our food; we must move our bodies, rather than sit for long periods (which is explored in the next section). If you can't take care of you for your own sake, also consider that you need great energy to be at your very best for your family, your friends and your work. What is lousy energy costing you?

The Impact of Sitting on Energy

Many adults spend most of their waking hours sitting, with studies showing that some spend an enormous 11 hours per day on their bottoms. Those hours tend to be clocked up working at a desk job, commuting to and from work, watching television, or at the computer. Whatever the reason, research shows that too much sitting isn't good for health or energy.

Even if you are in the small proportion of people who do the recommended amount of at least 150 minutes of exercise per week (preferably a combination of walking — just being mobile — muscle-building resistance training, stretching and breath-focused restorative practices), you still need to move more regularly throughout the day. In other words, it is the sitting itself — not necessarily a lack of exercise — that adds to the undesirable impact on energy and specific health parameters. The amount of time spent sitting must decrease.

Physiologically, distinct effects are observed between prolonged sedentary time and too little physical activity. It seems likely that there is a unique physiology of sedentary time, within which biological processes that are distinct from traditionally-understood exercise physiology are operating. The groundbreaking work of Professor Marc Hamilton and colleagues provides a compelling body of evidence that the chronic, unbroken periods of muscular unloading associated with prolonged sedentary time may have deleterious biological consequences. Physiologically, it has been suggested that the loss of local contractile stimulation induced through sitting leads to the suppression of skeletal muscle lipoprotein lipase (LPL) activity, which, put simply, is necessary for triglyceride (free fat in the blood) uptake and HDL-cholesterol production, as well as reduced glucose uptake.

Hamilton's findings suggest that standing — which involves isometric contraction of the anti-gravity (postural) muscles and only low levels of energy expenditure — elicits skeletal muscle electrical changes as well as LPL changes. In other words, when we sit for too long, the body's ability to both utilize (burn) energy and create and experience energy is compromised. Think about it. If you sit for five hours straight, do you bound up with energy or begin to droop over your desk and feel sluggish, lethargic and fatigued? Typically, it's the latter.

Get moving

All of the health and poor energy risks that come from prolonged sitting can be reduced by taking regular breaks from sitting. Frequent, small amounts of movement have been shown to improve some blood markers for cardiovascular disease and type 2 diabetes. Plus this has been shown to help clear some of the inflammatory products from the body and reduce the risk of weight gain that can occur through inflammatory processes.

Research has also shown that regular movement breaks across the day reduce back, neck and shoulder pain, plus boost mood, all factors that contribute to us experiencing better energy, both physically and emotionally.

To reap the health and energy benefits, it is best to get up (from your desk) every hour for about three to five minutes. You might like to set an alarm. Make it a gentle one or an inspiringly enlivening one (rather than one that grates your nerves, irritates you and activates the fight-or-flight response) or find an app to remind you. Or you might like to get up each hour on the hour. You might like to walk up and down a flight of stairs a few times or walk the length of the office. Or get up to get yourself a glass of water from a location distant from your desk. If you have a choice, you might choose to invest in a standing desk or create one from objects around your home or office. Be sure to stop sitting and move every hour, and notice if more motion enhances your energy.

Five ways to move

※ Take the stairs instead of a lift or an escalator.

※ Swap sitting meetings for walking meetings at work, using your phone to record the meeting. Spend five minutes at the end sitting and consolidating it all.

※ Get up during television commercials and go for a walk around the house.

※ Engage in active travel to and from work or school, bike riding or walking, standing instead of sitting on public transport and getting on and off a stop earlier so you have to walk further to your destination.

※ Swap sedentary family time for active family time. This might mean playing hide-and-seek or going to the park instead of watching television.

Remember it is what you do every day that impacts on your health and energy, not what you do sometimes. Just be conscious about how much you sit. Embrace more motion preferably once each hour for three to five minutes. Your health, energy and ability to focus may all be enhanced in the process.

Sitting is not the only consequence of an office-type lifestyle. Another major factor in fatigue for countless people today — office or no official office — is what I refer to as open loops in their head. The next section explores precisely this.

Open Loops

What else depletes energy? What I have come to call "open loops". Or you might prefer to think of them as "open tabs". Consider this analogy. We all know that our computer or smart phone slows down and burns more battery, the more programs we have open and the more things we are asking it to do. Twenty-three open tabs of web pages, spreadsheets, documents and presentations, the photo editing, movie playing, music, software updates ... our mind can feel very much the same. The more things you have open and unresolved, the bigger the drain on your mind power and energy, from all of these open loops.

How many times across a day, a week, a month, a year, decades even, do tasks or situations open up, yet they are never resolved, finalized or closed? How many emails do you read that you don't immediately reply to, and they hang in your mind and add to your task load of what's not yet done? It is as if you walk around each day with so many tabs open — like websites sitting open on your computer screen — that you never feel like you have got it all handled. You never feel like you can rest. So you don't, not properly, even if you try. Plus you might judge yourself for this. You might subconsciously tell yourself that you are a failure for not getting more done. Or that you are lazy, or hopeless or a fraud. Yet you may be completely unaware that you are judging yourself in this way.

Do you think these statements to and about yourself energize and uplift you, and empower you to take care of what's on your plate? Unlikely. Usually such harsh self-talk zaps the wind from your sails and you live most days proving yourself right — that you don't get enough done in a day, you procrastinate, and then the judgment begins all over again (if it ever paused) — and this depletes your energy further. Significantly.

You could consider that these open-loop scenarios offer you endless opportunity. But most people see them as an utterly exhausting pile of stuff that they wish they could hand over to someone else.

The solutions? Scheduling your time. Following through on what you say you will do. Delegating, if you are in a position to do this. Accept, as Oprah famously said, that you need to "Do what you have to do, until you can do what you want to do." When you fight with what is, when you battle with the ways things are, you suffer. So schedule what you will complete today and start closing some of those loops.

You can try closing some tabs using these four steps, which are employed by many people who like using this system:

* Identify and capture in writing everything that is open in your mind, that you are thinking about that needs resolution.

* Organize these into simple headings that relate the importance of each task and its urgency; cluster the topics in categories.

* Schedule times to consider, reflect, decide and execute the idea.

* If it is not time to perform step 3 on the task or idea yet, then just know you have captured it and the time will come for you to schedule it.

Keep an eye out for open loops. They can be a major drain on your energy without you being aware that they are doing so.

Further to this concept, while I was writing this book I met with and interviewed people from all walks of life and I also continued to read widely. You will find some references and resources at the back of this book. And with the open-loops concept in my mind I wanted to know how some of the (literally) busiest people in the world manage their time and get so much done! The concept of time management was discussed a great deal with many people.

Time Management: To Help Ease the Fatigue That Tasks Can Bring

Part of my goal in writing this book was to share with you what experts in their fields do to maintain and better support their energy. That meant conducting interviews and reading a lot. A time-management strategy I was taught many years ago involved dumping everything on my plate into a notebook (or later an app) and then coding it A1, A2, A3, B1, B2, C1, etc, based on how high up my priority list it was. This is helpful to some degree. But do you really think the people in the world who have to be the most time-efficient, and juggle more than we could ever wrap our heads around, use such a system? Kevin Kruse, who writes about whole-hearted leadership and researches time management and productivity, interviewed over 200 billionaires, Olympians, straight-A students and entrepreneurs. He asked them to give him their best time-management and productivity advice. And none of them have ever mentioned a to-do list.

There are three big problems with a straightforward to-do list. First, a to-do list does not account for time. If you have a long list of tasks, you tend to tackle those that can be completed quickly in a few minutes, leaving the longer items left not done. You want to tick them off to feel good, to feel like you have achieved. Fair enough, but have you actually nailed what *needs* doing?

Kruse found research from the company iDoneThis indicated that 41 per cent of all to-do list items are never completed. And when I wrote *Rushing Woman's Syndrome*, I found that this bothers more women (and possibly men;

however, I didn't survey men) than it does not. And if a to-do list that is not all crossed-off does bother you, this is a sure-fire way to make stress hormones. And as you now know, this can be a fast a furious road to fatigue.

Secondly, a to-do list does not distinguish between which tasks are the most urgent and important. Once again, our impulse is to fight the urgent and ignore the important. For example, how many people put off having medical tests that are actually extremely important? Or going for a walk, because you would have to have your head buried in the sand for your whole life to not know that moving your body is critical to your health, energy and longevity. Let's face it, if exercise were a pill we'd all be taking it. A colonoscopy and a walk may be in different leagues but they might be incredibly important, yet most people put them off.

Thirdly, to-do lists contribute to stress. In what is known in psychology as the Zeigarnik effect, unfinished tasks contribute to intrusive, uncontrolled thoughts. It's no wonder so many people feel so overwhelmed in the day, and then fight insomnia at night.

When you explore time-management research, including Kruse's, one consistent theme keeps coming up: highly productive people do not work from a to-do list — they live and work from their calendar.

When you have a huge amount of tasks that need completing in a day and/or you have other people relying on you, the only way the ultra-busy can pull it all off is to prioritize and keep a schedule that for some of them is almost minute-by-minute.

Other people in the time-management research, when asked to reveal their secret for getting so much done, included: "If it's not in my calendar, it won't get done. But if it is in my calendar, it will get done. I schedule out every 15 minutes of every day to conduct meetings, review materials, write and do any activities I need to get done. And while I take meetings with just about anyone who wants to meet with me, I reserve just one hour a week for these 'office hours'." Another quote was: "I simply put everything on my schedule. That's it. Everything I do on a day-to-day basis gets put on my schedule.

Thirty minutes of social media — on the schedule. Forty-five minutes of email management — on the schedule. Catching up with my virtual team — on the schedule."

The bottom line on much of what I read was, as obvious as this is: if it doesn't get scheduled, it doesn't get done. So here are some suggestions from all I read if you feel that your biggest energy-zapper is a sense of being overwhelmed and poor time management — a constant case of the feeling that there's not enough hours in the day. The ideas won't be everyone's cup of tea, as I know that scheduling every last thing can feel tedious and creativity-killing. It can also feel that there will be a great big lack of spontaneity in your life if you embrace such an existence. And I personally get that. Only thing is, if you want to feel more spacious in your life, try scheduling even three days out of seven and see how that creates a far more spacious headspace for creativity and innovation to flow. But for some of you, scheduling every day will end your to-do list, you'll get more done, and the energy-zapping stress will lessen as you have a sense that you are handling what's on your plate.

> *If* you want to feel more spacious in your life, try scheduling even three days out of seven and see how that creates a far more spacious headspace for creativity and innovation to flow.

1. Time-management research results suggest that you make the default event duration in your calendar 15 minutes. Most systems automatically schedule new events for 30 or 60 minutes' duration. Highly productive people only spend as much time as is necessary for each task. When your default setting is 15 minutes, you will automatically discover that you can fit more tasks into each day.

2. Try time-blocking the most important things in your life, first. Don't let your calendar fill up randomly by accepting every request that comes your way. First get clear on your personal and work priorities and pre-schedule sacred

time-blocks for these items. That might include two hours each morning to work on the strategic plan your boss asked you for, or 20 minutes of time for meditation in the morning. Mark your calendar to include time-blocks for things like exercise, a date night or other items that align with your core life values.

3. Time-management principles suggest that you schedule everything. Instead of checking emails every few minutes, schedule three times a day to do this. Instead of writing "call Sarah" on your to-do list, put it on your calendar or establish a recurring time-block each afternoon to "return phone calls".

What is scheduled actually gets done. Would you feel less stressed and more productive if you could rip up your to-do list and work from your calendar instead? Consider utilizing this as an energy-creating resource in your life.

If you do something out of duty it will deplete you.
If you do something out of love it will energize you.

Dr Libby

Sick of Saying Yes When You Mean No?

Clearly there are countless things we do or believe that can drain our energy. And saying yes when you really mean no is one of them. It is such a common occurrence today that it deserves its own section in this book.

But there's a story behind this part of the book that warrants a mention and that brings home to me — and I hope it will to you too — just how much of an energy-drainer this can be. I was sitting at my desk in New York City with the following headings written on my page of the topics I wanted to cover that day in my writing. It said:

Energy book today …
Finish dopamine section
Finish the role of infections in energy metabolism
Open loops
Open loops are energy-draining
Saying yes when we mean no is energy-draining.

And as soon as I'd written that, "Saying yes when we mean no is energy-draining", I knew it was where I wanted to start writing next, so I stopped the list. While I write books, I don't have my emails open, so I don't get distracted. And after I had finished the dopamine section and the part about infections, I made lunch, and checked my emails before I returned to write about what happens to energy when we say yes when we really mean no.

And there at the top of my inbox, was an email sharing a

new blog post by the beautiful, talented, witty and insightful
Kate Northrup, whose work I love. And the title of her blog
post? "Sick of saying yes when you mean no?" I laughed out
loud at the serendipity. And I read her blog post. And there
is no way on the planet I could say any of this any better. So
I contacted Kate to ask whether I could share it in this book.
And, thanks to her graciousness, here it is …

Sick of saying yes when you mean no? _____

By Kate Northrup
www.katenorthrup.com

Since being pregnant my internal "no's" and "yes's" have gotten
significantly louder. Waffling barely exists anymore. I'm not trying
to talk myself into things I don't really want to do. The boundaries
are loud, proud, and clear. I thought I was getting pretty good at
saying no before getting pregnant. But the clarity I have now around
what's good for me, my body, the baby, and our family makes my
previous version of boundaries look like chalk lines on the sidewalk
after a rainstorm.

One of my desires/intentions is that the volume of my "no"
and "yes" stays turned up to the same level after the baby is out.
I love knowing what I do and don't want to do beyond a shadow
of a doubt. And I love feeling less guilty about it than I ever have
before.

I know that we all have this clarity inside us. While pregnancy
might make it more pronounced, listening intently and acting
accordingly can also make the internal voice louder. Pay special
attention to that acting accordingly part. Listening to the truth that
bubbles up inside and then ignoring it is a good start, but it won't
produce the long-term, life-lived-on-purpose-and-amazingly-well
benefits that you're after.

For me, saying yes has never been a stretch. It's the "no's" that
have tripped me up.

If you're a recovering "yes-aholic", too, read on.

Here are my go-to strategies for saying a clear "no," which is a gift
to you and those around you. Because remember: Saying yes just to

please someone else isn't a true yes. It's not good for them, and it's not good for you.

DON'T SAY YOU'LL DO THINGS THAT YOU'RE NOT GOING TO DO

A woman walked up to me and asked me if I would review some of her work to give her my feedback. She was delightful, and I'm sure the piece she wanted my eye on was equally wonderful. However, I knew it would sit in my inbox, and I would delay looking at it. And it would bug me. And cause mental friction. And after all the delaying and hemming and hawing, if I did get around to reviewing it, I wouldn't give it my best attention.

Why? Because it's not a priority for me. Because I have several of my own projects that I'd like to finish before the baby comes. Because it felt like a no. (By the way, something feeling like a no is reason enough. Those other justifications are nice if they're true, but they're not necessary.) A no is a no is a no. No reason required.

In the past I would have told her to email me and I'd see what I could do. Then I might have let her down over email. Instead, I told her the truth in real time. I said that, while I loved what she was up to, I didn't want to tell her I would do something that I know deep down isn't a priority for me right now. It felt uncomfortable to say, but it felt freeing, too. We both knew where we stood. I wished her the best and gave her some other resources she might find helpful.

Take home message: if someone asks you to do something and you immediately know that you won't, don't say that you will. It doesn't serve you and it doesn't serve them. Keep it clean, people.

THERE'S NO NEED TO GIVE A REASON

Your no does not require justification. Here's a great sentence you can use, inspired by my friend Andrea Equihua: "Thank you for your invitation/offer/request. I'm not able to do it at this time, but if that changes, I'll let you know."

Gracious. Kind. Simple. Clear. *Non-apologetic.*

You don't have to apologize for not being able to fit into someone else's agenda. You don't have to give 57 reasons why it doesn't work. You can be kind while still giving a simple no.

GIVE YOURSELF TIME

There are moments when someone asks you to do something, and you don't know whether or not you can or want to. There are also moments when you're caught off guard when someone asks you to do something in person, and a direct "no" feels like too much of a stretch. (This is often the case when your "no" muscles are still developing.) These are moments when asking for 48 hours to get back to the person is ideal.

They feel acknowledged. You don't feel cornered. Then you can give yourself a moment to check in while you're not in their presence and see if you get a clear internal message.

You can also take the time to compose a response that's respectful, kind, and clear if it is indeed a no. When you're just starting out practicing saying no, coming up with this kind of response in the moment can be quite challenging. Giving yourself a day or two helps you get your wits about you.

IF IT'S NOT A HELL YES ...

You've likely heard this one before, but it's one I remind myself of nearly daily, so it's worth repeating. If it's not a hell yes, it's a no.

That's it. It works the same on choosing where to eat dinner as it does who you're going to marry.

THE GIFT OF YOUR NO

The gift of your no is that everyone in your life knows that when you do say yes, it's real. They know where they stand with you. It puts everyone at ease. And you honoring your "yes's" and your "no's" means that you get to trust yourself more and more, each and every day. Since you're the only one you'll be spending your entire life with, that's a pretty big deal.

May we all have the cojones to say no when we mean no and yes when we mean yes. And may we all have the courage to keep the volume turned up on that voice that always knows. It serves us, and it sure serves the world.

★ ★ ★

Really reflect on those sentiments and identify whether you struggle to say no. Consider the energy drain on your body and mind when you agree to something when you'd prefer to be doing something else, or with other people, or by yourself, or catching up on some much-needed rest. And reflect on why you do it. Is it to please the person asking? But is it coming from a place of genuine wanting to assist that person, or from a fear that they may not like you as much if you say no? The reason matters. Because the more your choices are fear-based, the more exhausted you tend to feel. When your choices come from love, they typically energize you. As Kate suggested with words that made me grin and appreciate, don't let your "boundaries look like chalk lines on the sidewalk after a rainstorm".

Stop, Keep, Start

Another useful strategy to adopt if too many tasks are over-whelming you, leading to regular, excessive outputs of stress hormones is *Stop. Keep. Start.* Take a journal or notepad and draw up columns with the following headings:

* Stop
* Keep
* Start

Fill in each column as you think of things by answering the following questions:

* What am I going to stop doing?
* What am I going to keep doing?
* What am I going to start doing?

You can use the suggestions on these pages to give you ideas. Here is a sample:

Stop: I am going to stop getting caught up in gossip as it is exhausting
Keep: I am going to keep eating a nourishing breakfast every day
Start: I am going to start walking four days out of seven for the next two weeks starting tomorrow morning at 6am

Stop, keep and start goals can make change fun, manageable and suitable for your lifestyle.

While I was travelling, I read a blog post written by the brilliant Danielle La Porte and it inspired me to ask people from all walks of life about things they had stopped, started or continued doing that have really served their life, and particularly their energy, in any area. Here are some of the answers that I particularly enjoyed from many different people, and in their own words:

- Started drinking warm lemon water first thing in the morning. It has really helped my digestion and skin.
- Got black-out curtains for my bedroom and removed anything that blinked or flashed. Welcome circadian rhythm contentment!
- Scheduled a weekly bush walk with a girlfriend. It gets me into Nature and we are happy walking in silence or chatting. I feel so much better after I do this each week, even though before I go, I never feel like I have the time.
- Started doing Stillness Through Movement classes (a form of restorative yoga) twice a week. Literally. Changed. My. Life. And I don't say that lightly.
- Started a computer course at my local technical college. I am 74 years old but I was missing out seeing my family on their Facebook page, not being able to use a computer. Now I feel more connected to them because I can use the computer and see their photographs. And I know how to type them a message now.
- Went gluten-free.
- Set up my office at home as if it is a real office, a real room, worthy of lovely treasures, rather than the "spare room made into an office". I feel organized and less stressed, and I look forward to going in there now.
- Found the courage to admit to my boss that I don't like managing people, and therefore I am not excellent at managing people. Thankfully, she changed my role to not manage people and I feel like I have a new life!
- Started getting up at 5am each morning and having an hour to myself.
- Started watching my children sleep (about an hour after they fall asleep) for 10 minutes each evening. Seeing them

so peaceful makes me feel so calm before I get more done into the evening. I feel like I approach my nightly tasks with a different attitude after I've watched them sleeping.

* Continued getting up at 5am and I meditate, give thanks for my life, read (learn) and watch the sun rise each morning. It changed my life and I don't plan on ever changing this ritual. I'm only sorry I didn't start doing this until I was 46.

* Started cleaning out my clothes cupboard every six months and I give what I haven't worn in the last chunk of time to a charity store so they can sell it and make money.

* Stopped responding to text messages immediately just because they were text messages. Remember when not that much was urgent? This gives me such a sense of freedom.

* Started taking voice lessons. It changed the way I breathe. And when I changed the way I regularly breathe, my posture and presence and hence my effectiveness and happiness all shifted in the most powerful way.

* Started meditating daily. No. Matter. What.

* Started and have continued to become harder to get hold of. [this person was very well known in the health and healing world] so I could have more spaciousness and ease in my life. I decided that if it interfered with me being home when my daughter gets home from school, then I'm a no, thank you.

* My son had been diagnosed with a mental health disorder. He loves music. So we got him a guitar and then went through guitar teachers until we found the one who said, "Forget scales. What song do you want to learn to play today?" I cannot tell you the truly wonderful impact this has had on our lives.

* I started going to bed before midnight. That danger zone between 11.30pm and midnight — when I get my second wind of the day ... I stopped pushing through that to do more emails or start another task — and I shut it all down. If I'm in bed before midnight, I fall asleep straight away. If I pass the warning zone and stay up, I fire up again and it

202 ★ *Exhausted to Energized*

takes longer to unwind for sleep. Anything I think I need to do after 11.30pm can wait until the morning. What I do (for home or work) is not more important than my sleep. No one will actually die if I don't start a new pile of emails at 11.30pm.

Your turn. How would you answer the questions:
    What am I going to stop doing?
    What am I going to keep doing?
    What am I going to start doing?

The results for your health and energy may astonish you.

Morning Rituals

One of the things you might decide to start doing, if you don't already, is a morning ritual that sets you up for your day. Part of my time writing this book was spent on Necker Island in the British Virgin Islands, home of Sir Richard Branson and his family. I was there as a speaker for a leadership retreat, a joint venture between Virgin Unite and an incredible Australian company called Business Chicks. It was such an honour to be part of the retreat. Over the week, I asked some of the world's foremost minds and hearts about their own personal energy, how they experience energy, and what they do to cultivate great energy (if they have it). By far the most common denominators of outstanding energy were:

* great rituals
* purpose for their life
* contribution — making a difference in the lives of others.

Within the category of rituals, the most common ones each person shared — regardless of their gender — were morning rituals. Often this was time spent on their own, and included meditation or prayer, reading, writing, restorative movement or vigorous movement. But almost every person had a non-negotiable morning ritual that set them up for the day, physically and/or spiritually, and rituals that often involved learning and growth.

Many of these people — both men and women — had children ranging in age from 12 weeks to 21 years. Some had four children under 10. Those who did and who had a morning ritual of solitude either got up before everyone else in their household or, if they rose later, they had taught the children to occupy themselves while they did their thing. Another key. however, was that they remained flexible so that if a child needed them it didn't "ruin" their morning. It was just what it was.

I want to encourage you to do the same. When you set up your day and get plugged into your natural, inner intelligence, you get more done. You also have healthier interactions, and, given poor-quality interactions are one of the fastest energy-zappers, this counts. When you set up your day, your mind is sharp, you hold your body more strongly, and you are more effective in your work day. You cope better with whatever comes your way. Those I spoke to also suggested that they are better colleagues, parents, partners and friends when they have set up their day. So the ripple effect of a morning ritual is significant. Not only do you experience better and more consistent energy, but those around you get the best version of you too.

> When you set up your day, your mind is sharp, you hold your body with more strength, and you are more effective in your work day.

Posture, Language, Focus

Some of the areas you may have identified as points for you to stop, keep or start doing may have involved how you speak to yourself or what you will focus on. Posture, the language we use, and our focus are three factors that we can immediately turn our attention to, to make a difference in our energy. And all of them are free. They simply take awareness and commitment from you to employ them regularly and to create some new habits.

Posture

This is not an anatomical conversation about posture, but is simply pointing out that how you hold yourself impacts your energy. Try it.

Slump your shoulders. Let your head hang forward and tilt your face down. Stay like that, and stand or walk around like that for a few minutes. Do you feel energized? Now pull your shoulders back, hold your head up, stand upright, open across your chest and face forward. Spend a few minutes like that. Which posture offers you more energy?

The upright posture, of course. Become conscious of how you hold yourself. Make it part of how you care for yourself to hold yourself well. Dr Donny Epstein, the genius who created Network Spinal Analysis (NSA), teaches that over time, due to the way our nervous system interprets the experiences we have — a raised voice, a failed exam, a car accident, the passing of a loved one — we develop defence postures. Each posture we have offers us a concurrent headspace, and the less defensive our posture is, the more resources (from within), including energy, will be on offer to us.

Become conscious of how you hold yourself. Stand up tall and lose the weight of the world off your shoulders. An NSA practitioner can take you further on this journey if that appeals or is needed. Different emotions will likely be present in each different posture, although you may not link them to how you are holding yourself. Posture significantly impacts on energy.

Language

The language you use, both habitually and sporadically, has the power to impact on your energy powerfully. Picture this. You set your alarm for 6am, planning to get up and exercise. When the alarm sounds at 6am, your first thought is "Hashtag, you're joking. How can it be six already?" You're weary. So you press snooze. And you are still pressing snooze at 7am when another family member wakes you fully from your slumber. Now being 7am, there's no time to exercise as you have other responsibilities and then have to get to work.

Perhaps the language you use inside your head, having slept longer than you intended and having not done your exercise, is that you are "lazy" or that you are a "failure" or "that's just typical", meaning that you already know you are a lazy failure and, well, you've just proven it again. What kind of energy does that language, that selection of words, and then the meanings they generate in your nervous system bring? Lousy.

However, perhaps your response to that scenario is to see it as it is, not better than it is and not worse than it is, just for how it actually is — you didn't get up and exercise. Full stop. If you see it in this latter way, your energy will be better than it would be for the first way, in part because the judgment you pass on yourself using the first set of language annihilates your nervous system, as explained in the next paragraph. And it's the judgment, the way we berate ourselves and put ourselves down, that usually creates the same pattern the next morning. When you are telling yourself that you are lazy and a failure, underneath it all you believe you are worthless. So why on

Earth would you take better care of yourself? And you just call it procrastination. And usually you keep judging. And that whole pattern is exhausting in itself.

What so many people do is put commas in sentences where there needs to be a full stop. "I didn't get up at 6am and exercise this morning full stop" for many is "I didn't get up at 6am and exercise this morning, therefore I am lazy and if I am lazy, well that's what my father told me every time I didn't want to help him in the garden and if I'm lazy and he values hard work then he doesn't like or value me". As crazy as that sounds, without realizing it, that's what you can trigger when you judge yourself. A process like that. Not always, but pretty often. And that judgment is stifling and exhausting because it scratches your oldest wounds. The only thing is, you won't know what you have done to yourself. It all happens in the ANS — remember? The part of your nervous system that you can't access with your thoughts.

> *B*ecome conscious of how you hold yourself. Make it part of how you care for yourself to hold yourself well.

When you see things as they are, and you put the full stop where it is supposed to go, it fosters better energy because you don't scratch the itch that you are "not enough". For every human's greatest fear is that they are not enough, and if they are not enough, then they won't be loved.

Become aware of the language you use. It can make or break the energy of your day. Stand guard at the door of your mind and become conscious of how often you judge yourself. The second you notice it, employ the full-stop strategy.

Focus

It's simple. What you focus on is what you feel. In any given moment, if you are focusing on what is missing from your life, what is wrong with your life, and everything you wish you could change about your life, does that foster great energy? Usually not. Usually focusing on this is exhausting and doesn't offer you the fuel to make the changes you wish for anyway. But the minute you shift your focus to what you do have, what is already present in your life — food, clothing, shelter and clean drinking water for a start, given that the basic needs of far too many people in the world are still not met — you shift your chemistry, you shift your energy and open up to possibility. It is not physically possible for the human brain to focus on two things at once. No matter how good you believe you are at multi-tasking, your actual brain can only focus on one thing at a time. And when you focus on what's good, what you appreciate, what you are grateful for, and you do this consistently, your energy shifts significantly.

Changing your focus to what you like doesn't mean you are wearing rose-coloured glasses or burying your head in the sand, avoiding or denying what you would like to change or what you want more of in your life. You will still know that stuff is there. It's just that when you always focus on what's wrong, you don't have the energy to change it. When you focus on what you appreciate, it gives you the energy to start to change what you would like to change.

I witnessed this very powerfully in a lady who had been diagnosed with depression and was taking three different medications for this. Her energy was low, she was prone to constipation — typically, she used her bowels only once a week until we did some work on this — and just sitting with her, you could feel her sadness. However, on another occasion I witnessed her (not in my clinic, but at an event) win a major prize and she jumped and squealed and smiled bigger than I'd ever seen her smile. It was delightful to watch, and I was so happy for her. It was just that, in that moment, her focus was elsewhere and her energy was far superior to what had become her everyday state.

When I first read the line "what you focus on is what you feel", it stood out to me. And I liked the simplicity of it. But then I thought some more and realized that life is more nuanced than that sentence by itself conveys. I am a huge fan of the concept that every emotion is here to serve us, and that what we feel gives us an opportunity to shine a light on something that may help us to grow and/or learn. Even when we meet real tragedy in life, we can react either by losing hope and falling into self-destructive habits, or by using the challenge to find our inner strength. And that can mean sitting with physical pain, emotional pain, loss, heartache, heartbreak, disappointment, broken trust, anxieties or fears, and allowing ourselves to feel. Because what you feel gives you the opportunity to become of even greater service to the world. Quite often it is a case of the greater the wound, the bigger the gift.

So, yes, I am a huge fan of shifting our focus to change how we feel on an everyday basis. It is a simple and fast way to improve energy. However, in saying that, don't always use this shift-in-focus strategy when feeling emotions that may be uncomfortable; sometimes we need to sit with sadness and the fatigue that can come with that and allow the insights from the pain to be revealed. When there is "purpose" to emotional pain, it is easier to bear and growth can result. Many adults, however, don't have the strategies to unravel emotional pain themselves. A psychologist or perhaps a wise friend can help you though. Support and guidance is always available, so please ask for help.

Remember: what you focus on is what you feel, and you have the power to change where your focus goes in any moment. Some people may not find this to be an easy option to employ consistently, but if you do, you will be rewarded with much-improved energy on a daily basis.

★

*N*otice if what you just said, did or ate fosters energy
or depletes it, in you and for those around you.

Dr Libby

Hydration

Another of the choices you may make in your "stop, keep, start" analysis is to drink more water. Too many people live their lives in a state of chronic mild dehydration, and this alone can lead to significant fatigue.

Water is the basis of all life, and that includes your body. The muscles that move your body are 75 per cent water. Your blood, responsible for transporting nutrients throughout your body, is 82 per cent water. Your lungs, that take oxygen from the air, are 90 per cent water, while your brain is 76 per cent water. Even your bones are 25 per cent water!

Most people are aware of the critical importance of great hydration for their health. Many link it to clear skin. It is also critical to great energy, and yet too many people spend too many days in a dehydrated state.

Scientists believe that when we are born we are about 75 per cent water, but by the time we are 30 most adults' total body water content has dropped to around 57 to 60 per cent. I will use 70 per cent as an average to make this discussion simple. Think about this concept: 70 per cent of your physical body is water. Wow. No wonder the impact of dehydration is significant on virtually every process in our body.

Our health is truly dependent on the quality and quantity of the water we drink. Unintentional chronic dehydration can contribute to fatigue, pain and inflammation in the body, and it can even be involved in the development of many degenerative diseases. Helping your body prevent such ills by ensuring great-quality water intake on a regular basis is a crucial step when you are seeking to cultivate good and consistent energy.

Next time you are feeling irritable, unable to focus and fatigued, think of water first. You might be surprised how far that goes to resolving — or at least improving — these challenges. A study published in the *Journal of Nutrition* tested mood, concentration and mental skills in a group of women who were given either enough fluids to remain optimally hydrated or were induced into a mildly dehydrated state. The women's mood and cognitive abilities were tested during exercise and at rest under the different hydration conditions. On most mental tests, the women's state of hydration didn't affect performance, but being dehydrated caused headaches, loss of focus, a sense of fatigue and low mood, both at rest and during exercise. The dehydration induced in the study was not severe — it was a measly one per cent lower than optimal. One per cent!

Although men weren't included in this particular study, the results are likely to apply to them as well. So if you are feeling a bit gritty or weary, drink some water, and this is even more important after a workout. Keep in mind that pure water or other non-alcoholic and caffeine-free drinks are best for hydration, as caffeine and alcohol both have a dehydrating action on your cells.

The wonder of water: the key to happy, healthy cells

When it comes to water, most people believe that they need to drink more than they currently do, and, without a conscious effort, this never seems to happen. The wonders of water are well documented, ranging from fostering glowing, clear skin and eyes to the prevention of kidney stones. Yet, as with most nutritional information, there is conflicting information out there, which makes it difficult for individuals to truly know how much is enough.

The science

Without water, a human will usually only live for a mere three days. So essential is this liquid to our survival that we need it more than food. Science currently tells us that we need 33 millilitres of water for each kilogram of our body weight. A 70-kilogram person, therefore, requires 2310 millilitres a day. We do, however, tend to forget that many plant foods have a high water content, and this contributes to our overall daily water consumption. Herbal teas and soups also add up. Foods and drinks containing caffeine and alcohol, however, draw water out of our body, so the larger their presence in our diet, the greater our fluid requirements.

Fruits and vegetables are almost always over 70 per cent water, so the more of these we eat, the less we need to consume as fluid. Naturally, perspiration and increased breathing rates generated by exercise increase our need for water, but the specific amounts necessary are difficult to determine and will be highly individual. Trust your thirst when it comes to this. Thirst is Nature's way of letting you know you need to drink!

Thirst and hydration

Some people rarely feel thirsty, while for others their thirst never seems quenched. Some people resist increasing their fluid intake as they tire of frequently running to the loo. For others, increasing their fluid intake makes them feel swollen and uncomfortable. With all of these different scenarios, it is not surprising that there is so much conflicting information out there. So what's behind these differences and what can you do about it?

Just because you drink water, or even enough water for adequate hydration, does not necessarily mean that the cells of your body are hydrated. Ideally, every cell of your body looks like a grape; this is the case when your cells are hydrated. A dehydrated state means your cells appear more like sultanas, and this can be the result of inadequate water intake, a lack of minerals, or poor adrenal gland function, often due to chronic stress, physical and/or emotional trauma, or excess caffeine or alcohol intake.

To absorb the water you drink into your cells, you need calcium, magnesium, sodium, potassium and chloride. Some of these minerals make their home inside the cell, while others reside outside the cell wall. These minerals all talk to each other, and if one has an excessively high level or, alternatively, if one of those minerals is lacking, it can be difficult for water to enter the cell. Physically, when water stays outside the cell, it manifests as a feeling of fluid retention, which, for some people, is so noticeable that clothing will cut into them as the day progresses. You can change this by improving the mineral balance of your diet and taking care of your liver.

One of the best ways to improve your mineral intake and balance is to base your diet on what I have come to call low HI food. Most plant foods get their minerals from the soil in which they are grown, so foods that come from organic, biodynamic, or permacultured soils tend to be superior in their mineral profile. Green leafy vegies have a broad mineral profile that includes calcium, magnesium and potassium. Nuts and seeds also pack a powerful mineral punch and make a great snack or addition to any meal.

> *Your body uses minerals, among other things, to create electrolytes. Often described as the sparks of life, electrolytes carry electrical currents through the body, sending instructions to cells in all of the body systems.*

Minerals

People with low blood pressure often feel better with a slightly reduced fluid intake, as excess water dilutes their blood levels of minerals. Increasing your intake of all of the minerals above can, however, make a significant difference in that low blood pressure feeling.

Your body uses minerals, among other things, to create electrolytes. Often described as the sparks of life, electrolytes carry electrical currents through the body, sending instructions to cells in all of the body systems. Electrolytes are also necessary for enzyme production. Enzymes are responsible for the biochemical processes that drive the function of the body, as well as for digesting food and absorbing nutrients, and they impact on both muscle function and hormone production as well. Poor mineral intake and/or balance, as well as dehydration, can therefore affect all body systems and functions.

Amp up your mineral intake
A healthy and balanced way to increase the amount of minerals in your diet is to amp up the amount of plant foods you currently consume, the green-coloured ones in particular. Add them wherever you can, and do your best to base your evening meal on vegetables, rather than them being a token effort on the side of the plate. You can also include Celtic sea salt or Himalayan pink salt. They typically contain 84 minerals (albeit in tiny amounts) that can help your body better absorb water into the cells. Adding good-quality salt to your food can be of particular importance if you eat limited or no processed foods, especially if you suffer with digestive system problems.

Juicing or blending fruits and vegetables is also a great way to increase the fluid and mineral content of your diet and ensure that water is absorbed into your cells. If fluid retention is an ongoing challenge for you, try juicing celery, cucumber, mint and a small amount of pineapple daily for a week. Supplementing with a "green drink" supplement made from ground-up green vegetables can also be highly beneficial.

Set up rituals in your day to flag your memory that it is time to drink. Start your day with a glass of warm water with lemon juice, for example. Make drinking enough natural water a habit in your life. It won't take long for you to feel the benefits. Water is a simple and wonderful investment in your long-term health and energy.

Support your kidneys

The primary job of the kidneys is to remove the waste products of protein metabolism from the blood. These include nitrogen, uric acid (urea) and ammonia. The kidneys also remove many other substances from the blood that could become problematic if left to accumulate, including excess hormones, food additives, vitamins, minerals and drugs. They also regulate the electrolyte balance of the body, which involves the minerals needed for healthy nerve function. These include calcium, magnesium, phosphate, sodium, potassium and chloride. The kidneys also help regulate healthy blood pressure.

The kidneys regulate the amount of water in the body, and your urine is the expended material after your blood has been filtered by the kidneys. Water also plays an enormous role in keeping the moisture content of our skin at a lovely high level. Consuming adequate water helps promote healthy elimination, and it reduces the likelihood of constipation, as one of the primary functions of the large intestine is to absorb water from digested food. When water consumption is low, stools tend to become dry, hard and more difficult to pass, and the longer this waste remains inside the body, the more waste will be reabsorbed back into the bloodstream. The importance of great elimination and detoxification for great energy are discussed throughout this book.

It is obvious, then, that if we are to have outstanding energy, or even just better energy than we have at the moment, we must take good care of our kidneys. Here are some strategies to help support their optimal function:

Drink adequate amounts of pure water each day. Keep a large glass at your desk to ensure you stay hydrated over the day. Be happy about getting up to refill it, as this not only means you have finished a glass, you are also taking a break from sitting, which we identified earlier as being essential to good energy.

Let your body guide you on how much water it needs by noticing your response to the water you drink. As you drink, observe if your thirst becomes awakened and your body actually seems to draw in the water. This is your body letting you know that it needs more water. Sometimes I start drinking and want another glass immediately. At other times, I am satisfied with one glass or a few sips. Give your

body all the water it needs throughout the day to ensure that the elimination of waste via the urine is well supported.

* Soft drink, caffeine and alcohol consumption is best minimized for good hydration. However, if/when you do consume these, drink a glass of water for each of these drinks you have.

* Sleep well! Really work to solve this if you don't currently sleep well. Not just for the direct impact sleep has on energy, but also because rest and sleep strengthen the kidneys. Seven to nine hours of restorative sleep per night allows the kidneys to adequately cleanse the blood, eliminating waste products in the morning urine that would otherwise be shunted to the skin for excretion. Do all you can to establish a consistent rhythm between your sleeping and waking hours, particularly if you would like more vitality. Consider taking a short nap on the weekends, especially when you are going through times of stress, which for many people these days is every week! Prioritizing sleep is essential if it is not currently of a good quality.

* Take part in regular restorative movement such as t'ai chi, qi gong, yoga and/or restorative yoga. These practices not only have specific poses or movements to support healthy kidney function, but the diaphragmatic breathing they foster is a powerful tool to decrease stress hormone production, as explained in detail in other parts of this book.

Histamine and Fatigue

As you now understand, hydration and healthy kidneys help to keep us energized. So does the immune system in a variety of ways. We touched on the importance of its optimal function when we looked at the way infections can influence everything from neurotransmitter production to gut function. So the immune system both directly and indirectly has an impact on energy. Another way the immune system plays a role in how fatigued we feel, though, is down to allergic responses. Here's what happens.

If people experience allergic symptoms, such as sneezing, a blocked or runny nose, sinus problems, itchy eyes, or hayfever, for example, they can feel fatigued after a particularly reactive day. Or it may be a time of year that is worse for them, such as spring. One of the substances involved in an allergic reaction is histamine, which is released from a type of immune system cell, called a mast cell, when its cell wall (its outside membrane) becomes unstable. The best way to picture this is as a circle and the outside line of the circle (the cell wall) starts to vibrate when it is unstable. When this occurs histamine is released, and this is one mechanism through which allergic symptoms can start to present. The level of exhaustion that this alone can cause for an individual is significant, and so it is important to address when someone is seeking improvements in their energy.

There are many aspects to histamine being released. For example, mast cell walls require vitamin C for their stability, so if someone has a poor dietary intake of this vitamin, histamine release is more likely. As an aside, many people with hayfever-type symptoms do well with larger doses of two to five grams of vitamin C per day supplemented into their diet.

Another reason histamine reactions, and hence fatigue, can become more likely is due to poor adrenal function. Not only is histamine released in many allergic reactions, but other substances that drive inflammation are as well. As you will understand from the adrenals section, cortisol, one of the hormones produced by the adrenal glands, is a powerful anti-inflammatory. In fact, reducing inflammation is one of its primary roles.

Inflammation can be created from a wide variety of scenarios in the body, one of which is long-term stress driven by adrenalin. Being the acute (short-term) stress hormone, adrenalin is designed to be produced for only very brief periods of time and in short bursts to get us out of danger. But we have seen that adrenalin production in modern times can be constant and relentless, for a variety of reasons. The body cannot sustain the metabolic consequences of these consistently high levels of adrenalin output, and so the adrenals release more cortisol to dampen down the resulting inflammation. As we saw in the earlier section on the adrenals, elevated cortisol comes with its own problems and also requires increased amounts of vitamin C to produce it. So if someone has a poor dietary intake, or their lifestyle induces the destruction of vitamin C — such as smoking or being exposed to other pollutants — the adrenals get to a point where they can no longer sustain the output of cortisol required to keep the inflammation at bay.

If people experience allergic symptoms, such as sneezing, a blocked or runny nose, sinus problems, itchy eyes, or hayfever, for example, they can feel fatigued after a particularly reactive day.

The individual then ends up with adrenal fatigue, and the subsequent deep, unrelenting fatigue this creates. When cortisol levels have fallen low, your ability to counteract the inflammatory, allergic-type reactions becomes poor and histamine release tends to increase, driving the allergic symptoms. People experiencing adrenal fatigue often notice that they become more sensitive or their allergies get worse when their cortisol is particularly low.

Conversely, the more histamine that is released, the harder the adrenals have to work to try to produce enough cortisol to dampen down the inflammation, and the more worn-out the adrenal glands themselves appear to become. This can establish a vicious cycle of reduced cortisol allowing histamine to inflame the tissues, leading to worsening adrenal fatigue, as well as more extreme allergic responses. And the fatigue that goes along with all of this can be debilitating.

Actively supporting your adrenal glands and the immune response through the use of specific nutrients such as vitamin C and bioflavonoids, and herbal medicine, as well as eliminating or reducing your exposure to foods and other substances that cause allergic or sensitivity reactions, can help break this cycle as well as strengthen adrenal function. Problematic foods for an individual can interfere with daily functioning and become a profound stress on the adrenal glands, so it is important to work with an experienced health professional to determine and trial an elimination of these foods to both decrease the load that the food reactions can bring, and to promote adrenal health. Dietary changes are best guided by a nutrition professional.

As an aside, my first job after my first degree in Nutrition and Dietetics was working as the dietician for an allergist (a doctor/medical specialist who has specialized in allergies). I will be forever grateful to him, as I learnt an exceptional amount from him and witnessed the power of dietary change in action every day. There was not a case of eczema, for example, that he didn't completely resolve. Not one.

I learnt during my time working alongside him that skin-prick tests are highly accurate for inhalant allergies, yet not for foods. You may get false negative and false positive responses to a skin-prick test for foods. One of the reasons for this is thought to be that the food itself does not end up in your blood. Fragments of the food do (as foods are acted on by the digestive system), and the structure of the fragments may be different for each individual based on their own digestive capacity and degree of gut permeability. In my time working alongside this gifted allergy medical specialist I witnessed first-hand that the only way we currently have to establish if someone reacts to a food is through a trial elimination diet. An exception to this is a blood test that can be done for what are known as immunoglobulin-E (IgE) mediated food reactions, which are true food allergies. But there are countless ways, many of which I don't believe we yet understand the mechanisms of, through which people can react to foods. Sometimes the dietary changes are temporary; sometimes they need to be permanent. An allergist and a nutritionist, dietician or naturopath experienced in allergic medicine can guide you with this.

For now, know that vitamin C, bioflavonoids, hesperidin, zinc, and medicinal herbs such as grapeseed extract, albizia, skullcap and feverfew can be highly nourishing for the immune system, and some of them play a role in stabilizing mast cells and alleviating some hayfever-type symptoms. And if this is something you experience and you are fatigued, it can make a world of difference to your level of tiredness.

Post-viral Fatigue

For some who have had glandular fever, also known as mono-nucleosis, which is caused by the Epstein–Barr virus (EBV), they will have experienced a fatigue so deep that they still don't feel like they are over it, even though the infection itself may have occurred over a decade ago. There are others who get this virus and don't even know they've had it. How can that be?

Before we get into the fatigue itself involved with EBV, I first want you to imagine how many infective organisms you think there are in the world. Millions? Billions? Trillions? Do we even really know? The short answer is, we have no idea, but the number would be almost infinite. Now, how many of those can we currently test for? A drop in the ocean of an almost endless number. There is still so much we don't know, and still so, so much we cannot yet test for.

With that said, a common scenario is when someone feels unwell but with non-specific symptoms, the major one being tiredness, they may visit their doctor to find out what's going on. If nothing shows up in blood tests, it is assumed that the person has a "virus" and they are sent home to rest and recover. And some people do recover. But some people never feel like they do.

A blood test can measure antibodies (markers in your blood) for current EBV infection and also past EBV infection. And often this is the only viral marker that is checked. Yet it is understood that most, if not all, viruses can cause fatigue, although not everyone experiences them this way. There must, therefore, be others factors at play.

Studies have demonstrated that a discrete post-infectious fatigue condition exists, and one that is not a mood disorder.

In a paper published in *The Journal of Infectious Diseases*, the author describes research that suggests that there appears to be not one but two specific post-infectious fatigue syndromes, one characterized by excessive sleep and the other by insomnia and muscle and joint pain. Having done my PhD in a laboratory where professors of immunology and microbiology were examining the role of infections in chronic fatigue conditions, I was privy to many experiments and to conversations around the morning-tea table, as well as presentations at global scientific conferences of the role infections likely played in myriad syndromes and diseases, including many autoimmune conditions. And in clinical practice, I have most certainly witnessed the debilitating fatigue that can result after an infection.

Possible causes

As I said, fatigue can follow any infective event, and in practice I have seen it regularly after an upper respiratory tract infection, usually caused by a *Streptococcus* species. I've seen it after Q fever, Ross River fever and what is considered to be a form of Lyme disease. As an aside, I acknowledge that Lyme disease (caused by the *Borrelia* species) is not recognized as being in Australia; however, I do believe that an infective organism of a similar nature to the *Borrelia* species will be identified and found to cause symptoms identical to, or similar to, those of Lyme disease. In my clinical experience, those who have been diagnosed as having Lyme disease are often the most unwell and need urgent support for many body systems.

> *G*ut bacteria are needed to detoxify and then help eliminate the numerous heavy metals to which we are exposed in our daily lives.

In clinical practice, fatigue can also be a symptom following what I call "Bali belly", where someone has had food poisoning

224 ★ Exhausted to Energized

or picked up a bug from water and, after the diarrhoea has resolved, they are left with what is diagnosed by their GP or a gastroenterologist as IBS. Some people experience a debilitating fatigue along with their gut symptoms. Many also describe a brain fog or a thick, heavy feeling in their head. Given that many neurotransmitters, such as serotonin, are predominantly produced in the gut and have most of their receptors in the gut, this is not surprising.

Clinically, with the latter scenario, I treat the gut first with antimicrobial herbs and then I see what symptoms remain. For the vast majority of people, their gut symptoms resolve with this. If energy is also disrupted, I will almost always use adrenal- and immune-supportive herbal medicine, along with coenzyme Q_{10}, vitamin C and zinc, a diet high in plant foods, no refined sugars and what I call a low reactive diet — often no gluten or casein is needed short term or long term, or sometimes a diet that is low in foods that can ferment in the gut is needed for a period of time. The dietary change that is required can be quite specific. I steer people in this state away from cold, raw food, and suggest they eat more warming, cooked foods, such as soups, stews and casseroles. The majority get well and get their lives back as a result — it can be an astronomical shift.

But there are those who don't get well after adopting these new ways. They may improve, but their energy is not back to where it once was. They have usually had multiple infections, and they've had to go to bed with them, sometimes for months. They usually have blocked sinuses and difficulty breathing through their noses. Their digestive system usually functions poorly, and they need additional stomach acid support and/or digestive enzyme support. Often they have had a long history of *Streptococcus*-based infections as children, such as recurrent tonsillitis or ear infections. They are typically low in zinc. As children, they didn't like red meat, but preferred chicken and white carbs. They loved salt-and-vinegar chips as children, which I believe was them trying to stimulate their stomach to make more acid (due to the vinegar). They are typically still zinc-deficient as adults, and this has compromised their immune response. Add on top of that the multiple rounds of antibiotics they had as a child, and their gut bacteria profile, has been far from ideal since then. When they pass wind it is not just a little odorous, but people leave the room (or wish they could). Gut bacteria are needed to detoxify and then help eliminate the numerous heavy metals to which we are exposed in our daily lives. You get the gist of the multi-system involvement and long-term "interior" stress for the body.

Often EBV or an infection like this doesn't come out of nowhere. There is a long history of minor or major health issues. It's just that too many people think chronic infections in childhood are normal. It's not. It's common, but it's not normal. If your child gets recurrent infections, there is so much that can be done to stop this. Please seek the guidance of a health professional highly experienced in nutritional support for the immune system.

Many of the people who end up with ongoing debilitating fatigue after a virus have typically also had massive family stress. Time and time again I have seen situations where one parent had an addiction, or a mental illness, or seemed highly irrational to the child, and the child (in their own words) experienced immense fear and/or rejection growing up. That was their perception. It may have been real, or it may have been how it felt to the child. The child may have been extremely safe and loved, but they didn't *feel* that way.

I share that with you because I have seen that scenario time and time again over the past 17 years. And that is why an holistic approach to so many people's health is required today, because there are usually (what I call my three-pillar approach) biochemical, nutritional and emotional components to people's wellbeing, and addressing all three is usually critical to supporting them to being well again.

Post-natal Depletion

Another area where fatigue requires an holistic approach is in what has become known as *post-natal depletion*. Before I begin this section, however, I want to be up-front and say that I am not a mother. I am writing this section as a health professional who has worked with thousands of mothers seeking help with their health and energy. I write it with immense admiration and respect for these women, and with the intention of offering insight and solutions into the mechanisms of a unique situation of what can be a deep, deep fatigue — that of motherhood.

Reading widely as I do, always wanting to support people as best I can, I came across what was for me, a new term — post-natal depletion — and what I read struck a powerful chord with me, having worked with so many depleted women, whether they have been mothers for a week or seven years. So this section is devoted to the fatigue that mothers may experience. What about the fathers you ask? They, too, tend to children's needs and get up to children in the night. And that is true. But what I am talking about here is not just the sleep deprivation that can occur with little ones in the house, but the physical and emotional depletion that pregnancy and lactation can create if the right supports — both nutritional and emotional — are not in place, and the concurrent journey of that type of depletion alongside the sleep deprivation and worry.

Post-natal depletion is a term coined by medical doctor Dr Oscar Serrallach (see notes in the references and resources section at the back of this book), and and is one I hadn't heard of prior to researching and writing this book. But given I wrote a book that I titled *Rushing Woman's Syndrome* in 2011, when

I saw the term "post-natal depletion" written up in an article, I was immediately drawn to learning more about it, with a strong sense that the likelihood of what this doctor was going to brilliantly describe would resonate for the readers of a book about energy. For some of the most truly exhausted people I have met are mothers.

Goop.com, Gwyneth Paltrow's very popular blog, also reported on post-natal depletion, opening their article with:

> Consider this: If you've had a child within the last decade, you might still be suffering some consequences — lethargy, memory disturbances, and poor energy levels, among other symptoms. And according to Dr Oscar Serrallach, a family practitioner based in rural Australia, it's not just because being a parent is hard — physically, the process of growing a baby exacts a significant toll.

Late pregnancy and early motherhood

Here's part of why. The placenta passes nearly seven grams of fat a day to the growing baby at the end of the pregnancy term, a much higher amount than in any other animal. Furthermore, about 60 per cent of the total energy that goes to the baby via the placenta is to feed the brain. For other primates, including gorillas, the figure is closer to 20 per cent.

The placenta serves both the growing baby and the mother. During the pregnancy, the mother supplies everything that the growing baby needs, which is why so many mothers become low in iron, zinc, vitamin B_{12}, folate, iodine and selenium. They also have much lower reserves in important omega-3 fats like DHA, and specific amino acids from proteins. The placenta also tunes the mother to the baby, and the baby to the mother. Of course this is no accident.

The placenta develops at the same time as the fetal hypothalamus, a hormone-producing gland in the baby's brain. The hormones produced by the placenta look very similar to the hypothalamic hormones — again, this is no accident. A beautiful example of this synchronicity occurs during birth.

Oxytocin, known as the love hormone, causes labour pains which are essentially contractions of the uterus. As the baby is squeezed through the birth canal, its hypothalamus produces oxytocin which ends up in the mother's bloodstream, causing more contractions. In what is in one way a magnificent symphony, the baby is assisting the mother in its own birth. Isn't that a miracle in itself?

Once the baby is born, there are enormous amounts of oxytocin in both the mother and the baby, literally creating a love-fest often referred to as the "baby bubble". Experts suggest that this needs to be encouraged and respected, and caregivers and fathers need to be aware of the importance of this time post-birth, when the bond between mother and baby is being established. This is Nature's design, so the further we drift away from this, the more the flow-on of challenges in the postpartum period and beyond can unfortunately occur for mother and baby.

It can be physically and emotionally challenging to get back on your feet after a baby arrives, and this can be more difficult if there are additional young ones at home and if the mother is not well supported. Hormonally, nutritionally and emotionally, things can take time to restore and rebalance. In my practice, I have noticed this readjustment getting worse and worse over the past 17 years.

Before I address this more fully, let's look at another physiological change that takes place with the mother during pregnancy in order to equip her for parenting. Studies suggest that (and sorry about this) on average, a mother's brain shrinks approximately 5 per cent in the prenatal period, as it supports the growth of the baby with so much fat, and much of the brain supplies that fat. Part of the actual brain shrinkage is also part of the physical and emotional rewiring that occurs to equip women for motherhood. It supports the creation of a "baby radar", where mothers become intuitively aware of their child's needs, whether they are cold or hungry, or if they cry at night.

However, this hyper-vigilance can become dangerous for the mother if she, in turn, is not supported. While there is plenty of prenatal support available, as soon as a baby is born the whole focus goes to the baby. There is often very little focus on the mother, who disappears into the shadows of her new role, which is often a more difficult transition if the woman has come away from a working role where she felt highly capable. This new hyper-vigilance is obviously vital for the survival of the child, but if the mother is living in an unsupportive household or society, it can lead to sleep problems, self-doubt, insecurity, feelings of unworthiness and a concerning, dangerous level of fatigue.

Note, too, that many mothers-to-be are already depleted leading up to conception and pregnancy. Nature's design is that the developing fetus will take all that it requires from the mother. The go-between to ensure that this happens safely is the placenta. The placenta is unique in humans in terms of how extensively the finger-like projections of the placenta reach into the lining of the womb, creating a large surface area. The reason for this is the fetal brain and its huge requirement for energy and fat, in the form of specific fatty acids such as DHA.

Enter post-natal depletion.

Symptoms of post-natal depletion

Dr Serrallach describes post-natal depletion as a common phenomenon of fatigue and exhaustion combined with a feeling of ongoing "baby brain". Baby brain is a term that encompasses the symptoms of poor concentration, poor memory and emotional lability. Emotional lability is where one's emotions change up and down much more easily than they would have in the past, such as crying for no reason. There is often a feeling of isolation, vulnerability, and of not feeling "good enough". This is experienced by many mothers, and is an understandable and at times predictable outcome associated with the extremely demanding task of being a mother from the perspective of both childbearing and child-raising. Along with these features, Dr Serrallach has identified a typical associated biochemical "fingerprint" that is partly the cause of, and partly the result of, post-natal depletion, and separate from post-natal depression.

Symptoms include fatigue and exhaustion, being tired on waking, falling asleep unintentionally, hyper-vigilance (a feeling that the "radar" is constantly on), which is often associated with anxiety or a sense of unease, feeling tired but wired, a sense of guilt and shame around the role of being a mother and a loss of self-esteem, which is often associated with a sense of isolation, apprehension and sometimes a fear about socializing or leaving the house. Frustration, a sense of being overwhelmed, and a sense of not coping are also common. Some women will read that and say that's how it is for all mothers, but that's not true. Not everyone feels that way — at least not constantly — and if you do, it can be highly worthwhile seeking support, both nutritional and emotional.

Causes of post-natal depletion

What creates the chemistry that allows post-natal depletion and the unrelenting fatigue that comes with it? There is no one factor, but let's look at a few of the main players.

Stress

We live in a society where people can feel continual and ongoing stress, and, if they haven't been taught tools to relax or switch off or manage their fears and concerns, then this alone can have a profound impact on hormones, immune function, brain structure, and gut health, as you have already read.

The tolls of pregnancy

Women are also having babies later in life. In Australia, the average age for a mother having her first baby is 30.9 years, and too many women are — from a physical health perspective — going into motherhood in a depleted state, trying to blend careers, social schedules, family needs and the chronic sleep deprivation that has become the norm in our society. Remember that humans have been on the planet for about 150,000 years and it hasn't even been 100 years since women (in significant numbers) entered the workforce. Of course we are capable. But our *body* has never had to juggle so much before. This experience for our nervous system and adrenals is relatively new, and we are still adapting. I did a TEDx talk about this in 2014, and you can watch it on YouTube if understanding more about what we are now asking of our bodies appeals.

Numerous child and maternal health experts believe that as a society we tend not to allow mothers to fully recover after childbirth before getting pregnant again or before they go back to work. And the demands this can bring, not to mention the new juggling act they have to engage to run their lives, can be overwhelming and exhausting and further deplete their nutritional and emotional resources. It is not uncommon to see the phenomenon of a mother giving birth to two children from separate pregnancies inside 18 months, particularly if they believe their "fertility window" is rapidly closing. Also, with assisted reproduction we are seeing higher rates of twins, which can physically exacerbate any depletion, having supplied two growing babies simultaneously with nutrition. You can do it. Of course you can do it! But additional support is required. And not enough people are aware of this or are taking actions to prevent or remedy the depletion.

Sleep deprivation

The sleep deprivation that comes with having a newborn can itself be depleting. Some research suggests that in the first year the average sleep debt is around 700 hours.

Lack of support and the advent of "Super Mum"

If you are reading this and you are thinking that this has always been the case, the biggest difference for too many women is the shift away from good family and societal support. A whole village, or certainly extended families, was often around to lend support not that long ago in human history. Multi-generational support groups for mothers have been part of indigenous cultures for millennium, although they are sadly absent in our culture. Now, too many women do everything on their own.

There is also a perceived notion that a mother has to be everything to everyone; something I have discussed in *Rushing Woman's Syndrome*. As a result, many mothers suffer in silence and are not receiving the education, information or support that they need to replete themselves of their exhaustion.

Nutrition and environment

Add to this that our food is becoming increasingly nutrient-poor, whether through the depletion of nutrients from the soil or through people choosing too may packaged and processed foods. Because we are so tired, convenience often wins out over nutrition — which is why, alternatively, slow-cooker and one-pot-wonder meals can be so practical, convenient and nutritious. Although poorly studied, there are specific aspects of the 21st-century lifestyle that may be contributing to post-natal depletion. These include environmental pollutants such as air pollution and "electrosmog", to name but two.

Treatment for post-natal depletion

To begin to address the depletion and fatigue that too many mothers are experiencing these days, it needs to be done gradually. Too much of anything, including information, can add to the feeling of being overwhelmed, so work needs to be done gradually while restoring nutritional health. Working towards hormonal balance and nutrient repletion are key steps to getting a woman back to experiencing energy, achieving better sleep quality, and feeling that she can cope again.

Nutritional support

In my experience, it is critical for a mum to work with a health professional experienced in this area, one who understands the way biochemistry, nutrition and emotions interplay. Typically, iron and zinc will be too low for the body to make the substances required for happiness and optimism, and these often need to be supplemented. Testing these levels first is important. Other nutrients that may need focus include vitamin C, vitamin D and magnesium. The omega-3 fat DHA is an essential supplement for a depleted mum. This is vital for nervous system (including the brain) support, as well as hormonal balance. Oily fish supply DHA, and there are now some good-quality supplements derived from algae. Also, the body can convert another omega-3 fat found in plants (such as flaxseeds and chia seeds), known as EPA, into DHA; however, the efficiency of the body to do this seems highly individual. Some studies suggest this conversion is up-regulated during pregnancy but not lactation. The focus for the depleted mum needs to be on easy, practical meals made from whole, real foods that are nutrient-dense.

Hormone rebalancing

It can also be highly beneficial to consult with someone experienced in helping women balance their sex hormones. Addressing specific nutrient deficiencies and establishing strategies around sleep, diet and lifestyle, often naturally improves sex hormone balance. Having your thyroid function checked (both thyroid hormones and thyroid antibodies) is also important, as for some women the thyroid needs support after childbirth. The thyroid gland and its function are explored in the next section. Appropriate, evidence-based herbal medicine can be invaluable at this time as well.

Emotional and psychological support

Seeking support is also critical. If you feel as though you may be experiencing post-natal depletion, let a friend know and seek professional support, such as the help of a psychologist. Restorative practices that activate the PNS are also a critical part of recovery from depletion. Restorative yoga, Stillness Through Movement, and acupuncture are all beautiful and highly effective. You need to make sure that you can actually

234 ★ Exhausted to Energized

relax, as I have found that many women today cannot. Even when they are trying to relax, they are still SNS-dominant and stressed. Often so stressed they can't relax! So, as crazy as it sounds, if you need help to learn how to relax again, then these restorative practices will be even more important. As I said, in the section on the nervous system, in my experience the most powerful way to activate the PNS is via regular restorative practices.

Although previous generations may not have outwardly discussed a mother's direction and purpose, for the women of today, it can be invaluable to have the support of a wise friend, psychologist, life coach, or mentor. Creating a life where there is opportunity for personal growth may be more important to some women than others. Identifying what matters to the individual is key, as there can be an avalanche of guilt that adds more weight to the depletion. This person may also be equipped to offer support for family dynamics, relationships, in-laws ... wherever they are challenges that the mother is facing. If these relationships have broken down, this may not only be an added stress for a mother, but will also mean that her support system is no longer available.

Psychologists specializing in supporting new mums suggest that the primary relationship between the mother and the other parent (if present) whether it is the father, stepfather or second mother, often needs some special attention during the early childhood years. There are psychologists and therapists who specialize in this type of "relationship rebuilding", and it can be beneficial to every element of the family dynamic.

Sleep and fatigue

Fatigue is the most common symptom in post-natal depletion. Having vitality or boundless energy is the end result of a series of body systems working optimally, as you are seeing throughout this book. Having deep and chronic fatigue is the end result of these systems being out of sync or functioning poorly.

Nutrition

Addressing micronutrient deficiencies along with the dietary intake, and opting for a wholefood way of eating with plenty of vegetables, are important places to start. The most important initial micronutrients include iron, zinc, vitamin B_{12}, vitamin C and vitamin D. Additionally, supplemental magnesium and good-quality appropriate herbal medicine can also be highly beneficial.

Prioritizing

Sleep is a conundrum for many mothers, as they are too tired, too stressed and too busy to sleep well. They will also tell me that they cannot possibly prioritize sleep. Yet they must, as it is a cornerstone of wellbeing and recovery from depletion. Alongside this, though, goes my earlier comment that there will be times when disrupted sleep is unavoidable. However, "sleep-support" houses now exist and allow new, sleep-deprived mums to sleep there, while nurses keep an eye on the baby, at the other end of the house. Make full use of these support services!

Environment

What is done in the hour before bedtime also needs to be addressed, and can make a huge difference, as you saw in the earlier section on sleep. Techniques to embrace for an hour or two in the lead-up to bedtime to help enhance good-quality sleep include not watching television or using a back-lit device, exposing yourself only to soft yellow lighting and calming music, and, as much as the children allow, treating your bedroom as a sanctuary. In fact, if there is only one room that can be kept tidy in the house, make it your bedroom. Once the lights are out, the room ideally needs to be cool and as quiet and dark as possible.

Stress

Emotional stress is best avoided in the hour of wind-down to sleep, if at all possible, as it tends to hijack sleep quality.

I also find that stressing about not sleeping is one of the worst things you can do. If you are up breastfeeding through the night, or attending to little ones, I encourage you to remember that your children are little for such a short period of time, and to remember that age-old piece of wisdom: "this too shall pass".

Sometimes the stress will be related to how you perceive your abilities as a mother and/or partner, with attached feelings of guilt and reproach. If you want to take things deeper, everything — and I mean everything — can be our teacher if we choose to see things that way. Instead of judging yourself for not being or doing enough, notice that you judge yourself and bring curiosity instead of judgment to the situation. Wonder why you are so harsh on yourself. Wonder why you are reacting with rage or resentment or withdrawal or immense sadness. Yes, seek support for these things, but also use them to get back in touch with truths and things that are welling up inside you. I say all this with love.

> *If* you want to take things deeper, everything — and I mean everything — can be our teacher if we choose to see things that way.

A cultural perspective

So is post-natal depletion really a new thing, or has it always been around? Really, how would we know? It has certainly become common these days and with more doctors becoming aware of it, thanks to Dr Serrallach, more and more women will begin to obtain the support that they need. We understand that most of the "primitive cultures" or first peoples of the world had very specific practices to ensure that mothers made a full recovery from childbirth. This is something that is not talked about much today. These are known as post-partum practices. From China to India, from indigenous Australians to the

First Nations peoples of America, there have been centuries of very deliberate practices in nutritional recovery, spiritual cleansing, and protection as well as elaborate social supports. For example, in traditional Chinese culture they observe the sitting month "Zuo Yue Zi" where the mother would not leave the house for 30 days, would not receive any visitors, and would have no duties apart from breastfeeding the baby. Special rebuilding, warm foods would be supplied, and the mother would not be allowed to get cold in that time. Ancient cultures have made the realization that Western society unfortunately has not: for society to be well and prosper, the mothers must be fully supported and healthy — in every sense of the word.

★

*R*emind yourself of the difference
between being alive and living.
It matters.
And great energy helps
you enjoy more of both.

Dr Libby

Thyroid Hormones and Energy: An Undeniable Link

When it comes to energy being produced inside the body so we can experience it, we've already explored contributors such as mitochondria, B vitamins and coenzyme Q_{10}, just to name a few. What also must be highlighted as a significant factor contributing to more and more people's poor energy is poor thyroid function and the subsequent challenges with thyroid hormones. To appreciate how thyroid hormones impact on energy, it is important to first understand how the thyroid gland works and what it requires for optimal function. I have explored the thyroid gland in most of my previous books: in *Accidentally Overweight*, thyroid function was examined in relation to weight loss; in *Rushing Woman's Syndrome*, it was explored in light of the stress response; in *Beauty from the Inside Out*, thyroid function was discussed for its impact on skin, hair and nail health (amongst other things); while *The Calorie Fallacy* looked at the importance of thyroid function on whether body fat or glucose is used as a fuel source for the body. This time, it is all about how thyroid hormones impact on energy and what the thyroid needs to function optimally.

When people think of the thyroid many simply link it to weight gain or loss; essentially, they link it to their metabolic rate. Yet the reason thyroid hormones are so intricately linked to weight loss or gain is because of the way they drive metabolic rate. This then impacts on whether you experience an availability of energy or not. As we have discussed previously, a deep, unrelenting fatigue or a "tired but wired" feeling can be the result of a wide variety of body systems or organs not working optimally. However, a tiredness-in-your-bones-type feeling can certainly be related to poor thyroid function. Here's how it all works.

A growing number of people in developed countries are experiencing thyroid problems. Some have a fully developed disease, such as hypothyroidism, Hashimoto's thyroiditis, hyperthyroidism or Graves' disease. With the latter two conditions, there is an increase in the metabolic rate, which can create an intense feeling of energy. (Some people describe it as a hyperactive or anxious feeling that they can't control.) For others, however, their thyroid gland simply isn't working optimally, which may be due to any of a variety of causes — nutrient deficiencies, the over-consumption of substances that can interfere with optimal thyroid function, oestrogen dominance, or infection. Autoimmune diseases of the thyroid have increased significantly in the recent past as well.

So let's explore this gland, how it works, how it impacts on energy and metabolism, and how to support yours best.

The thyroid gland

The thyroid gland is a little butterfly-shaped gland that sits in your throat area. It makes hormones that play an enormous role in whether you feel energized or not, your metabolic rate, and temperature regulation. Every day of my working life, I meet people who exhibit virtually every symptom of an underactive thyroid, yet their blood test results demonstrate that everything is in the "normal" range. More on "normal" ranges later.

The production of thyroid hormones involves a cascade of signals, and glands other than the thyroid are involved. This means that if there is a problem with thyroid hormone levels, or with debilitating symptoms indicating something with thyroid function is awry, then it is essential to get to the heart of the matter so that treatment can be appropriately targeted. Understanding the road into a dysfunction in the body is critical, as correcting *this* is the road out.

The thyroid function cascade begins with the *hypothalamus*, a gland that makes a hormone that sends a signal to the *pituitary gland,* a tiny gland that sits at the base of your brain. The pituitary then makes a hormone called *thyroid-stimulating hormone* (TSH) that signals the thyroid to make one if its hormones, known simply as T_4 (*thyroxine*). T_4 is found in the blood in two forms, namely "T_4" and "free T_4" (FT_4). They are the same hormone, except that FT_4 is "free" to enter tissues while the other is bound up and unable to enter tissues, which is where the work needs to be done. However, as T_4 and FT_4 are inactive hormones, they must be converted into the active thyroid hormone called T_3 (*triiodothyronine*). It is T_3 that helps you feel energized, drives your metabolic rate, and contributes to your capacity to burn body fat. The flowchart below illustrates the hormonal cascade.

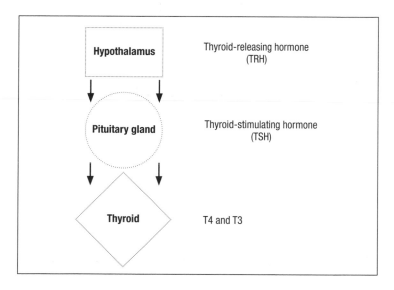

The thyroid hormone cascade: Signalling begins with the hypo-thalamus, followed by the pituitary, which then in turn signals the thyroid gland to make its hormones.

Thyroid nutrients

A number of nutrients are essential to the production of optimal levels of thyroid hormones. Iodine and selenium are both vital minerals to this process of conversion, which helps generate an energized feeling and literally lights up your metabolic rate. Many people today get very little iodine and selenium in their diets, as the majority of soils in the Western world do not contain these essential trace minerals. And if a nutrient is not in the soil, it cannot be in the food in which it is grown.

Iron is another mineral critical to the creation of healthy thyroid function, but iron deficiency is the most common nutrient deficiency in the world. There are numerous reasons for this, including: inadequate dietary intake; poor absorption due to (for example) poor gut function; gluten intolerance; coeliac disease; a diet too high in calcium-rich foods, as iron and calcium compete for absorption and calcium wins each time, as it is a bigger molecule; or regular, excessive menstrual blood loss. When someone is iron-deficient, instead of T_4 being converted into the active T_3 hormone, it gets converted into *reverse* T_3 (rT_3), which creates an additional problem for great energy, not to mention a healthy metabolic rate. To recap: the nutrients needed for healthy thyroid function are, in particular, iodine, selenium and iron.

The role of the mitochondria

Thyroid hormones are like the spark-plugs of the body. They ignite the fuel in the mitochondria of each cell, which is necessary to produce the biochemical energy with which the body performs all of its functions. For this reason, any problem with the thyroid gland leads to energy problems and often an unrelenting fatigue.

Thyroid hormones increase the metabolic rate, as well as speed up the rate of oxidation occurring in the body. (Remember, the oxidation process generates free radicals, and antioxidants are required to stop the free radicals from damaging body tissues.) The metabolic rate, in turn, impacts on every process of body functioning. This includes the metabolism of fats, carbohydrates and proteins, digestion and cardiovascular health. It affects DNA and protein synthesis, body weight, heart rate, blood pressure, respiration, muscle strength, sleep and sexual functioning, to name, in particular, a few. Thyroid hormones impact on every body system, and energy levels are compromised when levels fall too low.

To be somewhat more specific and yet still keep this description relatable, the mitochondria must respond to the active thyroid hormone T_3 by making *adenosine triphosphate*, or ATP, in the biochemical pathways known as glycolysis and the carboxylic acid cycles. These processes require many nutrients, including the B-complex vitamins and iron. This amazing process produces ATP, the actual substance the body uses to power its many actions.

Once ATP is formed in the mitochondria, the cells must also be able to use it effectively. So the ATP is converted to another substance called *adenosine diphosphate* (ADP), which must then be recycled back to ATP. Yet again, many nutrients are needed to utilize ATP efficiently and recycle it properly. If any of the nutritional factors are deficient, thyroid hormones will be ineffective in increasing energy production. Nothing in the world can replace consistently eating nutrient-dense food.

Thyroid diseases

The thyroid gland can become overactive, which is known as *hyperthyroidism*, or underactive, which is known as *hypothyroidism*. The latter can lead to fatigue and, for some, weight gain that can be difficult to shift until the hypothyroidism is addressed. The thyroid gland is also susceptible to auto-immune diseases. This is when your immune system, which is supposed to defend you from infection, starts to see the thyroid gland (which is obviously part of you) as a foreign particle, like a germ, and attacks it, leading to a change in its function. This can lead to either the overactive picture (with autoimmune involvement, which is known as Graves' disease) or an underactive picture (known as Hashimoto's thyroiditis with autoimmune involvement), a key symptom of which is a deep, unrelenting fatigue.

244 ★ *Exhausted to Energized*

Causes of poor thyroid function

Infection, what I refer to as "congested liver detoxification pathways", iodine, selenium and iron deficiencies, calorie intake that is too low for too long, as well as oestrogen dominance, elevated cortisol or adrenal fatigue are all major factors that can initiate this process. It is important to work out the path that leads someone to altered thyroid function, for behind the "why" lies most of the answer.

Which factors stand out for you? Sometimes many of the above apply, in which case it is about finding out where to start.

Hyperthyroidism: overactive thyroid gland function

Because this book is about explaining why you may be exhausted, I will only briefly address hyperthyroidism. In my experience, stress, specifically the pace of life and what people demand of their body, is a major factor in the development of hyperthyroidism. The people I have worked with who have successfully returned their thyroid function to normal and had a complete remission of their symptoms have literally changed their life. In all honesty, they usually change their job, and, if that is not possible, they completely change their headspace and their attitude to life. It has been incredibly inspiring to witness this in my clients.

Hypothyroidism: underactive thyroid gland function

Back to hypothyroidism. The classic symptoms of hypothyroidism are:

* a feeling beyond tired — deep fatigue
* a gradual weight gain over months for no obvious reason
* often feeling cold, sometimes cold in your bones and like you cannot get warm
* a tendency to constipation
* a tendency towards a depressed mood, forgetfulness, confusion

⁜ hair loss or drier hair than previously

⁜ menstrual problems

⁜ difficulty conceiving, and

⁜ headaches.

Let's explore the roads to an underactive thyroid and where to begin to support your thyroid health and hence experience better energy.

Infection and poor liver detoxification

A history of glandular fever (EBV, also known as mono-nucleosis), for example, is a common road to hypothyroidism. Another is congested liver detoxification pathways; remember, this is where the liver has become overloaded, with too many substances and not enough enzymes or nutrients for the liver to deal with the load, particularly in phase 2 detoxification. Treatment of both of these roads involves taking excellent care of the liver, as outlined elsewhere in this book. Additionally, astragalus is an excellent herb to use for a chronic infection background if a herbalist agrees that this will meet your needs.

Nutrient deficiencies

Eat Brazil nuts daily for selenium. Use Celtic sea salt with iodine and/or cook with seaweeds from clean waters for iodine. Food sources of iron include beef, lamb, eggs, mussels, sardines, lentils, green leafy vegetables and dates. There is a small amount of iron in many foods, so eating a varied diet is important. Absorption is enhanced if foods containing iron are consumed with foods rich in vitamin C. If you do not eat animal foods, do not assume that you are iron-deficient. For some vegetarians, their body utilizes the iron from vegetables sources very efficiently. For others — whether meat-eaters or vegetarians — there will be an iron deficiency, which has dire health consequences, not only on thyroid function. A simple blood test will let you know.

The other option is to take a supplement that covers these

nutrients. There are some excellent thyroid support tablets/ capsules on the market, so seek out one of these if that route appeals, but only under the guidance of an experienced health professional. Regarding iron, test before you begin taking any supplements, but if you are deficient, supplementing will be essential. Note, though, that many iron supplements are constipating. Most people find that this does not happen with liquid iron supplements, and there are now some tablets on the market that are highly effective and non-constipating.

Zinc and vitamin A are also critical to healthy thyroid function.

Oestrogen dominance

Too much oestrogen suppresses thyroid function, while optimal progesterone levels support its function. Dealing with oestrogen dominance (something I spend hours discussing at my women's weekend events and which is also explained in my other books *Accidentally Overweight, Rushing Woman's Syndrome, Beauty from the Inside Out* and *The Calorie Fallacy*) is the critical first step if this is the basis for your challenge with your thyroid gland.

Elevated cortisol due to stress

Elevated cortisol as a result of stress decreases the levels of the active, energy-generating thyroid hormone T_3, which consequently slows down your metabolism. Added to this scenario, remember that high levels of cortisol urge your body to break down muscle to provide glucose for your brain, and the less muscle you have, the slower your metabolic rate as well. In the absence of stress, a healthy body converts FT_4 into T_3, but with elevated cortisol levels the conversion of FT_4 to T_3 is compromised.

Poor conversion of FT_4 to active T_3 also occurs if you restrict your food intake. Your body assumes that you must be starving, and therefore it must have a way of slowing down the metabolic rate to preserve those precious fat stores to get you through the perceived famine. This may be frustrating, but your body's primary goal is for survival.

Elevated cortisol also inhibits TSH production from the pituitary. With less TSH, the body produces less FT_4. Review what you can do to deal with elevated cortisol, based on the information offered in the section about the stress hormones, if this scenario rings true for you. Poor thyroid function can also lead to elevated cholesterol, and once thyroid function has been treated, the cholesterol returns to normal. I have witnessed this countless times in clients.

Iodine

Iodine is a trace mineral so essential to our health that our body begins to shut down without it. Our thyroid gland loves iodine, and it cannot make thyroid hormones without it. Symptoms of an underactive thyroid were outlined above, and if iodine deficiency is involved in the thyroid becoming underactive, increasing the dietary iodine intake can make a difference.

Thyroid hormones significantly drive our metabolic rate, our experience of energy as adults, and our growth as children. Iodine is also essential to the IQ of the developing brain *in utero*, and, sadly, studies are now showing that some children in the Western world are suffering from such low iodine levels that their IQ is being detrimentally affected.

Sources of iodine

Soil is a poor source of iodine, and if a nutrient is not in the soil it cannot be in our food. New Zealand, for example, has volcanic soil, which has never contained any iodine, and Australian soils are deficient in iodine too.

While the soil may not be a good source of iodine, the sea is somewhat better. Food sources of iodine include all of the seaweeds, which you can add to soups, stews, casseroles and salads to give them a subtle salty flavour while imparting all of the nutritional value of the minerals. A form of seaweed commonly eaten is nori, and it is used frequently in sushi. Iodine is found in small amounts in some seafood.

Salt was first iodized in 1924; however, iodized salt has tended to go out of fashion with the advent of rock salts and

Celtic sea salt. Although Celtic sea salt offers the additional benefits of a broad range of trace minerals, many brands on the supermarket shelves lack iodine unless it has been fortified. Always read the label. The only concern with conventional iodized salts is that most brands contain anti-caking agents that are potentially not ideal for human health due to some of their ingredients.

The impact of iodine therapy for the maintenance of healthy breast tissue has been widely reported, although it is rarely discussed. The ovaries also concentrate iodine, and studies have shown that a form of oestrogen associated with breast cancer is produced by the ovaries in an iodine-deficient state. This has been shown to be reversible once iodine levels are optimal again.

Substances that can interfere with thyroid function and iodine utilization

There are also substances in food and the environment that can interfere with thyroid function for a variety of reasons. Vegetables belonging to the *Brassica* genus, such as broccoli, Brussels sprouts, cauliflower, kale and cabbage, contain substances in their raw state that are known as *goitrogens*, which suppress thyroid function. Cooking or fermenting these vegetables breaks down the goitrogens, meaning you can still get their valuable oestrogen detoxification properties and other benefits.

Some substances in the diet and environment can interfere with the thyroid's capacity to take up iodine, as any substance that can bind to the same place where iodine is supposed to bind can displace the iodine. These substances include fluorine, bromine and chlorine, all of which make their way into processed foods and drinks.

Fluoride displaces iodine. What that means is that, instead of the thyroid gland taking up iodine, if fluoride is present the thyroid will take it up instead. And fluoride doesn't behave the same way as iodine in the body, nor is it able to drive the necessary biochemical reactions for optimal thyroid function.

If this happens too regularly for too long, or in too large a dose, thyroid function may be compromised, more so in an iodine-deficient person.

Iodine requirements and supplements

Iodine is a difficult mineral to test for. Accurate tests require you to collect 24 hours of urine, and, remarkably, not all countries offer this testing.

Adults require 150 micrograms (μg), of iodine per day to prevent deficiency. It is far more beneficial, however, to individualize doses. Often significantly larger amounts are initially necessary to treat a deficient state, and this can be easily done with one to three drops of a good-quality liquid iodine solution per day. These solutions are available ready-made from some health food shops, or they can be made up especially by a compounding pharmacist. It is a trace mineral you can overdose on, though, so it is essential that any supplement intake be guided by an experienced health professional.

Thyroid medications

Typically today, if someone has been diagnosed with an underactive thyroid, they are prescribed thyroxine (T_4). Some people feel brilliant on this medication, and all of their hypothyroid symptoms disappear, including their fatigue. If this has not happened for you despite taking this medication, it may be time to try a different approach. After years of taking thyroxine, it will not suddenly start to work if it hasn't yet.

There are numerous brands of thyroxine on the market. If you want to stick with conventional medicine, tell your GP you feel lousy on your current medication and that you would like to try a different drug. I have hundreds of clients who had been happily taking one form of thyroxine, but, when the government subsidy was changed to a different brand and they swapped over accordingly, many of their hypothyroid symptoms returned. Explore trying some form of thyroxine even if your blood levels of TSH, FT$_4$ and T$_3$ are "normal", but you have symptoms.

When it comes to hypothyroidism, another treatment option is *whole thyroid extract* (WTE). This is taken instead of any synthetic medication; unlike the synthetics, which provide only one of the thyroid hormones, WTE provides all of the thyroid hormones. It is essential that you see your GP about this, and, if you choose this option, be guided in the transition from a synthetic medication to the WTE, which is made by a compounding pharmacist. WTE doesn't suit everyone, so be guided by a medical doctor who is experienced in an integrative approach to thyroid health.

> *W*ork with a health professional who will treat the symptoms rather than rely solely on the bloods, and who will monitor both your symptoms and the blood work as you explore treatments.

If you have not been diagnosed with a thyroid illness, but you exhibit numerous symptoms, do not rely solely on your blood test results to determine the diagnosis. Work with a health professional who will treat the symptoms rather than rely solely on the bloods, and who will monitor both your symptoms and the blood work as you explore treatments. I learnt this in a powerful way with a client whose story melts my heart. I shared this case study in *Accidentally Overweight*, but it is so powerful that I feel it important to bring it to life here as well. See below.

Thyroid antibodies

The importance of testing thyroid antibodies is best demonstrated with the following case study.

Patricia's Story

Patricia arrived at my practice seeking assistance with her health, and when I asked how I could help she burst into tears and said she knew she'd had an underactive thyroid for about 30 years. However, her blood tests had always come back as normal, and no one would treat her. She had gained over 100 kilograms in weight over 30 years, and it all began when her dear mum had passed away. Patricia said she had eaten poorly for about three to four months after her mum had passed, but her grief gradually eased and, as it did, she started to eat better again, as she always had. Nothing changed, however: her size kept increasing. So then she didn't just eat well, she signed up for a gym membership, and she started to eat even better. Still, her clothes grew tighter.

When I saw her, Patricia was unable to exercise due to knee pain from carrying so much weight (her description, and she thought she was 168 kilograms), but she still ate in a way that did not warrant her size.

Sure, this precious lady had a huge amount of unresolved grief, and, sure, there had been times when she hadn't eaten amazingly. She had, at times, become incredibly frustrated that despite her efforts nothing would shift. But she had also had plenty of years and months of making consistent efforts with food and movement, with no reward.

Given that Patricia ticked every box for an underactive thyroid, from a symptoms perspective, I decided to request fresh blood tests and include thyroid antibodies, specifically anti-thyroid peroxidase and anti-thyroglobulin. Having been taught at university that it was highly unlikely for thyroid antibodies to be elevated and an issue if thyroid hormone levels were in the normal range, I could understand why Patricia's autoantibodies had not been tested, but from a symptoms perspective I could not.

To cut a very long story short, despite her latest thyroid hormones levels being in the "normal" range, albeit skewed one way (discussed below), Patricia's antibodies were the highest I have ever seen. To put this in context, the "normal" range for both antibodies in this national laboratory is less than 50 (<50). My client's anti-thyroid peroxidase and anti-thyroglobulin levels were both >6500. Off the scale and through the roof.

When I telephoned her to tell her, she was at first thrilled that all along there had been a reason for how lousy she had felt. Patricia told me later that the anger then surfaced for a life she felt she had missed out on because this situation had not been picked up. She had remained very shy, which she blamed on her size, and on reflection was very sad that she had not met a partner with whom to share her life. She decided to seek out the most natural approach she could for her very underactive thyroid, and, after considerable weight fell off her over the first three months, Patricia booked her first overseas holiday.

There is always a why. You just have to find it.

Blood tests and "normal" ranges

The whole idea of a normal range is necessary, as cut-off points help indicate when something may be abnormal, and it would be chaotic without them. They are a wonderful guide; but I choose the word "guide" with purpose, because for some parameters they are not definitive.

Ranges and what is "normal"

I have great concerns when we base the future of a person's health on blood tests alone. According to Dr Karen Coates, an insightful and pioneering GP and co-author of *Embracing the Warrior: An Essential Guide for Women*, the normal range for some blood tests is calculated periodically by each pathology laboratory to ensure that the reference range printed on the test results is "accurate". On the morning of this day, the first 100 blood samples received are tested for their (in this case) TSH levels in order to determine the reference range. The same could also be said of iron levels, for example. But why do people usually have blood tests? Because they are feeling particularly spritely that day? No! Most often, the precise opposite is true! Yet we base our "normal" ranges on these figures.

Furthermore, it is also important to understand how the "average" amount of a particular nutrient or hormone is calculated. Mathematically, the top reference point is calculated to be "two standard deviations" above the average, while the bottom figure is "two standard deviations" below the average. The arbitrary rules of this method dictate that 95 per cent of the 100 blood samples taken must fall into the "normal" range. The statistical definition of standard deviations insists that only four or five results may fall outside this reference range, two samples below and two above.

The three points I want to make are these. First, the reference ranges for some blood parameters are getting broader. I have seen the normal range for TSH broaden from 0.4–4.0 to 0.3–5.0 and then return to 0.4–4.0. I have also seen it in recent times, from one particular lab, broadened out to 0.3–5.0. As mentioned below, people at either end of this blood range will potentially look and feel completely differently, and they will more than likely exhibit symptoms. If they are symptom-free, no problem; but my concern is that if we base treatment on the blood work alone and leave people to live with their symptoms, with their result skewed to one end of the normal range, we are risking, not optimizing, their health. And continuing to broaden the range means that more and more people who are actually unwell fall onto the "normal" range and don't get the help their body is crying out for.

This brings me to my second point, which is that you can see from the start that this process is flawed, given that it is based on unwell individuals. It is more challenging to create optimal health, prevent disease and maximize quality of life for people when they are being guided with their blood tests to fall into a potentially unhealthy normal range.

Thirdly, often the first time you yourself get a blood test for a particular parameter is when you are unwell. For example, you might not know that when you are optimally healthy your TSH is 1, even though the first time you have it tested, it is 3. However, as 3 is inside the normal range, you don't get a call-back, because based on "normal" blood ranges your thyroid function is fine. However, in this case, your pituitary gland is having to churn out three times more TSH to call out to your thyroid gland to get it to make its hormones, when in the past it only took one unit of TSH to get that outcome.

Your blood tests

I urge you to get copies of your own blood tests and look for results being skewed to one end of the normal range. Let's look at this further.

The normal range for TSH where I live is currently 0.4–4.0. Although those numbers may seem small, someone with a TSH of 0.4 feels and looks completely different from someone with a TSH of 4. Additionally, if your results are not actually outside the normal range, you will usually be told (well-meaningly) that there is no problem with your thyroid.

A common picture I see is a TSH of 2.5 or greater screaming out to the thyroid gland to make FT_4. Normal levels of FT_4 are 10–20, whereas usually, for someone with symptoms of hypothyroidism, their FT_4 will be 11. This person typically feels exhausted, has trouble naturally using their bowels daily, has dry skin, very low motivation, brain fog, and their clothes are gradually getting tighter. Their thyroid needs support. In this case, once I have taken a diet history to establish poor trace-mineral intake, I will usually start with iodine and selenium, and sometimes iron (once tested), along with adrenal support, a grain-free diet, and a big chat about their beliefs and what their perception is of what life is like for them.

The third prong to holistic healing

As you have heard me describe, the third pillar to my holistic approach to health — after the biochemical and the nutritional — is the emotional. Louise Hay teaches that thyroid problems represent feelings and beliefs around humiliation, feeling like you never get to do what you want to do, and that subconsciously they ask: "When is it going to be my turn?" She suggests you develop a new thought pattern of "I move beyond old limitations and now allow myself to express freely and creatively." Underneath diagnosed hypothyroidism, Louise Hay suggests, are feelings of hopelessness, a feeling of being stifled, and a sense of giving up. She suggests you develop a new thought pattern of "I create a new life with new rules that totally support me." Apply this concept to your life if it rings true for you. Park it if does not.

The whole picture

I include this information to offer you a whole picture of your thyroid health, from the conventional function of hormones and glands and blood tests, through the nutritional supports that are essential, including iodine, selenium and iron, to the metaphysical — for somewhere among these three approaches lies your answer. Not necessarily in any one or the other; I urge you to explore all three.

You can see from this explanation that the thyroid gland plays a powerful role in whether we experience energy or not, and, with the nutrient deficiencies, stress and hormone imbalances of modern times, this is another reason why the approach to restoring people's energy must be holistic and consider the whole person, not just one body system in isolation. Plus, when your choices stem from taking better care of yourself because you believe that you are worthy of such care, that alone is one of the greatest gifts to your energy, health and happiness.

Iron — The Mineral that is Critical for Energy

Iron plays a multi-factorial role in energy. As you have just read, good iron status is critical to excellent thyroid function and hence energy, but iron alone also impacts on energy, predominantly via its role in oxygen transportation. Yet iron deficiency is the most common nutritional deficiency in the world. It particularly affects children, menstruating women, and pregnant women. In New Zealand and Australia, it is estimated that up to 25 per cent of children under the age of three have some degree of iron deficiency, a deeply concerning statistic, given that iron deficiency anaemia in early life is related to altered behavioural and neural (brain) development.

Studies (see the references section) in infants suggest that this is an irreversible effect that may be related to changes in the chemistry of the production of certain neurotransmitters (such as dopamine), and/or the organization of part of the brain's network of wiring, or even myelination (the process of forming a myelin sheath around a nerve to allow nerve impulses to move quickly). The acquisition of iron by the brain is an age-related and brain-region-dependent process, with tightly controlled rates of movement of iron across the blood–brain barrier. Dopamine receptors and transporters are altered, as are behaviours related to this neurotransmitter. There is a growing body of evidence that suggests that brain iron deficiency in early life has multiple consequences in both biochemistry and behaviour in adult life.

According to the World Health Organization (WHO), a staggering two billion people in the world, in both developing and industrialized countries, are iron-deficient. Research suggests between 20 and 30 per cent of women of childbearing age in Australia and New Zealand are iron-deficient. This concerns me immensely, as the consequences are significant, and tiredness is just the beginning.

Many people are confused about the difference between iron deficiency and another term you may have heard of, anaemia. Immature red blood cells require iron to be converted by the body into a form they can use in order to mature. When fully mature, they will become the oxygen carriers of the body, distributing oxygen from the lungs to all of the other cells throughout the body. They have a big and important job to do, and this is part of how we feel energized when we have good iron status.

Iron deficiency is the first step towards a decrease in the amount of oxygen-carrying, iron-rich haemoglobin within each red blood cell. As red blood cells are deprived of the quota of iron, they become contracted and smaller, known in medical terms as becoming microcytic. Anaemia develops when the immature red blood cells, deprived of their quota of iron, fail to survive their infancy. A formal diagnosis of anaemia is made when there is a consequent and significant decrease in the number of mature red blood cells.

Iron-deficiency anaemia can be caused by:

* inadequate dietary intake of iron
* poor absorption of iron, or
* loss of iron due to bleeding.

Heavy menstrual blood loss is a common cause, as are increased demands for iron during pregnancy. In pregnant women, iron stores have to serve the increased blood volume of the mother, as well as the needs of the growing baby.

The condition can also be caused by blood loss from the digestive tract due to the long-term use of aspirin, or due to gastric ulcers, duodenal ulcers, bowel cancer, or untreated coeliac disease. I am now seeing more "silent" coeliac disease, where people are not presenting with the typical bowel symptoms. Sometimes iron deficiency, and often vitamin B_{12}

deficiency, are the only signs of what is later diagnosed on biopsy as coeliac disease. Once gluten is removed from the diet, iron levels return to normal. Fibre also interferes with the absorption of dietary iron, so the fibre content of the diet must also be taken into account when determining the basis of the iron deficiency.

Calcium and iron compete for absorption in the digestive tract, and calcium always wins, as it is a bigger structure. So if people consume their only iron-rich foods at a meal that is also high in calcium, iron absorption will be poor. Iron is critical for great

Research suggests between 20 and 30 per cent of women of childbearing age in Australia and New Zealand are iron-deficient. This concerns me immensely, as the consequences are significant, and tiredness is just the beginning.

energy and a vitality that lasts all day. The main symptoms of iron deficiency include exhaustion, shortness of breath, especially on an incline, muscle aches and cramps, rapid pulse and heart palpitations, increased anxiety, brain fog, poor memory and concentration, headaches, depressed mood, hair loss and an increased frequency of infections. A simple blood test from your doctor will establish whether you are iron-deficient or not. Testing is important, because some people have a tendency to store too much iron in the body and this needs to be avoided, or treated if it already exists.

The same nutritional advice we saw in the previous section applies here. Good food sources of iron include beef, lamb and eggs. Other food sources of iron include mussels, sardines, lentils, dates and green leafy vegetables. Variety is key, as there is a small amount of iron in many foods. If you do not eat animal foods, do not assume you are iron-deficient. For some vegetarians, their body utilizes the iron from vegetables sources efficiently. Vegetable sources of iron are better absorbed in the presence of vitamin C.

It is best to have a test before you supplement. If you are deficient, you will need an iron supplement to replenish your stores; diet alone won't do it fast enough for your energy recovery. It can take 18 months or longer to replenish stores if they are deficient, and by then you will have dragged yourself around and potentially damaged or interfered with other body systems for too long, adding to the recovery work that will be needed for you to get your spark back. In clinical practice I am careful which iron supplements I use, as they can be constipating to some people. Iron liquids and some good-quality tablets don't disrupt bowel function, however, and they return iron stores to normal very effectively.

If you know you are iron-deficient and you don't respond quickly or at all to iron supplementation, there is usually something else going on that needs to be addressed. For example, dietary changes such as a gluten- and/or a casein-free diet may need to be made to maximize absorption. A nutrition health professional experienced in this area can guide you with this to ensure you are still getting all of the nutrients you need … including iron! If you are iron-deficient and you are exhausted, replenishing your iron is sometimes all you need to get back your get-up-and-go. It can sometimes be that simple.

Teenage Girls

The fatigue that can kick in for teenage girls deserves a section all of its own, as it is so common. It is another one of those scenarios that I like to say is common, but is not normal. In other words, it doesn't need to be this way. Described below is what I have seen in clinical practice over 17 years in thousands of girls, where lethargy can be a major sign that something that isn't right has begun.

The scenario

A girl might be 10 years old and life is good. Her energy is fine. There might be some challenges with girls at school at times, but otherwise everything is okay. As times goes on, the breasts start to bud and the hips start to broaden, and to do this the body usually has to start to store some more body fat. This is the result of an increase in oestrogen production. Some girls feel a bit "puffy" or swollen as this occurs, and this is distressing to some of them as they feel or are told that they look "fat". (Please note that her food and movement intake won't have changed to generate this change in her body shape and size.) After a few months of her family noticing that she has started to become somewhat moody — not every day, but a few times a week she might be snappy, for example — everyone writes it off as "stress" at school or jokes that the "hormones must be starting".

Then menstruation begins, and for so many girls today the loss of menstrual blood is heavy, painful and clotty right from the outset. Days at school are missed each month. Sport is interrupted too. Sometimes menstruation is regular; other times, months are missed. But when it comes, it is so very painful.

She is oestrogen-dominant, and her iron and zinc may also be low, because as her body fat has increased one of her strategies has been to eat less meat and this decrease in iron intake has not been addressed. Moreover, many girls love animals and become vegetarian at about this time for animal welfare reasons. However, for others this reasoning sometimes masks a fear of body fat increases and they use the label of "I'm a vegetarian" to eat less or to have cause to be highly selective about what they eat. It is important to identify why she has made this choice. I say this without judgment, but simply to offer insight. Yet since the lead up to menstruation beginning, and even more so since it began, her energy is declining.

The sex hormones

Pituitary gland

When a girl first starts to menstruate, it is the first time that her pituitary gland, at the base of her brain, has ever really communicated with her ovaries. It does this predominantly via the production of the *follicle-stimulating hormone* (*FSH*) and *luteinizing hormone* (*LH*). Each month, these hormones, respectively, stimulate an egg to ripen and enable ovulation to occur. The only thing is, the pathway of communication between the pituitary and the ovaries is initially more like a goat track. Sometimes the messages get through; sometimes they miss. It takes about five years for these pathways of communication to become like a five-lane highway.

Progesterone

Progesterone, another sex hormone, plays a role in main-taining the lining of the endometrium in the second half of the menstrual cycle. Oestrogen lays it down, and progesterone holds it in place until menstruation begins again. But please really take notice of the other roles progesterone plays biologically in the body: it is an anti-depressant, an antianxiety agent, and it is a diuretic, meaning that it allows a female to get rid of any excess fluid. Once a female has started to menstruate, the main place from which she makes progesterone is her ovaries, but only after she has ovulated. The crater that remains on the surface of the ovary (the corpus luteum) behaves like a gland once the egg has been released.

Adrenal progesterone
The other place her body will make progesterone from is from the adrenal glands; however, it will do so only if the body believes that she is "safe". So if she is churning out adrenalin and cortisol because she is worrying about her grades, what her friends are saying, boys, fitting in, that her clothes don't fit the way they used to, or she hears her parents regularly arguing, for example, then her body will get the message that her life is in danger and that there is no food left in the world. Moreover, the female body links progesterone to fertility, so the last thing it wants is to bring a baby into a world where it perceives she is not safe and where there is no food. So her body will shut down the adrenal production of progesterone, thinking it is doing her a great, big favour.

Park the fertility aspect of what I have just said and consider the other biological consequences of low or no progesterone production: low mood, anxieties, fluid retention. As an aside, this can be playing a major role in adult women's low energy and other health challenges, and I discuss this in detail in *Rushing Woman's Syndrome*.

Oestrogen

An excess of oestrogen is often what makes periods heavy, clotty and painful in the first place, and this can be common when a girl first starts to menstruate, because, as we saw above, it can take some time for the pituitary hormones to reach the ovaries in a regular cyclic pattern and generate ovulation, and therefore good progesterone production. So often when a girl first starts to menstruate, she is oestrogen-dominant. Add to this what you learnt in the liver section about how too many liver-loaders (such as some of the substances found in processed foods and drinks) can lead to oestrogen being recycled. Even a good progesterone producer won't be able to match the high levels of oestrogen that are created when the liver is recycling it.

Management versus resolution of the symptoms

The most well-meaning adults in the world want to see her out of pain and not missing school, worried that she may fall behind, and that this may impact future happiness and opportunities. It is all so well-intentioned. She is not sexually active, but due to the pain she is started on the oral contraceptive pill (OCP) to "manage" her periods. The mechanism of action of the OCP (and the reason it is so effective

> *Even a good progesterone producer won't be able to match the high levels of oestrogen that are created when the liver is recycling it.*

at preventing pregnancy) is that it shuts down the ovarian production of hormones. That is its job. So if it is taken by a young woman soon after she begins menstruating, it sorts out the immediate discomfort, but it also means that the pituitary never gets the time to set up its pathways of communication with the ovaries.

Biochemical consequences

It is likely that an excess of oestrogen and a lack of progesterone created the heavy, painful periods in the first place, and that issue has not been addressed. Instead, it is being managed. Please hear this. I am not anti-medication nor am I anti-OCP. All of these options can be gifts, necessary at times, and options we are fortunate to have access to. What concerns me, though, is that the biochemistry that created the problems and the pain in the first place has not been addressed. Plus, this girl's body now relies completely on her adrenals for a small amount of progesterone to be made, because she is not ovulating. However, if, as explained above, she is busy churning out stress hormones, this won't be happening. So there is still an excess of oestrogen. Only now that she is on the pill, it is coming from the synthetic version the pill provides as well as from her body fat cells.

Emotional consequences

It is well-documented in the medical literature that an excess of oestrogen is one of the causes of a depressed mood (in people of any age). And what I have seen time and time again is that, although the OCP may "manage" the pain, it does not deal with the oestrogen dominance that created the problem in the first place, nor does it deal with the anger or the sadness and withdrawal that may have started to gradually creep in. Of course this can be due to social issues at school or in the home, but it can also be due to the oestrogen excess (relative to progesterone).

A family may start to notice that their once gregarious and happy girl is now sullen and moody and withdrawn. And again, with the very best of intentions and so much care for her wellbeing, the family takes her back to the doctor because they are concerned that she is depressed. And again, well-meaningly, she is put onto an anti-depressant medication. So by the time she is 15 years old she is on two of the most powerful medications in the Western world. Her energy is low, and her family will usually say at this point that she is a shell of her former self.

Potential long-term consequences

Thing is, now she has created the belief that she has a disease and that she needs these medications to be "normal". So she stays on them until she meets the love of her life and wants to have children. And she may be 30 before this happens. But remember, her pituitary gland hasn't spoken to her ovaries for 15 years, and the pathways of communication between the two glands were never set up. And so she doesn't fall pregnant quickly, and this is just another stress in her already high-stress life, of which excessive and regular outputs of adrenalin and cortisol are a daily occurrence. And because she has been hammered by the media to believe that her fertility is all but gone at 30 (which isn't true), she panics and believes that assisted reproductive technology (ART) is the only way for her to have a baby, because time is not on her side. So she spends a huge amount of emotional and physical energy in this ART process, and sometimes it has a happy outcome and sometimes it doesn't. But through it all she believes she is flawed in the most feminine of ways; she'll say to me "I can't even conceive".

This entire scenario does not have to eventuate. The cascading effects of that life path can be altered if the hormonal picture that initially created the heavy, clotty painful periods is addressed. And that would change the course of her energy and the course of her life.

Teenage Boys

I touched on some of what I describe here in the post-viral fatigue section. This expands on it with a focus on teenage boys. Granted, I have seen fewer teenage boys in clinical practice. Teenage girls come more often. But still I have seen thousands of boys with this health picture. And, oh boy (pardon the pun), can their fatigue be deep and unrelenting. Ask any parent trying to get them up for school!

The scenario

Here's a typical scenario. Not every fatigued teenage boy has this history, but usually some of it is true for him. And just for the record, not every teenage boy is tired. Some have wonderful energy that serves them across their day.

Often, he will have had recurrent *Streptococcus*-based infections as a baby, toddler or young child, such as ear infections, tonsillitis, bronchitis and/or croup. As a result he had multiple rounds of antibiotics. Hundreds of boys I have met have had between 10 and 20 scripts before the age of five. He may have been a fussy eater. His poos were likely extra smelly. In his early years, he wouldn't eat red meat. He loves white-coloured foods, such as pasta and other white carbohydrates, dairy foods, and he'll eat fruit. He becomes iron- and/or zinc-deficient, as evidenced by his pale face. Nothing is usually done about this at this young stage. Sometimes you can see the blood vessels near his eyes, as they appear as a bluey-purple colour through the skin. Sometimes even the whites of his eyes appear to have a blue hue. This is indicative of severe iron deficiency, the consequences of which you have already read about.

Getting older now, he craves salt-and-vinegar chips. I believe this is to try to stimulate his stomach acid production for better digestion. Remember from the digestion section that stomach acid is needed to do the chop, chop, chop work of breaking the circles (food) apart? He will eat chicken now (it's white, after all), plus he is prepared to chew a bit now. He is still iron- and likely zinc-deficient. If he is made to eat red meat, he has to have bucket-loads of tomato sauce on it. He continues to eat a lot of white carbs and dairy foods. Mouth-breathing is well established now, due to the recurrent *Strep* infections blocking and, for some, altering the airways through the sinus cavity. Poor blood oxygenation, iron deficiency and low zinc status are all potentially occurring. And you have already read about the consequences of these factors.

As puberty approaches, more testosterone starts being made. This requires zinc, so any zinc he does have gets used for the production of testosterone. The fatigue begins. He feels like he has been hit by a bus every morning. And his feet stink. His family members complain about it. They tell him to shower and wash his feet properly, which he does, and then five minutes later they smell again. This is a classic sign of zinc deficiency. Worrying about how they smell can be a big deal for some boys, and they will openly admit that they are embarrassed and stressed by it.

Nutrient and biochemical deficiencies and their consequences

Zinc

Zinc is also required for the function of another substance in the body called *metallothionein*. This structure plays a significant role in our ability to rid heavy metals from our body, soon after we are exposed to them, rather than them ending up being stored in our body in places like the brain or the bones. Metallothionein has seven zinc fingers in its makeup, and when, for example, cadmium (a heavy metal) comes along, a unit of zinc drops off and the unit of cadmium binds to the metallothionein, halting it from doing any harm. When we are

zinc-deficient, metallothionein function — among hundreds
of others processes — is impaired, and this can have significant
long-term health and energy consequences.

Gut bacteria

Gut bacteria are also critical for the detoxification of heavy
metals. However, these bacteria populations will have been
significantly altered during childhood due to the recurrent
Strep infections and use of antibiotics.

On top of the changes in gut bacteria that antibiotics drive,
another process that has often occurred for these boys (and
of course girls in the same circumstances) is that with ears,
noses and throats full of mucous from the *Strep* infections
as children, they don't cough up all of the mucous and spit
it out. They swallow it. The stomach acid is supposed to kill
anything nasty — like *Streptococcus* — when it reaches the
acidic conditions of the stomach, but, as you have learnt in the
digestion section, the pH of the stomach acid for some children
(and adults) is not acidic enough to kill the *Strep*. So it survives
swallowing and makes its way to the large intestine where it
takes up residence. *Strep* is a lactic-acid-producing bacterial
species. And when you have large numbers of acid-producing
bacteria in your colon, the lactic acid they produce changes the
pH of that part of the gut to be too acidic for the good bacterial
species to stay living there. So the good guys die off. So now you
have the double-whammy of problematic gut bacterial species
in residence and a lack of good guys, and the good guys are
needed for many processes critical to nourishment, immune
function, mood, heavy metal detoxification, gut health itself
and energy. Yes, it's major. And again, it is common but it's not
how it is supposed to be.

Streptococcus

Furthermore, many types of *Streptococcus* have become
resistant to what was our first line of defence against them:
penicillin. Part of the reason for this is that each species on

the planet, *Streptococcus* included, wants to survive to the next generation. And, over time, *Strep* worked out that penicillin works by destroying their cell wall. The best way to imagine how a bacterium appears is as a circle with a squiggle inside of it. Penicillin was such a highly effective antibiotic when it was first released because its mechanism of action is to break open the cell wall of the bacteria, killing it. So after many exposures, a species works out that to survive they have to evolve to beat or overcome the mechanism or substance that is doing the killing. So there is evidence now to suggest that some organisms, *Strep* included, have evolved to be cell-wall-deficient organisms. Which is one reason why the penicillin-based antibiotics have become ineffective at dealing with a species they once killed very effectively. I digress. My point here is that gut bacteria profiles that are high in *Strep*, low in beneficial flora such as *Escherichia coli (E. coli)* and *Bifidobacterium*, and potentially (but not always) contain some problematic species, which may include Clostridia or *Klebsiella*, play a significant role in poor health and lousy energy for anyone who has this health picture. And I see it mostly in boys.

Acne

Pimples or acne might begin appearing around this time, because, as well as with the increase in steroid hormones, comes an increase in sebum production in the skin. The extra sebum gives the bacteria that live on top of our skin even more to feed on. So they multiply in numbers. They may start to infect the pores, initiating redness, inflammation and become infected. And there still isn't enough zinc in his body to heal the wounds on his skin that the infections are creating.

Liver function

The increase in hormones requires the liver to step up its detoxification pathways to change and help eliminate the hormones. Often, however, the liver cannot keep up with its load, due to his poor-quality way of eating, which is not supplying the body with what it needs to make the liver enzymes necessary for detoxification. Added to that, the number of problematic substances (or "liver-loaders") is too high for the liver to keep up with, even more so with the increase in testosterone requiring detoxification.

Self-esteem and exhaustion

So now the congested skin may affect his self-esteem, and his energy falls even further. He says such mean things to himself inside his head. And whether he is quiet and withdrawn or full of bravado, he believes he is not okay the way he is.

Meanwhile, this teenage boy is exhausted. Throw in on top of this challenges with his family, at school, and perhaps with sport or girls. Many boys worry that they aren't big enough or strong enough. Pitch all of this in together and you have a mixture for a deep, unrelenting fatigue.

Management

Layer upon layer of internal disruption to the optimal function of countless body systems now needs to be addressed piece by piece. The (psychological) beliefs in his own deficiencies also usually need to be addressed, too, as by now he will be telling himself that he is lazy, a failure and worthless; exhausting self-talk in itself.

> The beliefs in his own deficiencies also usually need to be addressed, too, as by now he will be telling himself that he is lazy, a failure and worthless; exhausting self-talk in itself.

Now to unravel it, for as you can see there is a lot going on. Let me first say that this process is best guided by a health professional experienced in this type of work. And patience is needed as it can take months for this to start to resolve. I will share with you, below, some of the strategies that I have seen make a difference to this scenario in my clinical practice. I don't do all of this with each person, and I don't do all of this at once. Sometimes only a few of these strategies are needed, which a health professional experienced in this area can guide you with. A nutritional rescue armoury may include:

* casein-free diet
* zinc supplement
* vitamin C supplement
* gut antimicrobial medicinal herbs; a medical herbalist needs to prescribe these and they need to be tailored to the individual
* liver support in the form of medicinal herbs; a medical herbalist needs to prescribe these (they can usually be added to the gut herbs so that only one dose of herbs is required) or a green vegetable powder
* apple cider vinegar before breakfast and dinner to stimulate stomach acid
* coenzyme Q_{10} supplement
* no refined sugars, as sugars feed the bad bugs
* iron studies blood test — if deficient, supplement.

This usually changes everything over (about) a six-month period. If energy is still low after this, his perception of where the stress in his life is coming from must be explored, or you can do this concurrently with the nutritional strategies above.

The Interplay of Fears and Energy

Some might say we are born with a baseline level of energy that we show up with each day. Some people inherently have more, some less. What I want to discuss is when energy changes from what you know to be your norm, or if you observe it and are concerned about it in a family member, as regularly occurs with teenagers. To demonstrate this, I will use a case study I was part of, a case I shared with a psychologist colleague. I will simply refer to the psychologist as Mrs M. All names and identifying information have been changed, and the family gave permission for me to share their story anonymously. I believe this case demonstrates a powerful point about energy.

Before I begin, however, please note that I am not anti-medication. My preference, however, is to be part of a team that gets to the heart of the matter and resolves the challenges that have led to the change in behaviour, mood, sleep patterns and energy.

A 15-year-old girl, Claudia, and her parents, Jill and Michael, saw Mrs M as they were concerned about the drop in Claudia's grades and her apparent lack of motivation. They were also concerned about the increasing number of medications she was being prescribed for her challenges.

Having been in the top three students for all of her subjects throughout high school, she was now close to failing two subjects and was doing poorly at the others. Instead of studying, Claudia had developed a tendency to stay up late and play computer games, as well as spending time on social media. According to what is known as the DSM-5,[†] she was

---

† This is *The Diagnostic and Statistical Manual of Mental Disorders, Fifth Edition*, used by psychiatrists and psychologists to diagnose what the Western world refers to as mental health conditions.

also showing signs of depression and anxiety — low energy, insomnia and angst about seeing friends. The family GP suggested taking Claudia to a psychiatrist, who subsequently prescribed an anti-depressant. After three months, nothing had changed, so he swapped Claudia to a different anti-depressant. He also prescribed dexamphetamine, a stimulant drug for what he thought was attention-deficit hyperactivity disorder (ADHD), which he believed was what was keeping Claudia from her schoolwork. When this combination still didn't help Claudia, the psychiatrist suggested adding a drug, which is usually used as an antipsychotic, typically used to treat bipolar disorder and schizophrenia in adults. This concerned Claudia's parents, which was how they had ended up seeing Mrs M, the psychologist.

When Mrs M met Claudia and her parents, Claudia had been on medication for almost 12 months, and all three family members reported to Mrs M that there had been no improvements in Claudia's mood, behaviour, energy or sleep. All three said that Claudia could barely get out of bed in the mornings.

Early on in their first session, Mrs M asked when Claudia's depressed mood had begun, and she replied that it was about 15 months ago. Mrs M's next question was "What was going on at school or in the family at that time?" According to Claudia, she said she had heard her parents start fighting, most nights. Because she was up late gaming and on the internet, she could hear everything. She said she had heard both of her parents mention getting divorced. Then Mrs M asked her how that would make her feel; because some children are relieved at the prospect of a divorce, some are frightened and some don't mind, it was important to know how this scenario would lead Claudia to feel. Claudia replied, "Like my life would end, I'd be so sad." In front of her stunned parents, Claudia went on to say that she thought that if she didn't do well in high school then she wouldn't have to go away to university — which, up until her grades fell, she had been on track to do, to study law — and that maybe then, because she would still be around, they wouldn't get divorced.

Mrs M shared that, although Jill and Michael were shocked at what Claudia had said, Mrs M herself was not surprised at all. She shared that regularly in the initial consultation, a teenager or even a young child will express their fears about their family, and she wonders whether they do this out of relief or because they are hoping that the consultation will help their family members.

Mrs M ended up working with Claudia on her own, seeing Jill and Michael as a couple to work on their family systems and their own relationship, as well as seeing the three of them together. I won't go into the detail of the psychology sessions that were done over a six-month period, but will simply say that Jill and Michael had challenges in their own lives that were leading to late-night yelling at one another and that they would threaten each other with divorce. But both said they didn't ever want to follow through on that. They said it out of frustration at the other person not understanding their point of view. Still, they didn't understand why their daughter's grades had fallen away so significantly, and why, even though she complained about being so tired each day, she would still stay up late gaming and on the internet.

Yet in Claudia's individual sessions with Mrs M, she said that she was actually worried about how much she was on the internet and she felt like she was almost addicted to it. She said she knew she needed boundaries on her gaming because she wasn't getting enough sleep. Yet she found it impossible to stop or cut back, because, without her mind being on the game, she would start to worry about her future, her parents and what some of the people at her school thought of her. She said "the screen blocks my worry". Claudia also reported that she would text two girlfriends late at night and they would text-chat sometimes until 2am or 3am. Yet in the mornings, she would feel exhausted and couldn't get up. She said she felt like she was addicted to a drug (she was referring to the internet), yet texting and gaming had started out as something fun.

Numerous experts on addiction suggest that addiction is not about the addictive substance or activity itself, but about a pain that people feel in their life circumstances. In my work with people who regularly over-eat or who start eating and feel like they can't stop, I share with them that I believe people use over-eating as a way to distance themselves from how things are, when they are not how they want them to be. It is not about the food. The food is just the thing they use. The same goes for Claudia with gaming. Addictions can stem from a real or perceived inability to deal with everyday occurrences or stresses, and this can be particularly intense at a variety of life stages, including the teenage years.

One of the strategies the family devised was that Jill or Michael would switch the internet connection to the house off at 8.30pm, to assist Claudia to stop gaming. She also gave her mother her phone at 9pm and her mother would return it to her the next morning. The arrangement also involved her parents not "hassling" her to do her homework as soon as she arrived home from school, and accepting her grades for what they were. Claudia didn't want to feel like she had let her parents down every time she received a result. She was allowed to game

Numerous experts on addiction suggest that addiction is not about the addictive substance or activity itself, but about pain that people feel in their life circumstances.

for an hour on arrival home from school. Then she would be asked once to commence her homework after that hour. For this family, this new arrangement worked.

At the request of Mrs M, I did some dietary change work with Claudia as she had been diagnosed with IBS, with a dominance of constipation, and she also said her skin itched constantly. I guided Claudia and her family to omit all preservatives from their food, which meant an educational session about reading food labels, and a diet based on whole, real foods. After four weeks the skin itching had completely resolved, but the IBS hadn't. Claudia had had eczema as a baby, and this had responded to a casein-free diet, so, based on her history, in the second session I guided Claudia to trial a casein-free diet for four weeks. By her third consultation, the IBS was resolved. The dietary changes were happening at the same time as the sessions with the psychologist so, as with many conditions, the interplay of these two modalities (nutrition and psychology) may have been key to the resolution of the IBS. We cannot separate them, so in essence, we will never actually know whether one modality resolved the IBS (the psychology or the dietary changes) or whether both together were needed for Claudia.

Mrs M continued seeing Claudia about the things she feared and that led her to feel anxious. During these sessions, she gave Claudia not only time to talk about them out loud and without judgement, but also offered her (what turned out to be) highly effective strategies to deal with her feelings and fears. Since what she feared was what had been keeping her wanting to game as a distraction, she started to sleep better. Over the course of three months, Claudia's energy improved significantly and her results at school also began to markedly improve. Given that she had felt no improvements on the medications she had been taking for the 12 months prior to commencing seeing Mrs M, and that she had only felt better after seeing the psychologist, under medical supervision Claudia stopped taking them all.

Claudia's problems were not illnesses. Her problems were anxieties triggered by family tension and her own fears. Being only 15 years of age, she hadn't yet developed or been taught any emotional strategies to understand any of this or to cope. So to escape from the tensions, she spent too much time on the internet, texting and gaming. This resulted in sleep deprivation, which according to the psychologist can be mistaken for ADHD in some teenagers. Claudia's insomnia led to a vicious cycle of gaming and internet overuse. Gaming at night can intensify a depressed mood in teenagers, and, according to published scientific literature, exposure to light at night from back-lit devices and electronic screens can increase levels of some stress hormones and lead to a depressed mood and learning problems. The best solution for Claudia was not a variety of medications, but rather giving her tools and strategies to help her with her fears and anxieties, as well as supporting and guiding her parents to address their challenges in constructive ways and away from Claudia or her earshot.

This case study ended very happily, with a teenager who had better sleep, better moods, improved schoolwork, better relationships, and an energy that was restored to its previous, higher level. I share this with you — albeit a simplified version of what occurred — to demonstrate the complexities that energy can involve. For some people, it truly requires a three-pillar approach of addressing the biochemical, the nutritional and the emotional elements of their bodies and lives. I take my hat off to Claudia and her parents for their authenticity and bravery in facing their challenges with each other's care at the front of their minds, and to Mrs M for her insights, professional skills and gentle yet powerful strategies that assist families with their fears and dynamics. It was a joy to witness Claudia return to such an energized, happy and playful way of being, through truly getting to the heart of what was bothering her. Was her renewed energy simply the result of better sleep? I doubt it, although of course this will have helped. I believe for Claudia it was the result of feeling safe and loved (for, although she had always been safe and loved, her perception was that this was threatened) and that she now had tools to cope with fears if and when they arose.

★

You have one body, and only you can be responsible for it.
So you have to decide
what you want to do with it.

Dr Libby

Why Are You Tired?

I asked people from a variety of Western countries why they believe they are tired, and here are some of their responses. My point is to show you how most people feel like their fatigue is due to physical factors such as their diet, while very few initially identify the mental or emotional factors that lead us to feel weary. I am including this here, in their words, so you can identify what may be behind your fatigue if it hasn't yet become clear, and before we explore more of the mental and emotional side of the fatigue picture. The responses were:

Too many responsibilities.

Eat badly.

Can't fall asleep.

Wake many times in the night, sleep poorly.

Urinate numerous times overnight, sleep poorly.

Kids wake me in the night.

Breastfeeding baby through the night.

Illness.

I worry about what people think of me and I know this exhausts me.

Monkey mind.

Have no purpose.

I am only tired after I spend time with certain people.

I hate my job.

I'm more tired in winter. I think the lack of sunlight affects me.

- I can never live up to people's expectations of me.

- I don't exercise like I once did.

- Just a plain old lack of sleep because I do emails late at night.

- Poor-quality sleep but I don't know why.

- Toxic food.

- Processed food.

- Preservatives.

- Dehydration.

- Air-conditioning.

- Lack of sunlight.

- Stress.

- Having young children.

- Studying.

- Long commutes.

- Money worries.

- Boring job.

- Not having any time to myself.

- Over-exercising.

- Discomfort — for example, a sore stomach disrupting my sleep.

- Poor digestion from eating late.

- Cramming too many activities into the day. To do this I get up at 5am and am late to bed.

- Giving too much time and energy to others. For example, I'm always trying to motivate others. I guess this ties into relationships.

- Emotions. I feel exhausted by feeling strong emotions, particularly those related to people close to me.

- Being an overachiever/perfectionist is so tiring.

- The expectations I place upon myself exhaust me.

- Boredom is exhausting, or just a general lack of interest or engagement in life.

* Societal pressure.
* Long work hours.
* Commuting.
* Night sweats.
* Shift work.
* Lack of routine — "reacting to life" instead of scheduling my days and weeks.
* Worry about the health of those I love.
* Business worries.
* Too much caffeine during the day.
* Pets/animals wake me during the night.
* Overstimulating my mind too close to bed[time] through television or computer.
* Noisy neighbours.
* Restless partner.
* Too much alcohol.
* Uncomfortable bed/pillow.
* Sore back/body.
* Too much travel/jetlag.

For the physical factors above, the different body systems you have already read about will likely need support to overcome their dysfunction to set you on the road to restoring your energy. You can do this! And the mental and emotional explorations are mostly (although some patterns have been touched upon already) still to come.

★

The Fatigue of Grief: A Friend's Personal Story

She literally turned off the computer and pulled back on everything relating to work. She said no to pretty much everything that came her way. This was the opposite of how she usually lived. She was one of the most caring and extroverted people I knew, and this had become her life. She was in shock and her heart was broken after her sister passed away suddenly from a medical condition no one knew she had. My friend's life conditions no longer matched her blueprint for how it was supposed to be.

Grief can be a powerful force. I witnessed it in her. It took away her voice, and the lights in her eyes went out for a while. As a friend, you want to "fix" it and make it right and help her get back in touch with her magical luminosity. But it was her journey, and time was needed for her to process this experience. Her friends just needed to love her, support her in ways that were meaningful to her, and listen when she wanted to talk. Besides, there was nothing to "fix". She just needed to feel.

The difference in her energy was extreme. She went from being one of the bounciest people I know to the most exhausted. Her posture changed, her head hung low. She looked as though the weight of the world was on her shoulders. She said it turned her super-computer of a brain into a muddy fog and to make sense of anything took ages. Plus thinking was exhausting. It was as though her life force went from 100 to 10 overnight. Thank goodness for the 10.

She stopped smiling. The only time I remember her smiling was when she relayed to me that her counsellor had asked her to tell her something she could do each day that would make her smile. This irritated my friend so much that she replied to her counsellor — whom she liked and appreciated very much, mind you — that "I'd rather put pins in my eyes, because that would be easier." She didn't mean it, but her own response made her smile. There was a trace of her wit still there.

I tell you this so that you can see more of the changes that the fatigue of grief can bring. For someone who had prior to her loss been quite the fashionista, now on the days when she had to leave the house she barely washed her hair. She said she didn't have the energy. It was all too much of an effort.

The only real thing that kept her going was her routine, she said. She'd get up, walk her dog (we all thank the stars for that dog), come home and make the dog's breakfast. Usually not her own. She'd do any urgent work if she had to. Her mum had stuck post-it notes throughout her house that said "remember to eat and drink". Then she'd walk the dog again, cook dinner and go to bed.

She had never lost anyone close to her before. She said she wished it could have been her and not her sister who had died. She said everything she felt was so hard to explain, and besides, she didn't have the energy. She just wanted to hide, so mostly she did. But no matter how much sleep she got, the fatigue of her grief was endless.

I share this with you for no other reason than to demonstrate the powerful effect of emotions on energy. Everyone handles the death of a loved one differently, and this person's experience is not designed to evoke judgment on how she could have done it differently or the inner workings of every part of her process. Nor for you to think that it was alright for her, because she didn't have a family to look after, and you can't take that time out to grieve if you have people for whom you are responsible. This is simply to share the impact on energy that grief can have. Sure, my friend felt guilty that she had lived and not her sister. Sure, she ate poorly for months after her loss. Sharing her story (with her permission) has simply been to show you the power of the fatigue that can come with grief.

After about five months, the fog started to lift and her care for herself as well as her energy started to return. Her counsellor was a huge support to her, as was her dear dog. Her friends took her food to eat and books to read that might help her. One book in particular did help hugely, she said, as it shifted her perspective on death. But the main thing that helped was time, and not numbing how she felt with substances, but simply being allowed to feel how devastated she was at the passing of her sister. She says it has made her more compassionate, kinder and more patient. And she likes these things about herself.

Joy

On my travels I met a lady who worked in the kitchen in one of the most beuatiful places on Earth. The view out across the ocean from the kitchen where she worked was stunning. When I remarked on this to her, she replied that she never sees it anymore, although she looks at it every day. She said she looks "straight through the beauty". At that moment, another staff member piped up and said, "I suppose you only get to keep what you let yourself have." At the time, I had no idea what he meant, but later that day, the sentiment the other staff member had offered hit me.

Even if it is right in front of you every day, and you don't let yourself have it — which means noticing it, taking it in, allowing yourself the pleasure of it — it is never yours. It never becomes part of the ground of goodness on which you can live, and this, the essence of this, forms so much of our foundation of energy that isn't really discussed. Because if you don't "let yourself have" a majestic view, then what else are you denying yourself? Why not let yourself have what you already have?

I love this quote from the brilliant Geneen Roth. "When we spend our days wanting what we don't have, we miss what we do have. We don't have the ability, the concentrated attention to focus on both. We get so convinced that life would be better if we had more, did it differently, that we sleep walk through the sweetness of what's here. Little things, ordinary things."

I have read that when people who are dying are asked what they will miss the most, they say, "the ordinary things. The smell of air. The feeling of my dog's fur under my hands. My partner's face. A freshly cut lemon. The night sky." We have those now. Let yourself have what you already have. It's what joy is all about. And joy gives us an irreplaceable depth of energy.

You Are Busy With
What You Say Yes To

I felt that statement deserved a section all of its own. Really
think about this sentiment.

Privilege and Perspective

Having worked with thousands of people over 17 years in practice, I have been privy to some horrendous experiences that people have endured. The resilience of the human spirit never ceases to break my heart wide open and blow my mind. I have also witnessed what are comparably little things that frustrate, sadden and exhaust people. On top of that I have gained an appreciation for the immense privilege in many people's lives — the privilege of having your basic needs met, when today still too many people in the world don't have this. And amongst all of that, I have witnessed many with such privilege who have been unable to see their lives this way, for a multitude of reasons. And one of those reasons is exhaustion, whether it be from chronic sleep deprivation, or an inability to say no, or any of the other factors we have explored in this book.

You may have created a life where all of your basic needs are met, and then on top of that you have a full-time job, you are doing some continuing education, you have three children and a partner, a house that needs cleaning, planes you have to catch on time, aging parents who need your help ... and that is the tip of the iceberg of your responsibilities and tasks. In such a space, if you cannot see the gift and the immense beauty in all of that — even amidst the chaos — then you are missing out on this extraordinary life you have created. Some of you can't see it this way. Some of you know this and it devastates you. For others, it elicits major feelings of guilt.

And when you complain to me about how hard your (privileged) life is — with all of the above in it — I get it, but I also know you don't really mean that. What I take you to mean

288 ★ *Exhausted to Energized*

is that it is hard to take care of the people you want to take care of with the depth of care you want to demonstrate, and still have something — some energy — left over for you, for you to do the things that you want to do or to simply be, instead of dragging yourself around (whether you let people see this part of you or not) wondering "When is it going to be my turn?" Pretending to have it all together is exhausting in itself. Wondering "When am I going get to do what I want to do?" Worrying constantly about what others think of you. Or, as mentioned earlier, you could take a leaf from Oprah's book — remembering that she hasn't always been the Oprah you know her to be today, but has the immense pain of her past — when she suggests you "do what you have to do until you can do what you want to do". Very few situations are permanent.

But if you had good energy, you would be able to deeply appreciate how extraordinary this incredible life you have created actually is. You would actually get to enjoy your life instead of feeling like it is hard. For if you have energy, if you have a spacious feeling about a life like this, and a calm and grateful heart — even if what you have to do in a day doesn't actually change — you enjoy your life and you are unstoppable.

When you fight with what is — the fact that you have a mortgage and bills and a demanding job, and challenges with your children and family, and people who need you — when you resist what is, you create a stress so deep within you that you no longer recognize the attitude you show up with every day. And how you have become saddens you. And the never-ending stress utterly exhausts you.

The biggest obstacle to taking a bigger perspective on life is that our emotions capture and blind us — the anger, the rage, the frustration, the disappointment, the sadness ... The more sensitive we become to the blinding capacity of our emotions, the more we realize that when we start getting angry or denigrating ourselves or craving things we don't have in a way that leads us to feel miserable, we begin to shut down. It is like sitting on top of a mountain with the most exquisite view laid out before your eyes, and you have wrapped yourself in black-out curtains.

You can experiment with this. You can go and sit where there is an amazing view. And the first hit is usually "wow!" and your mind opens. Yet if you sit there long enough, you will start to worry about something. Then you realize that it feels as though everything is closing in and getting very small. We all do this all day, every day. The skill is to catch ourselves and come back to the view, to the beauty, be open to the big picture. Do this moment after moment after moment.

> *B*ut if you had good energy, you would be able to deeply appreciate how extraordinary this incredible life you have created actually is. You would actually get to enjoy your life instead of feeling like it is hard.

Which do you think fosters greater energy? The opening or the closing? The "wow" or the worry? I'm not denying there aren't things to be concerned about; I am simply wanting to offer you a new perspective that encourages you to open to wonder. To the wonder and gift of life, with all of its messiness and chaos and unpredictability. Embrace uncertainty, for some of the most beautiful chapters in our lives won't have a title until much later.

To paraphrase Viktor Frankl, we must never forget that we may also find meaning in life when confronted with a hopeless situation, when facing a fate that cannot be changed … When we are no longer able to change a situation, we are challenged to change ourselves.

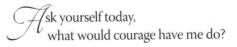

*Ask yourself today,
what would courage have me do?*

Dr Libby

The Fatigue of Failure

"Every man is proud of what he does well; and no man is proud of what he does not do well. With the former, his heart is in his work; and he will do twice as much of it with less fatigue. The latter performs a little imperfectly, looks at it in disgust, turns from it, and imagines himself exceedingly tired. The little he has done, comes to nothing, for want of finishing." So said Abraham Lincoln on 30 September 1859 in an address to the Wisconsin State Agricultural Society.

There is no better way to open a discussion about the debilitating fatigue of telling yourself that you are failure, or that you are worthless, or unworthy (of love or success), or unloved, or unlovable.

Without perhaps realizing it, we all have standards in every area of our lives. From how we eat, to how we think we have to look, to how much kindness we show others ... we all have standards. Trouble is, most people don't know that they have them, as they are stored away in their subconscious. But if you don't meet the standards you have for yourself, you immediately judge yourself, and it is this judgment that exhausts you from the meanings you create.

When you judge yourself, as corny or boring as it may seem, you run the judgments you believe were placed on you as a child, and the meanings you took from those judgments back then are still the ones you create today.

The pattern of behaviour

Here is a common example I have heard time and time again. If you feel like you weren't listened to as a child, if you didn't feel heard, the meaning you likely took from that experience or perception may have been that you are worthless — not worth listening to. Not important. And if you felt unheard by a parent or primary caregiver, the one(s) who meet your basic needs for survival of food, clothing and shelter, you cannot see (at that young age) that they behaved the way they did due to *their own* challenges. Because through a little person's eyes, you rely on them for survival. For love.

And if they don't listen to you, you create a meaning that you are worthless, not valued and not worthy of love. You create the meaning that they don't love you. So now as an adult, when you feel like someone didn't listen to you, your biggest itch — your greatest wound — gets scratched. And the cascade of self-judgment and subsequent meanings gets expressed. You might explode in anger temporarily, leaving a wake of (emotional) destruction on those around you, only later being able to see this, because anger makes you (temporarily) blind. And when you witness that destruction or simply berate yourself for overreacting or for displaying behaviour where the "punishment didn't fit the crime", you judge yourself again, create more (harsh and unresourceful) meanings and sadness about who you now perceive yourself to be — a failure as a mother/father, partner, friend, colleague — and you withdraw in a depressed mood, with the lowest energy you can imagine. Yet 10 minutes beforehand you had so much (albeit somewhat destructive) energy. So what has occurred here?

Crazy eights

It's what I call a "crazy eight", which when I am explaining it I represent with the infinity symbol:

At the left end is low energy, depressed mood, shallow breathing, slumped, poor posture, a focus on the past. At the right end is the explosion; the anger, the forceful energy, the expression of pain, anxieties and fears, but there's energy. And at the midpoint is happy, content and functional behaviour. Yet for people who run crazy eights, they spend very little time at this midpoint.

They can spend days, weeks, months or longer in the low-energy state, passing judgment constantly on themselves, telling themselves that they are a failure moment to moment. But no one can stay in that place forever. So to feel more, to have more energy, to pull themselves out of the low state, they explode, instead of seeing the emotional trigger for what it is: an opportunity to learn, grow and transform the wounds of the past and leave the crazy eight behind for good.

The power of created meanings

People who experience this tell me that the energy of the explosion feels good. They just hate themselves for their behaviour, and they believe that how they behave is who they are. Please note, I am not talking about abuse here. I am presenting a method of communication, which, granted, can in some situations have an element of verbal or emotional abuse. I am simply wanting to paint the picture of how powerful the meanings we create are on our energy. And the fatigue that comes with the belief that you are a failure, and therefore not lovable or loved, cuts deeper than any other. If your fatigue is the result of the meanings you create about who you are, the work you need to do to recover your energy is emotional.

Turning it around

As adults, I believe we not only have a responsibility to take care of our physical health (cooking is non-negotiable if you want great physical health!), but we are also responsible for our emotional landscape. We are not taught how to cope or how to decipher this landscape at school. But what I have witnessed in my time working with people is that if we resolve situations like the one I have just described, many challenges involving poor energy are resolved. (Please note I am not referring to fatigue from physical illness or disease here.)

Sure, dopamine is likely to have been involved in this crazy eight: low dopamine at the depressed-mood end, and dopamine levels through the roof at the anger end. And this can be addressed. But what I have found is that until the meanings that were established in childhood are seen for what they are — the way you made sense of or survived your environment as a very young and precious human — the fatigue won't truly lift. You will have moments or days when you will feel a bit better, but it won't go until that internal tug-o-war, that you instigate every morning about three seconds after you open your eyes, is resolved.

You might choose to see a psychologist to assist you with this. Or you might choose to bring awareness to now. And now. And now. And to now. Because then you will be present to what is, to the dance that goes on when she said *x* and then all you know is that now you want to yell. If you can use your breath and feel the anger that's there, and then, instead of releasing that energy, breathe, walk away, go wherever you need to, to create the moments for yourself to examine the "WHAT JUST HAPPENED", not the "MEANING" you created — that because she said *x* that meant she hadn't listened to what you had said five minutes ago. Look at the *what happened*. She said *x*; I wanted to yell. Explore what went on inside your head to get you from her statement (and I'm referring to a genuinely innocuous statement here, not a loaded statement) to intense anger. And there you will see what you did to yourself. The judgment you passed on yourself, how little you think of yourself and how little you value yourself. And you will see that behind that anger is the biggest tidal wave of sadness, and that, my friend, is what exhausts you so much.

Every day you fight the sadness, the devastation that you aren't okay the way you are; how could you be, you sub-consciously wonder, when your mother never listened to you? You weren't even worthy of her attention and love (your perception) and attention means love when you are five. How could anyone else ever love you if she didn't? And yet this belief in your own deficiency is why you contribute to the world.

Every human does this to themselves — no one escapes it — for if we perceived that all of our needs were always met, we would never do anything. Our task, as adults, though, is to get to the heart of what we do to ourselves and find the peace and happiness that's really there.

> *W*hat we do is we merge the "what happened" with the "meaning", and then we live our lives as if the meaning is what actually happened. And living the meaning can be utterly exhausting.

Merging "the what happened" with "the meaning"

Imagine a whiteboard in front of you. Imagine I draw on it a big circle and in that circle write *what happened*, and then beside that circle I draw another circle and in that circle I write *meaning*. What we do is we merge the "what happened" with the "meaning", and then we live our lives as if the meaning is what actually happened. And living the meaning can be utterly exhausting. This is best described by using an example.

The family consists of mum, dad and two daughters, aged 14 and eight. Dad phones home near the end of the day and suggests that he meet the three of them at a restaurant for dinner. So mum tells the girls that this is what is happening, and asks them to go and get changed, ready to meet dad and have dinner. The 14-year-old appears later wearing a crop-top. Mum says: "You need to go and get changed." A few days later, Mum overhears Ms 14 on the phone to one of her friends saying, "Well, my mum thinks I'm fat." After Ms 14 gets off the phone, Mum approaches Ms 14 and asks her why she said that to her friend, to which Ms 14 replies, "Because you said it the other day." Mum says that she did not say that, and that she would never say that. She says that she knows she didn't say it because she doesn't even believe it; in fact, the opposite is true and she is actually worried that Ms 14 is too thin. Mum finishes with the question: "When do you think I said this?"

Ms 14 replies: "The other day when you told me to go and get changed before we met Dad for dinner."

So in the circle with the words "what happened" I would now write: *Mum told me to go and get changed.* In the circle with the word "meaning" in it, I would now write: *Mum thinks I'm fat.* Had mum not overheard Ms 14 on the phone, Ms 14 would have carried that belief (that her mother thinks she is fat) into her future years. For how long? Who knows? But this is one way an eating disorder can be created. Not through malice or harshness or through it being anyone's fault. Just because our brain is set up to merge what happens with the meanings we create about what happened. And one of the ways you can create more energy in your life is to "un-merge" the "what happened" from the "meaning".

The fatigue of your belief in your "not-enoughness" probably feels like a never-ending tangle of string and you don't have the energy to unravel all of this. All you need to begin, though, is an awareness of these patterns and a desire to live in another way, with new tools and strategies and a new level of self-care and appreciation for yourself and for life. When you judge (for we all do), whether yourself or another person, simply notice that you did and work out *why*. For inside those whys are your freedom and your energy.

Purpose

We discussed purpose earlier in the book. Some people are clear on theirs, some aren't. This bothers some people, others it doesn't. Some people believe you need a purpose to have energy, others believe that the purpose of life is to be present to what is here in each moment. And this is where the juice is — the meaning of life, the purpose, the love.

So when I sat down to write this piece, I remembered something I had written about 25 years ago. And I decided to share it, which surprised me, as it's very personal. But when I feel called to share something highly personal, I do so with the sole intention that it assists you in some way. For I know my purpose, but it's not a "Rah, rah! This is my purpose — let's do this!" kind of vibe. It's basically what I really care about, and I do what I can do towards it. I don't think about. I just live it.

My purpose

I have no idea where this came from — there was no book I read or conversation that prompted it — but since I was 15 years old, my deepest concern has been that civilization is on the road to destruction, unless we create significant change. But as a 15-year-old I wanted, as I still do now, to trace everything that I wanted to solve to its source — with health, with people's pain, with the planet. I can clearly recall the "creative writing" piece I wrote at this age where we were instructed to write about "conflict". I remember considering everything from burning coal for electricity to the escalating population of planet.

And my solution to the conflict between people and planet that I felt was brewing was to want less. It was to shift our focus from ourselves and personal gain and how we appeared to others, and instead to see ourselves as part of the whole. I felt that unless we gave up thinking in linear and material ways, there would be no Earth left to inhabit.

I believe that one of biggest challenges humanity now faces is this: on the one hand, we (a collective "we") want to preserve our natural environment; on the other, everything we do to grow the economy and preserve our standard of living disrupts the natural environment and our relationships with it. We must raise our consciousness and learn to think in new ways. To quote Einstein: "No problem can be solved from the same level of consciousness that created it." We must give up making arbitrary distinctions between human beings and the rest of Nature, and instead start thinking in terms of the interconnections between all living beings. And to do that, I hope my books and events help you to get back in touch with the magnificence that you are, because when you know you *are* enough, then you know you *have* enough. And from this knowing, the children you raise inherently spend very little time out of touch with their enoughness, and they make their choices accordingly — wanting less, knowing they are enough. And that creates the next generation. And that's how I do my bit to stop the destruction. That's what I do to create more love. That is why I do what I do. That is why I get up in the morning.

What is *your* purpose?

What is your purpose? Or maybe an easier question to answer is: What do you care about?

Maybe you feel lost or as though something is missing in your life, or perhaps you want to make a bigger difference in the world than you feel you are now doing, but you aren't sure how. So many of us walk through life, feeling numb and desperate for a deeper connection, but are not sure how to get it.

I have heard people say (and, although I don't actually agree with this, it does communicate a point) that the two greatest days of your life are the day you were born, and the day you find out what your purpose is. But if you don't know what your purpose is, then you don't know why you are here, and it can be hard to keep going, and that can feel exhausting. "What's the point?" you regularly wonder. And your deflated feeling continues.

But maybe the problem is *not* that you don't know what your purpose is. Maybe it is the way you are trying to find your purpose. We can't often think our way into our life's passion and purpose. We have to "do" our way in.

This means taking steps towards what you want and removing the things in your life that you don't want. And that might require minor or major changes that allow you to take one step at a time and explore many different passions. If you are searching for your purpose and some passion, try the strategy "stop looking and start doing".

Take action

So, you can't *think* your way into finding your life purpose, you have to *do* your way into it. The more we act, the more we get clear on things. So instead of overthinking it with fears (Will this work out? Should I try that? What if I don't like it?), start taking steps towards being able to try new things. The experience is the reward; clarity comes through the process of exploring.

It can also be a good idea to break up with the idea of "the one". Many of us struggle because we try to find that one thing that we are meant to do; but trying to find only one thing can be the reason why we feel like something is missing. The notion that we have only one thing that we are meant for limits us from fulfilling our greatness. So start getting in touch with your passions and what you care about. When you lead a passionate life, you are living your life on purpose.

Try letting go of thinking that there is only one purpose for you, and try embracing the idea that our purpose in life is to love life fully by being our authentic selves. To love and be loved. The need to seek our purpose can sometimes come from a lack of passion. When you don't feel connected to your life or to others or a community or a faith, you can lack passion and purpose. To resolve a feeling of emptiness, if it is there, add more passion — work out what you care about and take action in those areas. If it helps, remember this:

Passion/Care + Daily Action = Purposeful Life

Consider that the real purpose of anyone's life is to be fully involved in living. Be present for the journey. Act on what you care about. If there are things in the world that are unacceptable to you, create a plan of action and take steps to making a difference in that area. While you focus on yourself, you will never find purpose. It has to be about others or there is no lit-up feeling inside. No matter how big or small, what is it that you really care about?

The Wrap-up ...

As you have seen, poor energy can unfold from such a wide variety of sources that there may be no one thing causing it. It can be the result of the interplay between your biochemistry, your nutritional status and your emotional landscape. For some, there are very specific things to do to treat; for example, low energy coming from adrenal fatigue, or poor energy resulting from liver congestion or thyroid dysfunction. It might mean addressing underlying infections. Those physical challenges with health and energy have specific roads of treatment to help correct and resolve them, as you have seen. Yet there are also some general considerations to help you on your road to living a life with more energy. Here we go:

1. Continuing to do what you have always done and expecting a different result is some people's definition of insanity. To change your energy, you have to change something or multiple things. You can't just do what you always do. That is creating how you feel now. Something or things have to change. The way you eat, drink, move, think, breathe, believe or perceive are common categories that need addressing.

2. If I had to choose four main areas that support great energy from a physical perspective, based on scientific research as well as my clinical experience, they would be: what you eat, how you move, how you breathe and how you sleep. If you have poor energy and you know that any or all of these areas need attention, then take consistent action on one of them, minimum. It will likely have a ripple effect on the others.

3. If you feel that stress is really at the heart of your low energy, then I urge you to consider this. Yes, stress can be incredibly

energy-zapping, particularly chronic stress. Yet the real word for stress is fear. Whatever you are stressed about — anything at all — it is usually what you are frightened of. Peel back the layers on what you perceive are your stresses and see what's really there. See what you are actually afraid of. Of being a failure, of being seen as lazy, of people not liking you, of letting others down … For most people, when they peel it all back, their fear is that they are not loved, or that there will be a loss of love. Everything — and I mean everything — comes back to avoiding rejection and obtaining or maintaining love. I don't know how else to say it. People think the opposite of stressed is relaxed or calm. I say it is trust.

4. You have inside you "a natural intelligence", as Marianne Williamson so beautifully shares. You can name this what you like, but for now let's call it that. An acorn grows into an oak tree. What does that? A human doesn't instruct that and make that happen. The acorn has a natural intelligence that grows it from its baby self into the highest, best version of itself as a beautiful oak tree. Same goes for a rose. Do you instruct the rose to open? No, its own intelligence grows and opens it. Do you really think you are separate from that? You have the same natural intelligence inside you, wanting to grow you to become your highest, best version of yourself. Natural intelligence wants nothing more for you than to be your best version of you. The thing is, most of us walk around as though we are lamps, busting to shine our light, but we aren't plugged in. We spend our time in houses where the electricity is connected, but we don't plug in, so our

> *Whatever you are stressed about — anything at all — it is usually what you are frightened of. Peel back the layers on what you perceive are your stresses and see what's really there. See what you are actually afraid of.*

light never goes on. And in your heart of hearts you know if this is happening. You sense there is more to life. You sense you have potential that you haven't yet tapped. And this gnaws away at you. You have boundless energy when you are plugged in. You trust. You trust the unfolding of life. You believe that life doesn't happen *to* you, but that life happens *for* you. So how do you plug in? The only way I know is meditation. That allows you to hear the natural intelligence that is always there, within you, waiting for you to listen.

$\mathcal{P}$art of having amazing energy comes from service.
Serve others with all of your heart.
Lift their burden and your own will be lighter.

Ezra Taft Benson

References and Resources

I have included this section for numerous purposes. First, if you enjoy science there are some fascinating publications listed here. These are written in a scientific reference format.

There are also books I have cited in the text, listed in full here if further reading in a particular area interests you.

After reading *Exhausted to Energized*, you may ask, what's next? I have received and been touched by countless emails from people all over the world saying that they feel like I have read their diary when it comes to describing how they feel in the pages of my books. People tell me that they want more of this type of information, which gives them further insight into their physical and emotional health. I cannot encourage you enough to check out the array of options on my website, including my weekend events and online courses. If you relate to the title *Rushing Woman's Syndrome* but you feel like you don't have time to read the book, you might enjoy the 30-day online *Rushing Woman's Syndrome Quickstart Course* where I guide you on how to retire from being a rushing woman! Take a look at the blog, too, at www.drlibby.com.

I also post health information each weekday on Facebook and Twitter. Connect with me there at:

www.facebook.com/DrLibbyLive

www.twitter.com/DrLibbyLive

And on Instagram, find me as "drlibby".

My passion is to educate and inspire, and to help people change the relationship they have with their bodies and their health, and put the power of choice back in their hands. It is an honour to assist you in your optimal health journey.

Books and articles

Beard, J. (2003). Iron deficiency alters brain development and functioning. *The Journal of Nutrition* 133(5): 1468S–1472S.

Bey, L. and Hamilton, M.T. (2003). Suppression of skeletal muscle lipoprotein lipase activity during physical inactivity: a molecular reason to maintain daily low-intensity activity. *Journal of Physiology* 551(Pt 2): 673–682.

Casey, Dr Lynne. (2013). *Stress and Wellbeing in Australia Survey.* Melbourne: The Australian Psychological Society.

Coates, Dr Karen and Perry, Vincent. (2007). *Embracing the Warrior: An Essential Guide for Women.* Burleigh Heads: Arteriol Press.

Epstein, Donny. (1994). *The 12 Stages of Healing.* San Rafael, CA: Amber-Allen.

Hamilton, M.T., Hamilton, D.G., and Zderic, T.W. (2004) Exercise physiology versus inactivity physiology: an essential concept for understanding lipoprotein lipase regulation. *Exercise Sport Science Review* 32(4): 161–166.

Hay, Louise. (2004). *You Can Heal Your Life.* Carlsbad: Hay House.

Horvath, K., and Perman, J.A. (2002). Autistic disorder and gastrointestinal disease. *Current Opinions in Pediatrics* 14(5): 583–587.

Horvath, K., and Perman, J.A. (2002). Autism and gastrointestinal symptoms. *Current Gastroenterology Reports* 4(3): 251–258.

Horvath, K., Papadimitriou, J.C., Rabsztyn, A., Drachenberg C., and Tildon, J.T. (1999). Gastrointestinal abnormalities in children with autistic disorders. *Journal of Pediatrics* 135(5): 559–563.

Jin, W., Wang, H., Ji, Y., Hu, Q., Yan, W., Chen, G., and Yin, H. (2008). Increased intestinal inflammatory response and gut barrier dysfunction in Nrf2-deficient mice after traumatic brain injury. *Cytokine* 44(1): 135–140.

Lipton, Dr Bruce. (2008). *The Biology of Belief: Unleashing the Power of Consciousness, Matter and Miracles.* Carlsbad: Hay House.

Northrup, Kate. (2013). *Money: A Love Story. Untangle Your Financial Woes and Create the Life You Really Want.* Carlsbad: Hay House.

Prandovszky, E., Gaskell, E., Martin, H., Dubey, J.P., Webster, J.P., and McConkey, G.A. (2011) The neurotropic parasite *Toxoplasma gondii* increases dopamine metabolism. *PLoS ONE* 6(9): e23866.

Roth, Geneen. (2011). *Lost and Found: Unexpected Revelations About Food and Money.* New York: Viking Penguin.

Salamone, J.D., and Correa, M. (2012). The mysterious motivational functions of mesolimbic dopamine. *Neuron* 76(3): 470–474.

Weaver, Dr Libby. (2011). *Accidentally Overweight.* Auckland: Little Green Frog.

Weaver, Dr Libby. (2012). *Rushing Woman's Syndrome.* Auckland: Little Green Frog.

Weaver, Dr Libby. (2013). *Beauty from the Inside Out.* Auckland: Little Green Frog.

Weaver, Dr Libby. (2014). *The Calorie Fallacy.* Auckland: Little Green Frog.

Weaver, Dr Libby and Tait, Cynthia. (2012). *Dr Libby's Real Food Chef.* Auckland: Little Green Frog.

Weaver, Dr Libby and Tait, Cynthia. (2013). *Dr Libby's Real Food Kitchen.* Auckland: Little Green Frog.

Weaver, Dr Libby and Tait, Cynthia. (2014). *Dr Libby's Sweet Food Story.* Auckland: Little Green Frog.

White, P.D., Grover, S.A., Kangro, H.O., Thomas, J.M., Amess, J., and Clare, A.W. (1995). The validity and reliability of the fatigue syndrome that follows glandular fever. *Psychological Medicine* 25: 917–920.

White, P.D., Thomas, J.M., Sullivan, P.F., and Buchwald, D. (2004).The nosology of sub-acute and chronic fatigue syndromes that follow infectious mononucleosis. *Psychological Medicine* 34: 499–503.

White, P.D. (2007). What causes prolonged fatigue after infectious mononucleosis — and does it tell us anything about chronic fatigue syndrome? *The Journal of Infectious Diseases* 196(1): 4–5.

Whitton, Tracy. (2011). *Stillness Through Movement.* Burleigh, Gold Coast: Tracy Whitton.

Online papers

In alphabetical order of the topic to which the reference relates.

Addictions information used in the dopamine chapter: http://www.huffingtonpost.com/johann-hari/the-real-cause-of-addicti_b_6506936.html. Accessed: 7 August 2015.

Hydration information: http://jn.nutrition.org/content/early/2011/12/20/jn.111.142000.full.pdf+html. Accessed: 30 July 2015.

Mitochondria information: http://fitstar.com/high-intensity-exercise/. Accessed: 25 June 2015.

Open loops section: http://www.forbes.com/sites/kevinkruse/2015/07/10/to-do-lists-time-management/. Accessed: 27 July 2015.

Oxygenation information: http://www.livestrong.com/

article/112789-effects-low-blood-oxygen-levels/. Accessed: 27 June 2015.

Post-natal depletion information: http://goop.com/postnatal-depletion-even-10-years-later/. Accessed: 27 July 2015.

Post-natal depletion information: http://oscarserrallach.com. Accessed: 27 July 2015.

Sleep apnoea information: http://patient.info/doctor/obstructive-sleep-apnoea-pro. Accessed: 27 June 2015.

Stop, Keep, Start ideas: http://www.daniellelaporte.com/28-best-things-i-ever-did/. Accessed: 5 August 2015.

Stress statistics: American Psychological Association, *Stress in America Report, 2011,* at www.apa.org. Accessed: 24 July 2015

CDs

Weaver, Dr Libby. (2012). *Restorative Calm.* Auckland: Little Green Frog.

Whitton, Tracy. (2011). *One With Life.* Burleigh, Gold Coast: Tracy Whitton.

My TEDx Talk

The Pace of Modern Life Versus our Cavewoman Biochemistry
https://www.youtube.com/watch?v=tJoSME6Z9rw

Dr Libby Live Events and Online Courses

Available at www.drlibby.com

I regularly do speaking tours, so check my website for topics, dates and venues. I also run weekend events that offer participants a wonderful restorative experience coupled with in-depth learning of holistic health: the biochemical, the nutritional and the emotional. The *Essential Women's Health Weekend* and the *Beautiful You Weekend* are two favourites that people love.

Online courses include:

Rushing Woman's Syndrome Quickstart Course

Condition the Calm Course

30 Essential Beauty Gems Course

New Year New You Webinar

Sensational Sleep Webinar

Understanding the Mysteries and Magic of the Female Body Webinar

Acknowledgements

Thank you to Chris and Kate for wanting this book written, and for encouraging me to write it. And thanks for your love, friendship and care. I am very grateful to have you in my life.

Thank you to Dr Merv Garrett and my professors from the University of Newcastle, who allowed me to be immersed in an environment where critical thinking and questioning what was currently accepted was encouraged, and who further fostered my love of human nutrition, biochemistry, immunology and microbiology. All play a role in energy.

Thank you to the wonderful humans in my team, Kate, Jenny, Dee, Georgia, Imogen, Karen and Lisa, for your care, passion and cleverness, and for all you do each day to make a difference in the world. Extra special thanks to Maddy for her love, laughter and presence while I wrote this book.

Thank you to Kate S. for her wonderful editing skills and for emails that delight me with the construction of language and the sentiments they convey. I am very grateful to work with you. Thank you to Amy for the layout, for your design, attention to detail and caring ways. Thank you to Stasia for the cover design and to Steven, Rae, Kelly and Steph for your genius and the laughs on the photo shoot day.

Thank you to the farmers who nurture the soil and grow great quality (for people and planet) food. We cannot have great health and energy without your efforts and care. Thank you to the growing number of health- and environment-conscious companies who enable people to have access to exceptional-quality, non-toxic products. You are all changing the world, and I deeply appreciate what you do and contribute.

Thank you to the teams at Business Chicks Australia

and Virgin Unite for inviting me to join you as a speaker on Necker Island while I was in the middle of writing this book. It changed the course of the book, and the experience impacted me greatly, and I thank you so much for both. And thank you to everyone who went to Necker on this trip, for all that we shared and for so much laughter that our faces hurt. I will treasure the experience forever. Extra special thanks to Kristina, Anna Carin and Marianne.

Huge thanks to the New York crew for sharing your magical home with me while I wrote part of this. Your hearts are bigger than the Universe and your care knows no bounds.

Special thanks to Tracy (Stillness Through Movement) and Neale (Five Elements Chinese Medicine) for supporting my health so gently yet so powerfully, and for being such beautiful souls.

Thank you to Karl for all that you are. Thank you to my parents for their love, for never quelling my curiosity, for my education, and for having parsley and chickens in the backyard. I am so blessed to have you for my parents and for the friendship that we share today. Thank you to Chris for helping me share these messages with the world. Thank you for being a visionary, for your insights, your authenticity, and for cracking me up. Thank you for being such a wonderful human.

And finally, thank you to the incredible people who allowed me to share their stories throughout these pages (with changed names). Case studies help people learn as they see that others who have suffered have transformed their health and energy. Thank you to the people I meet at my live events who share their challenges, stories and achievements with me. You inspire me to do what I do.

Meet Dr Libby

Dr Libby is a nutritional biochemist, holistic health specialist, a seven-time number-one bestselling author and an international speaker. She combines 14 years at university with 17 years of clinical practice in all that she shares. Her mission is to educate and inspire, enhancing people's health and happiness, igniting a ripple effect that transforms the world.

Dr Libby's three-pillar approach to health looks at the biochemical, the nutritional and the emotional factors behind what might be driving the body to behave in a certain way. She also helps you answer the question: "Why do I do what I do, when I know what I know?" She believes that the body is an extraordinary barometer and that the parts of it that frustrate or sadden us are simply messengers asking us to eat, drink, move, think, breathe, believe or perceive in a new way. She helps you decipher the gifts that these are.

Armed with an abundance of knowledge, scientific research and a natural ability to break down even the most complex of concepts into lay terms, Dr Libby has true desire to help others get back in touch with their own magnificence. Actors Deborra-lee and Hugh Jackman describe Libby as being a "one-stop shop in achieving and maintaining ultimate health and wellbeing".

Accidentally Overweight

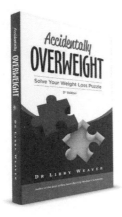

Accidentally Overweight, Dr Libby's first number-one bestselling book, explains what is necessary for the body to be able to access body fat and burn it. So many readers say that *Accidentally Overweight* could easily be called Optimal Wellbeing, as the information is relevant to everyone regardless of their health goals.

Whether consciously or subconsciously, many people are frustrated by how they feel about their body and this frustration can take up their headspace and influence their moods. Many people eat well and exercise regularly, yet their body fat does not reflect their efforts. This book explains the biochemistry and emotions of weight loss to help free people from their battle with their bodies. It includes strategies to explore emotional eating and specific herbs and nutrients to support optimal biochemistry for the effective utilization of body fat.

What to eat and how much to eat for optimum health and ideal body shape and size can seem like confusing and, at times, overwhelming areas to explore. Right now you could walk into a bookshop and pick up a book that tells you to eat plenty of carbohydrates, as they are essential for energy, and right beside it on the bookshelf will be a book that tells you not to eat carbs because they make you fat and tired.

How on Earth are you supposed to make sense of this well-meaning, but conflicting, information? How do you work out a way of eating that fuels you with great energy all day long while burning fat? What do you do if you feel like you have tried everything to lose weight only to gain it back? Have you ever put your mind to losing weight and made an enormous effort to eat well and exercise regularly for little or no reward? Or perhaps you are actually OK with your weight but you just don't *feel* right? *Accidentally Overweight* answers all of these questions, and more.

To learn more visit: www.drlibby.com

Rushing Woman's Syndrome

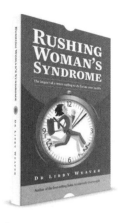

Dr Libby's second book, *Rushing Woman's Syndrome*, became another number-one bestseller. *Rushing Woman's Syndrome* describes the biochemical and emotional effects of constantly being in a rush, and the health consequences that urgency elicits.

It doesn't seem to matter if a woman has two things to do in her day or 200; she is in a pressing rush to do it all. She is often wound up like a top, running herself ragged in a daily battle to keep up. There is always so much to do, and she rarely feels like she is in control and on top of things. In fact, her deep desire to control even the smaller details of life can leave her feeling out of control, even of her own self.

Rushing Woman's Syndrome examines the nervous system, endocrine system (including sex and stress hormones, the thyroid, and the pituitary gland), and the digestive system, as well as the emotional aspects of why women rush. Dr Libby can simplify even the most difficult biochemistry effortlessly, making this book equally educating and inspiring. *Rushing Woman's Syndrome* takes you on an emotional journey to help you decipher just where your beliefs are coming from and how those thoughts affect how your body behaves. So come on a journey of food and hormones, thoughts and perceptions, energy and vitality. It is impossible not to see your life and body from a whole new perspective after reading this book.

After a multitude of requests for coaching and requests from women who were too busy to read the book(!), Dr Libby created two 30-day video coaching programmes called *The Rushing Woman's Syndrome Quick Start Course* and the *Condition the Calm Advanced Course*, which guide you on your journey from rushing back to calm. These courses have achieved phenomenal results with women across the world who are now enjoying life without the rush.

To learn more visit: www.drlibby.com

Beauty From the Inside Out

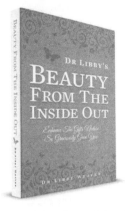

As a society our relationship with beauty is in crisis. We are told that beauty exists only in certain forms, images and at certain ages. We can feel bombarded with images that lead us away from our own unique beauty and encourage us to try to look like someone else rather than accepting more of who we are. While adults can be affected by such messages, these messages can be particularly damaging to teenagers who so desperately want to be loved, approved of, considered special and seen as beautiful. There is so much beauty on offer to us 24/7, at any age, inside us, around us, and shining from us. For so many a veil just needs to be lifted so you can experience your own radiance. Let's see what we can do!

When most people think about improving their appearance, they usually focus on a product, another "quick fix". Yet when you consider that the skin cells on your face are a small percentage of the total number of cells in the whole body, it seems crazy that we don't spend more time getting the majority of the cells functioning optimally, leading us to the outcomes we seek.

Through *Beauty From The Inside Out*, Dr Libby expertly explains your outer world, the food you choose, the nutrients you ingest, hydration, posture, movement and what your body needs to create lovely nails, lustrous hair, sparkling eyes and clear, luminous skin. Be guided to deal with very specific bumps in the road, such as dark circles under the eyes, eczema, pimples and hair that is falling out, to name only a few. Just as importantly, Dr Libby explains your inner world, sex hormones, stress hormones, detox, digestion, elimination pathways, thyroid and pituitary functions. Both worlds relate to your sparkle as does taking a heart-opening look at your emotional landscape. For many, that is where the real elixir is.

Beauty From The Inside Out is a must-have beauty bible for all women. Enjoy radiating your own unique sparkle, from the inside out. Dr Libby has also released an online course called *Dr Libby's Essential Beauty Gems*.

For more information visit: www.drlibby.com

The Calorie Fallacy

How many of us have been told that if we burn more calories than we eat, weight loss will be inevitable? How many of us have discovered that this century-old philosophy does not seem to apply to our body, no matter how hard we work, in this modern world?

In a world obsessed with calorie counting, as evidenced by the widespread listing of calories on food items and menus, claims of the latest low calorie miracle food, diet and exercise regimes guaranteed to burn calories fast, we find ourselves instead watching the waistlines of the Western world continually increasing.

What if the foundation nutritional philosophy that the calorie equation is the sole determinant of weight loss is completely outdated and in many cases wrong?

Bestselling author Dr Libby's book *The Calorie Fallacy* is designed to help you stop dieting and start living. It is time to stop counting calories. It's time for a new model of how to manage body shape and size. No longer are energy equations satisfactory in the information they provide. The concept that as long as you eat fewer calories than you burn you will lose weight is well overdue for an update.

Dr Libby explores the fundamentals of weight loss like never before in this groundbreaking book, that challenges the very core of weight-loss convention and dogma. Sharing her own personal journey that led her to explore and uncover the biochemistry of sustainable weight loss, Dr Libby presents countless case studies of clients she has worked with over the past 16 years, along with her two decades of scientific research into the principles of body fat loss.

Dr Libby contests the assumption that you have to lose weight to be healthy, instead replacing it with a paradigm-shifting statement that in fact you have to be healthy to lose weight. This will transform how you view your body and enhance your understanding of what your body requires to lose weight.

So for all of you who have been making an enormous effort and commitment to weight loss with little or no sustainable outcomes, and for those who simply want to understand how to live happier, healthier lives, allowing your body to efficiently use body fat as a fuel, Dr Libby will arm you with the wisdom to stop dieting and depriving yourself and start thriving. Stop dieting and start nourishing yourself, and watch the transformation occur.

To learn more, visit www.drlibby.com

Real Food Chef

After noticing her clients struggling to come up with ideas for quick and nutritious meals, it seemed a natural progression for Dr Libby to create a series of recipes that have her seal of approval. And so the *Real Food Chef* was born.

The recipes appeal to a broad range of people, from busy mothers to teenage boys. Good, honest food that could be made by anyone; these recipes are sure to impress even the fussiest of eaters and offer nutrient-dense alternatives to your favourite foods. From blueberry cheesecake to satay chicken, *Real Food Chef* is bursting with ideas and images to inspire.

The *Real Food Chef* system focuses on using food in its whole form, including all the food's vitamins and minerals and the natural plant compounds known to support human health; after all, it is nutrients that keep us alive. The recipes are free from refined sugars, dairy products, and gluten, with few exceptions; they are, therefore, suitable for those with some of the more common food allergies or intolerances. Anyone who wants to optimize their nourishment would benefit from this book.

The *Real Food Chef* concept is a dynamic combination of Dr Libby's nutritional expertise with chef Cynthia Louise's gift for transforming everyday meals into nutrient-dense and incredibly delicious versions of their former selves. As a team, they bring you the why, and the how, to eat real food and amp up the nutrition in your world.

Filled with delicious, nourishing recipes, quotes to inspire, and food education, the *Real Food Chef* is designed to enhance your quality of life and give you more energy to live the life you love.

To help you create these incredible recipes, Dr Libby and chef Cynthia have returned to the *Real Food Chef* kitchen to show you how to make every dish in the *Real Food Chef Video Tutorials*. Chef Cynthia shows you step-by-step how to create your *Real Food Chef* masterpiece and Dr Libby provides the nutritional support, reminding you how each ingredient supports your body, mind and soul.

To learn more, visit www.drlibby.com

Real Food Kitchen

Following on from the phenomenal popularity of the *Real Food Chef*, the second cookbook in this series takes family favourites and applies the *Real Food Chef* principles to ensure maximum nutrient density of every meal and every mouthful. With 90 recipes covering breakfast, drinks, lunch, dinner, snacks, dressings and desserts – the *Real Food Kitchen* will inspire you to take better care of yourself with the delicious and nutritious recipes featured.

This way of eating has a wide-reaching effect for it is not just about the outstanding nourishment that comes from each recipe, it is also about what we've left out... refined and artificial ingredients that have the potential to take away from your health such as refined sugar, white flour and preservatives. The recipes are also dairy-free and gluten-free, with few exceptions.

This book provides you with amazing recipes such as Macho Nachos, Spaghetti Carbonara, Coconut Ice, Caramel Slice and Banoffee Pie that serve your health and happiness, and brings it all to life in an easy to use, quick to prepare, delicious tasting recipe book, that also contains nutrition information and inspirational quotes. Continue your journey to outstanding health, energy and vitality by embracing the *Real Food Kitchen* way of eating, and witness the transformation as your body, mind and soul responds to true nourishment.